Advance praise for:
YOU LOOK TOO YOUNG TO BE A MOM

"When children bear children, they rise to the challenge of turning their lives around. And when they tell their stories as they have in this remarkable book, they will make you laugh and cry, rage at injustice, and mostly they will inspire you with the belief that you, too, can accomplish anything. Read this book and be thrown into the company of the world's most unexpected heroes." —Beverly Donofrio, author of *Riding in Cars With Boys*

"In this rare and evocative collection, women defy pervasive 'teen mom' stereotypes and other social conventions, challenging all of us to rethink things we learned about love, struggle, and success." —Vickie Nam, author of *YELL-Oh Girls! Emerging Voices Explore Culture, Identity, and Growing Up Asian American*

"*Finally* a book that bares the authentic voices of teen parents and shows the world what those of us who are privileged to work with them already knew: These young women are strong, resilient, and love their children fiercely. They are worthy of our respect and our support, nothing less." —Lisa Goldblatt Grace, LICSW, MPH, former director of Just a Start House, a long-term shelter for homeless pregnant and parenting teens and national consultant working with agencies to develop Second Chance Homes in their home states

"The writers in *You Look Too Young to be a Mom* have busted through fifty years of prejudice to come to the truth: Motherhood is lovely and difficult and life-altering, no matter what age it comes to you. Let's hope this groundbreaking anthology removes teenage motherhood from the category of social ills and puts it back where it should be—real life." —Jennifer Niesslein, coeditor of *Brain, Child: The Magazine for Thinking Mothers*

"*You Look Too Young to be a Mom* is a testament to the power of love, and to the enduring good that comes from having faith in oneself."
—Linda Wolf, coauthor, *Daughters of the Moon, Sisters of the Sun: Young Women and Mentors on the Transition to Womanhood*, www.daughters-sisters.org

"A rousing, assumption-busting read, delivered in bite-sized portions well-suited to the needs of harried moms of all ages."
—Ayun Halliday, author of *The Big Rumpus* and sole employee of *The East Village Inky*

"Meeting teen moms through reading *You Look Too Young to be a Mom* will destroy any stereotypes you may have about very young parents. Here are unique and wonderful young parents—just as most teen moms, in my experience, are unique and wonderful."
—Jeanne Lindsay, author and founder of Morning Glory Press, publisher of resources for teen parents

"Teen pregnancy and parenting is often castigated and reviled, cited as a pivotal point of ruination for an individual young woman and for society as a whole. In Ms. Davis's excellent book, these teen moms are personalized. Through their stories they reveal their intelligence, wit, feelings, and gumption as they describe their personal experiences . . . There are no stereotypes here."—Susan Straub, Read-To-Me Program

"If you're a teen mom who dreams and despairs of becoming a professional, this is the book for you."—Pat Gowens, editor of *Mother Warriors Voice*

You Look
Too Young
to be a Mom

Teen Mothers Speak Out
on Love, Learning, and Success

Edited by
Deborah Davis

A Perigee Book

For my mother, Betty Lou Davis,
and mothers of all ages everywhere.

A Perigee Book
Published by The Berkley Publishing Group
A division of Penguin Group (USA) Inc.
375 Hudson Street
New York, New York 10014

Copyright © 2004 by Deborah Davis
Cover design by Ben Gibson
Cover photo copyright © by Gari Wyn Williams/Photonica
Text design by Tiffany Estreicher

Perigee trade paperback edition: April 2004

Visit our website at www.penguin.com

Library of Congress Cataloging-in-Publication Data

You look too young to be a mom: teen moms speak out on love, learning,
and success / edited by Deborah Davis.
     p. cm.
   ISBN 0-399-52976-4
     1. Teenage mothers—United States. 2. Unmarried mothers—United States.
3. Teenage pregnancy—United States. 4. Self-realization. I. Davis, Deborah.

HQ759.4.Y68 2004
306.874'3—dc22   2003064784

Printed in the United States of America
10 9 8 7 6 5 4 3 2 1

Contents

PART 1: Are You Still With Me?
ON FINDING SUPPORT FROM FAMILIES,
LOVED ONES, AND MENTORS

PART 2: Two Pink Lines
ON PREGNANCY, BIRTH, AND LEARNING TO MOTHER

PART 3: Growing Up Together
ON SEXUALITY, RESPONSIBILITY, AND PARENTING

PART 4: Growing Belly, Shrinking Brain?

ON DROPPING OUT, GETTING BACK IN, AND FINISHING AN
EDUCATION—IN SPITE OF THE STATISTICS

PART 5: Encounters That Empower
ON BEING CHALLENGED AND STANDING FIRM

PART 6: Toilet Paper or Milk?
ON WORK, MONEY, AND FINDING A CAREER

PART 7: Emerging From Darkness

ON HEALING FROM ABUSE AND ADDICTION, AND
LEARNING TO LOVE AGAIN

PART 8: Mama Power

ON FIGHTING FOR OUR RIGHTS, KNOCKING DOWN
STEREOTYPES, AND CHANGING LIVES

CONTENTS

Acknowledgments

My deep thanks goes to the hundreds of mothers who sent me their stories, encouragement, and suggestions and to the dozens who answered my questionnaire. It is an honor to be entrusted with the details of your astounding and courageous lives.

I am grateful to all the teachers, counselors, social workers, organizers, nurses, writers, midwives, and staff at innumerable social service and educational organizations who saw the need for this project and helped to publicize the call for submissions.

Specifically, I wish to thank Ariel Gore and Bee Lavender at *Hip Mama* magazine; Pat Beresford at Inwood House; my mother-in-law, Susie Wilson, for connecting me with many individuals and organizations dealing with teens and young parents; Patricia Henley; and my sister and brother-in-law Susan and Les Gerber for housing, food, and fun on my trips to New York.

I owe gratitude to many others as well:

To my agent, Faye Bender, and my editor, Michelle Howry, for your vision, enthusiasm, and clarity. Working with each of you has been a joy.

To my friends and fellow writers, especially Virginia Lore,

Peggy Christian, Pamela Powell, Jaylon Niekras, Linda Wiley, Cheryl Ann Brown, Adam Smith, and the Hedgebrook gang, for your advice, critiques, and companionship. Extra thanks to Christine Castigliano for her Web site expertise and Jaylon for teaching young moms with me and sharing her valuable insights.

To my son, Eli, for making me laugh, inviting me to play when I sit at my computer too long, and inspiring me to grow as a mother by leaps and bounds.

And to my husband, Dwight Wilson, for his ongoing love, encouragement, and keen ability to reorient me in the forest when I am lost among the trees.

Ariel Gore

Foreword

When I got pregnant at eighteen, I'd been on the road for the better part of my adolescence—traveling through Asia and Europe, sleeping in train stations and squats, sheltered by lifestyle and distance from the American political rhetoric about "the breakdown of the traditional family."

When my tits swelled and I started throwing up outside the soup kitchen I knew I'd be a mother, but I didn't know about all the prefixes that would be used to describe my motherhood. I knew I didn't want to get married, but I didn't think about the fact that I would be an *unwed* mother, a *single* mother, procreating *out of wedlock*. I knew I was young, but I didn't identify with the phrase *teen* mother. I knew I was broke, and I figured that if I came back to the States I would get on some kind of public assistance, but I never considered the fact that I was about to become a *welfare* mother.

When I got home to California, three-month-old baby on my back, I applied to college, applied for Aid to Families with Dependent Children, and inherited a television from my grandparents. After *Sesame Street,* I watched the news. I started hearing about all of these mothers products of "the breakdown of the American family." The *single* mothers, the *unwed* mothers, the *teen* mothers, the *welfare* mothers—bloodsucking leeches, all. Irresponsible. Promiscuous. Lazy. Their chaotic homes were breeding grounds for criminals and drug addicts. As one columnist put it in *Newsweek*, "Every threat to the fabric of this country—from poverty to crime to homelessness—is connected to out-of-wedlock teen pregnancy." Every threat to the fabric of this country? Who were these women? Did they live anywhere near us? Would they hurt my baby?

Of course, there was something fishy about the premise of the whole news story—*The breakdown of the American family?*

I'd grown up in the San Francisco Bay Area in the '70s and '80s. The only kids I knew whose parents stayed married were black, Asian, or Latino. White people divorced. Or they never married. *Leave It to Beaver* was a rerun and a joke. Still, it took a while to sink in—blame it on culture shock or the sleep deprivation that defines life with an infant, but my girl was taking her first steps before it all crystallized in my mind: *Unwed. Teenage. Welfare. Mother. Oh my God. They're talking about me!*

Here I'd thought I was just some low-income mama, smitten with my child, trying to put food on the table, trying to find a baby-sitter so I wouldn't have to take my girl to college classes with me anymore. And now I was every threat to the fabric of the country? *Every* threat? Unbelievable. I sat in front of the television with my mouth hanging open. I'd always wanted to be a one-woman revolution. Now here I was on the nightly news! A political issue. A statistic, maybe, but a *critical* statistic. A member of an allegedly burgeoning army of one-woman revolutions. There were thousands of us—maybe millions. I envisioned us marching on Washington, taking over the White House. All we'd done to become every threat to the fabric of the country was to get pregnant and keep our babies. Imagine what we could do if we followed up on all those threats. . . . The possibilities boggled the mind. Mama power! We could rule the world!

I shared my enthusiasm with friends and mentors, but folks seemed less than excited. I was an exception, they told me. The brave mamas in my small circle of friends were also exceptions. We were going back to school. We were good mothers. We were "pulling ourselves up by our bootstraps." Unlike . . . those *others*. The ones on TV. The irresponsible. The promiscuous. The lazy. I didn't believe them—but what did I know? I still couldn't legally buy alcohol. I lived in a small suburban community in Northern California. I spent most of my time in school or taking care of my growing girl. I wondered.

Junior year, I moved to Oakland. My circle of mother-friends grew and, yes, I met several teen moms who believed the statistics, who found themselves beaten down by economics and circumstance, by the rhetoric and the very real lack of support in the high schools, colleges, and workplaces. But I also met dozens of women who refused to believe the hype, women who were— maybe ironically—*inspired* by all the negative images and discouraging words. Undaunted by what they saw and heard on TV, the young moms I met responded to every "You can't" with a bold "Just Watch Me."

As young moms, we knew the decks were stacked against us. We set to work unstacking those decks. We fought for our right to stay in school. We worked night and day. We were sometimes promiscuous. But we were never idle. We mothered our children fiercely. If we were every threat to the fabric of the country, all the better!

The voices in this collection are the voices of those mothers. The one-woman revolutions. We are not exceptions. We are the real thing, our hearts on our spit-up-stained sleeves. Our homes are the chaotic breeding grounds for the next generation of artists, of doctors, of politicians, of soulful human beings. We show our kids by example how to fight for their rights, how to follow their dreams, how to turn off the TV, and how to respond when anyone dares to tell them they "can't."

Mama power! Just Watch Us.

—Ariel Gore,
editor of *Hip Mama* magazine

Introduction

"Teen mom."

What image comes to mind when you hear this?

Do you see a courageous, loving, resourceful young mother accompanied by her family, teachers, boyfriend, husband, friends? Probably not. But that is the image this book will leave you with.

In creating *You Look Too Young to be a Mom*, I have been privileged to work with a remarkable group of women. Nevertheless, I didn't always view young mothers in the positive light I now see them.

Fresh out of college in the early 1980s, I worked with abused and "at-risk" teenagers. It is embarrassing even now to recall my first involvement with a teen mother. I had heard that Julie (not her real name), a longtime participant in a community service program I directed, had gotten pregnant by a friend's boyfriend. When she stopped coming to my program, I went to visit her at the friend's apartment, where Julie had been living to escape beatings at home.

Sitting across the kitchen table from a silent Julie, I felt stunned, and questions shot through my mind: *Is she a slut? Did she want to have sex with her friend's boyfriend? Did she seduce him, as her friend accused? Did he rape her? What really hap-*

pened? But I couldn't bring myself to mention the pregnancy. It wasn't just that she'd been having sex or that she'd had sex with a man in his twenties; as a teenager, I'd done that myself. Julie had crossed that psychologically abhorrent line: The result of her sexual activity was going to be *visible*. I could no longer fit her into the neat and innocent category of "Abused teen trying to make good of her wretched life." And I was disappointed. She was to be one of my success stories, but she'd gone and ruined her life—and, consequently, a portion of mine.

Still, I wanted to hear her side of the story and offer my support, but with my twisted thinking, I had no idea how. Finally, I blurted, "You look like you've gained a little weight." She shrugged and remained silent. Embarrassed and ashamed, I left. I never saw Julie again.

Years passed, and I turned to writing novels for young people and teaching writing classes. At age thirty-five, having just completed my second novel, I gave birth to a son. I was as unprepared for the disruption to my carefully crafted writer's life as I was for the avalanche of maternal love and devotion that consumed me. My worldview shifted. Writing and teaching were still important, but they moved to the back burner.

In the writing lull that followed my son's birth, I trained as a childbirth educator and doula.[1] I provided labor support to birthing women, several of whom were in their teens. I was struck by the young moms' intense love for their children—so like my own; their awareness of the challenges they were up against; and their efforts to be good parents while continuing to grow and to lead full lives. I was impressed with how attentive

---

[1] *Doula* refers to a woman with training and experience in childbirth who provides continuous emotional, physical, and informational support to the mother before, during, and just after childbirth.

they were to their babies. I also witnessed the relentless emotional pummeling they received from doctors and other hospital staff, not to mention from myriad insensitive strangers on the street. I recognized people's feelings of discomfort around pregnant or parenting teens. I'd certainly had them myself.

I remember sitting in 1998 with Paula (not her real name), a sixteen-year-old pregnant client, and her nineteen-year-old boyfriend as they preregistered at the hospital where she would give birth. After asking many questions and recording Paula's answers, the intake worker looked up. "Who will be taking care of the baby?"

Paula looked confused. She glanced at her boyfriend and back to the woman. "We will," she answered.

The woman laid her pen on the desk and leaned forward. "Taking care of a baby is a big job. Who is going to help you?"

Paula's face darkened. She looked wary. "My boyfriend and I are going to take care of the baby."

The woman sighed and wrote something on her form. I wouldn't have minded questions about support. *Every* new parent needs support; my own midwives had asked if my husband and I would have extra help after the birth of our child. But this intake worker hadn't simply asked about help for the couple. She'd clearly implied that the couple was not capable of caring for their child, although none of their answers to her routine questions had indicated that.

The insensitive treatment Paula and my other young clients received angered me. I funneled that anger into my work. I urged my clients to be assertive in seeking the information, support, and resources they needed. I helped them write lists of questions for their too-busy obstetricians, hooked them up with La Leche League and WIC [the Supplement Food Program for Women, Infants, and Children] and other young moms, and smoothed hair out of their sweaty faces as they pushed their babies into the world.

As my son grew older, my energy for writing and teaching returned. With a friend, I volunteered to teach a weekly writing class to pregnant and parenting young mothers in a local alternative high school. The stories they wrote and read aloud saddened and inspired me. One woman described feeling too ashamed to reveal her pregnancy until she went into labor. A new mother wrote about saving money by living with an older sister who criticized her daily. Some described getting up at 5 A.M. to shepherd themselves and their children through dressing and breakfast and two or three bus rides to get to child care and school, then reversing the process at the end of the day.

As my respect and admiration for young mothers grew, I wanted to offer them a forum for sharing their voices and experiences so that others' eyes might be opened and their prejudices and preconceived ideas questioned. I decided to seek out women who had birthed in their teen years, engage them in a writing project, and from their work compile an anthology.

In October of 2000 I began posting calls for submissions on the Internet, mailing queries to high schools, colleges, and social service organizations, and placing magazine print ads. I asked for stories that showed the positive side of becoming a mother at a young age: What has worked for you? Who and what has helped you in your mothering journey? How do you cope with the prejudices you encounter, in yourself and in others?

I received two hundred submissions, plus a barrage of enthusiastic E-mails. The contributors wrote with infants asleep in slings in their laps and toddlers playing at their feet; they revised after long hours at jobs and during semester finals. I received notes saying, "Here is my revision. Tell me if anything else needs fixing." Music to my ears!

I asked for details, details, and more details. "I want readers to be able to put themselves in your shoes," I urged, "to hear, smell, feel, taste, and touch what you experienced." I had to remind some writers to tell their *own* story, not their boyfriend's, not their mother's.

I tried to include writers from across North America, women representing a range of ethnic, socioeconomic, religious, and political backgrounds. They don't see themselves as unique, just awakened. All have learned how to sidestep the unending onslaught of dire predictions and criticisms that impede their way. Every woman in this book has combined resourcefulness with a large measure of hope and confidence to forge a path for herself and her children. Some have relied on religious faith, some on renewed ties with family. Some got married. Some got divorced. Some simply learned how to ask for help.

The essays are grouped by subtopics—from the process of pregnancy to the trials of parenting, from the work of staying in school to the rewards of defying stereotypes—though some of the stories would fit well in several chapters. The topic of support, for instance, repeats like a drumbeat throughout this book. Each chapter closes with one question excerpted from a questionnaire I sent to several hundred current and former teen mothers, followed by a sampling of their varied responses. I didn't include stories by women who placed their children for adoption. That is a courageous and appropriate choice for some mothers, but I wanted to keep the focus on the positive experiences of young women who raise their children. They represent 90 percent of the roughly half-million teenage women who give birth each year in this country.

There have always been women who birthed in their teenage years, and there always will be. The beauty of the stories in this book—and the value for all of us—is that they show the gradual triumph of love and self-esteem in the face of relentless prejudice and discrimination. For those who find themselves on the path of motherhood at an early age—and for those who know or work with young mothers—it is my hope that *You Look Too Young to be a Mom* will offer encouragement, validation, and inspiration.

Deborah Davis
Seattle, Washington
July 2003

PART 1

Are You Still With Me?

ON FINDING SUPPORT FROM FAMILIES, LOVED ONES, AND MENTORS

I broke the news to Jared over chow mein at the China Clipper, a seedy Chinese cocktails and dance club. If there was a reason I later had a happy birth, it had its beginning right there in that booth with the peeling paint and yellowed walls, within earshot of the waitress with the grown-out roots. I don't remember what Jared said, only that his eyes didn't leave mine and he entered my lonely and fearful world with the warmth and courage to carry us through.

From then on, Jared's quiet strength was a part of every moment. If he was fazed by people's shocked responses and unsolicited opinions, he never let me know. He held me through my late night sobs and tolerated my early morning rants. He quit smoking as a show of solidarity with me. When our child, the picky customer, sent up an order, he promptly cooked it for me as I sat lethargically on the couch, breathing through another bout of nausea. He left his job at the gas station to come to my prenatal appointments and washed the smell of gasoline off his hands before touching my growing belly. He revered my changing shape and never complained about my erratic sex drive. And when I went into

*labor, he stayed with me the whole twenty-some hours, up to the emotional
climax, when he tearfully cut our baby's umbilical cord.*

—Jade Souza,
21, doula, homeless-youth worker,
mother, Olympia, Washington

For three and a half months during the making of this book,
my family and I lived in a small town in south India—a
country of one billion where for a large percentage of
women, marrying and becoming a teenage mother is the norm.
As is traditional in her culture, my young next-door neighbor
Bharti left her mother-in-law's home when she was eight months
pregnant with her first child to spend the last month of her pregnancy in her own parents' home, an hour's bus ride away. She
would stay there until she gave birth in a nearby hospital, then
continue living with her parents for three to four months after
the birth before returning to her husband and his family.

I visited Bharti when Balendra, her robust new son, was five
weeks old. Bharti looked calm and rested. "They do everything
for him," she explained, referring to her mother, grandmother,
three sisters, and assorted "aunties"—older women who may or
may not have been related to her.

Although I missed seeing the aunties give Balendra a massage,
I got to watch the baby's great-grandmother bathe him. She
hoisted her sari up over her knees, sat on the concrete floor of
their bathing area, and doused him with water scooped from a
barrel as he lay squirming on her bent legs. Then she dressed
him and, with his grandmother's help, slipped an ancient
Ayurvedic remedy into his grimacing lips.

"Do they let you do *anything* with him?" I asked the baby's
mother.

Bharti laughed, answering that they brought Balendra to her
for feeding and, at night, for sleeping.

North America isn't India, of course, and if you don't have a large, helpful extended family nearby, how do you find support?

I heard from one writer whose family turned her out when they learned she was pregnant but whose boyfriend's family embraced her. Another writer made it through a vigorous film school program by creating a surrogate family with her closest friends, one of whom repeatedly took care of her daughter when she had to edit her films late into the night. Some young mothers have found aid and encouragement through public or private agencies, Internet message boards and chat rooms, or school programs for pregnant and parenting teens. All, it seems, have had to be willing to seek out and ask for the assistance that they wanted and needed. One mother in my teen parent writing class said, "There's plenty of help if you have a good attitude. It comes if you are open to it."

The women in this chapter found—or gave—support in ways that they least expected. Jennifer Bottoms Bryant turns fearfully to a mother she'd frequently disappointed. Mindy Diehl takes a risk with a parent she'd deemed entirely wrong for the job of providing emotional support. Chris Vitale encounters a mentor whose respectful manner sets her on a whole new path. Donna Dahlquist offers wise thoughts on how to reply to a teen who tells you she's pregnant, and Pat Beresford discovers that revealing her own teen mom story to a struggling new mother can have a profound and positive outcome.

Jennifer Bottoms Bryant

Mother Love

graduated from high school on a hot day in June 2000. Sitting on an uncomfortable metal folding chair, wedged in between two hundred other eighteen-year-olds, I silently counted my pregnant classmates. Six. *Seven,* I reminded myself, discreetly brushing my fingertips across my stomach. Two weeks ago, when everyone else I knew was planning graduation parties and trips to visit colleges, I sat alone in the bathroom, a small white plastic stick in my trembling hand.

I decided to wait to tell my mother until after graduation. Two nights past the ceremony, I stood in the kitchen doorway, watching my mother wash dishes. I was tense, anticipating her reaction. I had disappointed her so many times—lying, sneaking out, failing classes at school, and more. Our relationship had improved and strengthened over the past year, but I didn't know how she would handle the news of my pregnancy. Would my news finally send her over the edge? What if she told me to leave? What if she stopped loving me? I cleared my throat. "When you're done, I need to talk to you," I said. "In private."

She looked up and smiled at me. "Okay." I walked past my younger brother and sister, who were watching television in the living room, and down the hall to my mother's bedroom. I sat on the edge of the bed and waited nervously. The minutes that passed felt like hours. Finally, I heard her footsteps in the hall. Mom walked into the bedroom, closed the door, and sat down next to me. "What's up?" she asked.

"Mom, I'm pregnant." There. I had said it. Now she knew I was a failure. I began to cry. "I'm sorry, I'm sorry. . . ."

She held me while I cried. "Shh," she whispered. "You don't ever have to apologize again." When I stopped crying, she asked, "Have you considered abortion or adoption?"

I shook my head vehemently. "No. I'm keeping it." I had already weighed my options. I knew that SUVs and picket fences weren't essential to being a good parent. My mother had raised me without either. Those kinds of things seemed insignificant compared to the magnitude of the love she had given me over the years. She was a single mother to my brother, sister, and me by the time I was eight. She worked full-time to provide for us, but no matter how tired she was, she always found a way to attend my school events, take us out for ice cream on hot evenings, and help us with our homework. Despite my age, I was ready to be this child's mother and to raise him with the same love and compassion that I had been raised with. I was prepared to hold my head high in the face of society's criticism and my own doubts. My baby wasn't even born yet, and already he was teaching me to stand up for myself in ways that mattered.

Mom made me an appointment with her OB/GYN. We went together. I stared in fascination at the tiny creature on the ultrasound screen. "Well, you're definitely pregnant," my mom said with a laugh.

In the months to come, my mother continued to attend my prenatal appointments with me. We shopped for maternity clothes together, wrinkling our noses at the frumpiest outfits and laughing in the dressing room at the ill-fitting maternity pants. When I decided to get an apartment with my boyfriend, she co-signed the lease for us and helped me pack and haul stuff from one place to the other. All of our friends and family pressured us to get married. Mom was the only one who didn't, but when my boyfriend became my fiancé, Mom came with me to pick out fabric for my wedding dress. Together, we found a seamstress skilled enough to sew a dress that would accommodate my ever-expanding belly. My mother helped me coordinate the wedding and reception. She knew we wanted to keep it simple, but she made sure we weren't lacking in the basics—a three-tier wedding cake, a decorated banquet hall, and lovingly hand-assembled bouquets.

During the last trimester of my pregnancy, my mother came over to help me assemble furniture for the nursery. As we worked side by side, Mom revealed bits and pieces of her life to me: what it was like for her to be married at seventeen, what her pregnancy and my early years were like, the challenge of balancing marriage and mothering. She didn't have me, her first child, until she was twenty-four, but she understood what it was like to be a young mother and wife. I felt as though we were moving into a new phase of our relationship. No longer simply mother and child, we were now equals, bonded by common experiences.

Although many of my friends had left for college or simply lost interest in me once I became pregnant, Mom managed to get enough people together for me to have a wonderful baby shower. Three weeks later I went into labor. I stayed at home with my husband until the contractions were strong and regular. Then I packed my suitcase and called Mom.

"We're on our way to the hospital!"

"I'll meet you there," she replied.

My mother held my hand, rubbed my back, and stayed with me throughout most of my labor. Her very presence was reassuring to me; after all, she had given birth three times, and she knew what I was going through. Mom, my husband, and I walked the fluorescent-lit halls together to speed up my labor. She held me close and talked to me to take my mind off the pain of the contractions. When I was exhausted after two hours of pushing, she encouraged me to keep going. After twenty-eight hours of labor, my sweet son was born. My husband, mother, stepmother, and mother-in-law were all there to welcome him into the world. Mom cut the umbilical cord when my husband declined the offer. As my baby lay on my chest, staring up at me with wise blue eyes, I fell in love. I understood fully why my mother had stood by me and supported me in all of my decisions. I smiled at Mom, and felt a new connection between us.

My mother continues to play a strong role in my life as I go about the daily business of raising my now eighteen-month-old son. She is proud of him and of me. My son always has a smile for his grandmother; he knows that she will be there for him, just as she was for me, to read stories, give hugs, and play together. I know that I can always depend on her when I am in need of help, advice, or a sympathetic ear. Our relationship is stronger than ever, and I am lucky to have her in my life. My son gave me my backbone and a desire to fly. But it was my mother who gave me wings.

Jennifer Bottoms Bryant *lives in Virginia with her son. She spends her time writing, attending college, and scraping Play-Doh off the carpet.*

Mindy Diehl

Dealing With Dad: From Fear to Family

The summer I was sixteen, I met a guy named Mark. He was new in town and he was an older man. Mark had been in the army, and he impressed me with his fascinating stories about being in different parts of the world. He was from another state and made it sound wonderful. Within a week of starting to date he asked me to marry him. He promised me a November wedding and a house out in Colorado and that we'd live happily ever after. I felt lucky and loved. Mark had promised me the world, and I was willing to take it.

Late that summer, my period was a week late. I had not used any protection with Mark. He claimed he didn't know how to use a condom, and I was so caught up in the relationship at the time that I didn't care what the consequences might be. When a pregnancy test showed positive, I began to cry uncontrollably. I had no idea who to talk to or what to do. My mother figured it out shortly thereafter. She knew I was late for my period because we always got them at the same time of the month. She asked me if I was pregnant, and when I told her yes, I saw a smile of satisfaction on her face. She told me she knew I would get pregnant, that she had been waiting for my promiscuous ways to catch up with me, that she knew I was a slut. She made me call my dad at work and tell him. It seemed she was satisfied that Daddy's little girl was pregnant, as if she finally had a reason to try to make my dad not love me.

Dad said we would discuss this when he got home. Nervously Mark and I sat on the couch and waited. Even before this, a wall had formed between my dad and me that neither of us had been able to break down. Now I felt guilty, and I was scared that this was the end of any reconcilable relationship with him.

When my dad arrived, he was calmer than I had anticipated. He said that no matter what happened, he'd be there for me. Little did I know then how much that promise would mean. He set some guidelines: I would continue my education and work after school. Mark was to get a good job, a nice car, and an apartment, and then maybe Dad would sign for me to marry before I was eighteen.

At first, it appeared to be working out. Mark seemed genuinely excited about having a baby. We picked out names and started a birthing class together. But Mark didn't live up to his promises. He started getting possessive, following me to work and watching my every move. He'd sit and stare at me while I was working. He had a job, but he didn't work regularly. His car was falling apart, and he seemed to have no intention of getting an apartment that would suit our needs.

I got sick of this real quick. I told Mark I needed a break. I needed to figure out what I wanted in my life. I can't remember ever being more confused. In some ways, I wanted our baby more than anything, but I was scared to death, knowing that I alone would be responsible for the new life.

After only a week Mark had a new girlfriend and was showing her off everywhere—attending my friend's funeral, making out in front of our house. I knew for sure now that I was alone. I felt miserable. I hated school, and my home life was terrible. I fought constantly with my mother and didn't really get along with anyone at school anymore, even the other pregnant girls. My mother gloated over the fact that I was pregnant and had committed the ultimate sin. She reminded me constantly of how terrible and useless I was.

I now had a birthing class to go to, but who would go with me? I had no close friends, and my mother could not handle it emotionally, nor did I want her to be there. After a brief family discussion, we all decided it would be best for Dad to take me. I saw this as my chance. I could show him that I wanted this baby and would do the best I could for it. I was determined that once and for all I would make something of myself.

So Dad came to my teen birthing class with me. There I was with a bunch of other pregnant sixteen- and seventeen-year-olds who had either their mother or their doting boyfriend with them. I had my father, a man in his mid-thirties, with graying hair and a mustache, who didn't talk much, the only grandfather in the class to attend—but those classes began to mean the world to me. Slowly, Dad and I began working things out. I began spending more time at home and confiding in him. I became less scared of him. Inside, he was just a person whose oldest child needed him.

Dad would work all day, then take me to my class. I remember once when we were learning infant safety. It seemed funny to me that this huge, scary-looking guy was holding a doll, learning how to save a choking baby. But I also realized that he was seriously going to help me with this child! In moments like that I really started appreciating my dad more.

When we learned I was to have a boy, Dad and I went shopping for the baby's needs. Dad liked to shop, but he was a guy and shopping for a baby was a new experience. Neither of us knew the difference between a crib sheet and a receiving blanket, but through our little shopping trips we learned together. We bought little boy outfits with trucks and tools on them. We bought baby toys and a Pooh crib set. We actually had fun. Dad was in the toy aisle one day and found a little musical Big Bird that attached to the stroller or crib. I felt touched and proud, because it showed me that my dad wanted this child in his life. My son still has it.

Dad and I continued our weekly birthing class, and on the last day he received a special diploma for being the only grandfather in the class. He was very proud of himself but told everyone that he was only being there for his daughter. I was also proud. We had accomplished the class together!

The pregnancy went along well until an ultrasound at seven months revealed that my son had an irregularity in the left side of his heart. His upper left chamber was smaller than the right chamber and he had a tiny hole in one of the ventricles. I was very upset. I thought, *How can I take care of a child who may not be perfectly healthy?* My parents were upset as well, but in different ways. My mother said she wouldn't be able to handle living with a baby who might need medical care. My dad was worried about my baby. We went to a specialist who did Level II ultrasounds and discovered that there was indeed a defect, but the doctors couldn't tell for sure how it would affect my son's life. I remember lying there watching my dad look at my son on the ultrasound. He was visibly in awe of the sight of my unborn son's tiny nose and little cheeks. He even took one of the pictures to work with him.

On the night of May 7, 1998, a week past my due date, I went into labor. Dad suffers from migraines that can leave him ill for days. Unfortunately, this night he had one of them. During a migraine, lights bother him and he often can't handle much noise. Dad and I made our way to the hospital, and he suffered with his own pain as I labored through the night and into the next morning. He could barely keep his eyes open and sometimes wore sunglasses to shield his eyes from the light, but he never left my side. He cracked jokes to make me laugh yet was very aware of the pain I was in. I had opted for as little medication as possible, so I tried not to let on how bad it hurt; still, he knew by the look on my face and he said later he could see the pain in my eyes.

He encouraged me the entire time. He told me he was proud of me and that I was doing a really good job and that he was right there and wouldn't leave my side. I did go without any pain medication until it was time to push. By then I was tired and just wanted a little Demerol to ease the pain. At 10:06 A.M. I gave birth to a healthy eight-pound, six-ounce boy named Taylor. Dad had the honor of cutting the cord and was the first person in the family to hold my son. I think that was only the second time I had ever seen my dad cry. He told me he was proud of me, and for once in my life I was able to believe it. He saw what I was capable of doing, and it seemed to amaze both of us that I could be that strong.

When Taylor was less than an hour old he had an EKG done on his heart. Luckily, the defect had corrected itself, and Taylor now had only a slight heart murmur. We were all very relieved with the outcome!

I am proud to be a young mom. The whole experience brought on a lot of changes for me personally. It was so hard for me to let my guard down and show my dad who I really was. I wasn't necessarily trying to hide myself; I just didn't think he'd understand me. I'd always wanted to go to my mother to talk about sex or how to dress stylishly or how to apply makeup or shave my legs, but I couldn't. I can't even define the moment I really started opening up and going to him for things like that, but I do know it took time. It's different to go shopping for baby clothes with my father. Or to ask for an opinion on whether to breastfeed or bottle-feed. Or to share my experiences in love and relationships. It makes things even more special, because now I can talk to my dad about anything. Kind of like an all-in-one parent.

Five years later my life is better. Taylor is now in preschool and a healthy, affectionate little boy. I have a dedicated and hardworking husband who is a wonderful dad to my son and is planning to officially adopt him. Three years ago I gave birth to our daughter, Adrienne Sierra, named after my dad's deceased mother. Dad got the easy part this time and baby-sat Taylor while my husband took my side as I gave birth. We kept in close contact over the phone, and as soon as our girl was born he was the first person we called. My dad has an incredible bond with my children and plays a very active role in their lives, babysitting and spending special time with each of them. My daughter loves to sit on my dad's lap after dinner. Oftentimes you'll see her curled up on his lap fast asleep. My parents have divorced, and my mother is no longer a part of my life or my children's.

I am no longer the daughter who needs to be reminded of what to do. I am a happy, secure wife, mother, and daughter as well as a strong young woman. My dad enjoys my kids but knows that it's my husband and my job to raise our kids. I see my dad in a whole new light, and I have more respect for him. I am no longer afraid to voice my opinion or go to him with a question. I feel as if we are now equals.

Mindy Diehl *is a twenty-two-year-old full-time mother. Married for four years, she lives with her family in a small town in northern Pennsylvania. Her hobbies include reading, fishing, walking, crafts, and playgroups with other mothers. She is an active member of her county's Head Start program as well as a moderator for a Web site that supports teen mothers. In 2001, her son Taylor was diagnosed with an Auditory Processing Disorder, a learning disability that impairs the way a child can communicate verbally and receptively. Mindy is active in finding out more about this disorder and the long-term effects of it.*

Chris Vitale

A Journey to Self

Being sixteen and pregnant was still pretty uncommon in my neighborhood in the 1970s—uncommon enough to take a fairly bright but quiet and nondescript young girl right out of oblivion and thrust her into the spotlight, a place she'd never been and never wanted to be. I was one of those teenagers who wouldn't get a second glance: kind of short, average build but rather flat-chested, curly, plain brown hair, and pimples. I always chose to be a silent member of the crowd, never drawing too much attention.

Becoming pregnant changed everything. Now I was on my way to a new school, Educational Medical, just for pregnant teens, to be out of sight and out of mind. The only thing I knew about "Ed Med" was that everyone there was either pregnant or had already had their baby. The program was designed to support girls through pregnancy and childbirth while maintaining their high school education. It was the only way I could see to continue my education, so I figured I'd give it a chance. As the car turned up toward the school, I caught my breath. It was hard to believe that one little baby could have tossed my life into the air in just a few short weeks. I had no idea what I was in for!

Changing schools never seemed like a choice; it was something I had to do. I felt so much support from my teachers and the administration at my regular school, yet I was almost ridiculed by my peers. I couldn't take the torture of their whispers and giggles or the absurd questions into my personal life, which now seemed to be an open book. I'd always done well in school and still had many dreams to strive for. In my heart I knew I really was still the same girl. I didn't just suddenly become a loser! I wanted to believe I could succeed, but I expected to have to do it on my own.

As my mom and I walked into the school, I remember thinking how much it didn't look like a school and how incredibly quiet it seemed. It was dim inside; there were hardly any windows at all. Mrs. Brown was waiting for us in her office. She was a sturdy-looking African-American woman who didn't smile much but didn't seem at all unpleasant. She sat across her desk from me and directed all of her questions to me, even when my mom tried to answer. She filled me in on all of the specifics of the school and then asked me what my plans were.

"Plans? Plans for what?" I had no idea what she was getting at.

"What are your plans for your life?" she asked.

Since the day I acknowledged my pregnancy, no one had asked me that! Everyone thought my life was over. I took a deep breath and said, "I always wanted to be a nurse."

Even though things were pretty bad between my mom and me, when I watched her walk out of the door and leave me behind I felt so afraid, like I was back in second grade. I wanted to run after her, but something stopped me. This was my first realization that I was alone and that now was the time to find the strength I had buried deep within. But mostly all I felt was a huge lump right in the center of my chest.

Within the first hour of being at the new school, I was surprised and a bit uneasy to realize I was the only white girl. Coming from a city school with a pretty diverse student population, I was truly in the minority for the first time. Once again, the girl who took extra steps to blend in was standing out. I tried to keep to myself, to look as though I was reading or writing, and definitely not make eye contact. This technique got me through the first class, but then I had to go to breakfast, which this school served in the middle of the morning in an effort to meet our prenatal nutritional needs. Before coming to this school I'd never even eaten breakfast! The cafeteria was about the size of two classrooms, with long tables instead of desks. Everything in front of me was fresh and wholesome— fruit, milk, cereal without added sugar, breads, peanut butter, and jelly. This was hardly what I was used to eating at school, but I figured they must know what's best.

I could tell by the lively conversation in the room that this was going to be a hard place to go unnoticed. I grabbed a seat in the corner and pretended to read my cereal box over and over again. A girl about my age walked over to me and said, "When are you due?"

Confused, I said, "What?" I didn't have a clue what she was talking about.

She smiled and pointed to her stomach.

"Oh." I laughed. "In March." I'd never been asked anything about my pregnancy in such a nonthreatening way. She sat down, and we started talking about being pregnant, being sixteen, being in a new school, teachers, boys, and parents. Her name was Mary, and although we'd come from different places with different backgrounds, we couldn't have been more the same. For the first time in weeks, I felt like I was me again—just a girl, moving through life.

Mary introduced me to a lot of the other girls. As with Mary, I felt a connection to them faster than I'd ever felt with another peer in my life. Because this was the only school of its kind in the area, the girls were from all over the county. It took me a few weeks to realize why I was the only white girl. I wasn't stupid, and I knew getting pregnant had nothing to do with race, so where was everyone else?

About every three to four days a white girl would come to the school. Consistently, she would keep her distance and build a wall between herself and the outside world. Usually, we'd try to let her settle in a bit, but at the end of the day we'd never see her again. Just like that, they never came back, not once! We weren't sure why they never returned; maybe they didn't feel like they fit in, maybe it was a race issue, or maybe they just gave up. One afternoon I asked Mary why she spoke to me on my first day. She told me I didn't have "the wall." Although I was keeping to myself I wasn't saying "Stay away," so she didn't.

As I became comfortable in my new school, I settled into a new perspective. I was already six months pregnant but was only just beginning to see the reality of my life without a dark shroud of shame. At school we were all one, and I began to see and feel the connection of motherhood in a way I never knew was possible. Despite our youth and differences, we were connected by the pain and disillusionment of many of the adults in our lives and by the loss of "being a kid"—and more importantly, by the life we each carried inside. As we learned about our bodies and our babies, the wonder of it all allowed us to feel positive. The outside world could be dark and grim, with lots of negative language and feelings—but when we came through the doors of our school, the whole atmosphere was different.

Nobody pretended our lives would be all smooth sailing, but everyone at that school gave us hope. We were allowed to dream, and we were assured we could succeed—in fact, it was an expectation. Mrs. Brown spoke to us as young women with responsibilities—to ourselves, our children, and society. She was direct and at times brutally honest. She never sugarcoated anything, and she never accepted anything but our best. Behind those walls we knew we would have to work much harder than other girls our age; we had responsibilities they didn't have. We had another life to consider. Everything we did focused on that one simple reality. . . . We were no longer one.

When I left Ed Med to do home schooling before my baby was born, I kept in touch by phone and letters with the school staff and the friends I'd made there. I knew that if I had not attended the school for pregnant teens, I might not have made it to graduation. I don't think I could have taken the pressure of being at my regular school. I did graduate with my class at my high school. It was awkward and uncomfortable, but I had a point to make. Even when one of my classmates said, "I didn't think they'd let you graduate, since you missed so much school," and I wanted to punch him and let him know how hard I'd been working, I didn't. I just smiled and said, "Yeah, it's amazing isn't it?" I was so far beyond these kids in my life; it was just time to move on.

I had a beautiful daughter, and we've been growing up together for twenty-seven years! I took everything positive from my school experience with me through the rest of my life, and to this day I keep those lessons close to my heart. I don't give up. If something doesn't work, I find another way. I don't allow anyone to beat me down. I find the people who are there for me and with me, and I stay close to them.

About twenty-five years after leaving the school for pregnant girls, I was sitting at a conference where I was a guest speaker, and one of the other speakers had just taken the podium. She was a sturdy-looking African-American woman who didn't smile much but didn't seem at all unpleasant. Her name was Mrs. Brown . . . and as I listened to her I realized she was *my* Mrs. Brown. The woman who knew I had a life, who knew I would be something, was right in front of me, and my heart was beating almost out of my chest! I sat there, watching her lips move but not hearing her words. In my mind I replayed the past twenty-five years—where I had been and what I had accomplished; painful situations and hopeless times; feeling afraid and feeling so proud—and in every one of my significant moments, Mrs. Brown was there. When I had cause to celebrate she was there smiling. When I wanted to give up she was there, not smiling but expecting me to move forward. This woman who had been a stranger had such a profound effect on my life because she was exactly what I needed her to be at exactly the right time.

I have to believe that we are all given those opportunities. If we are open to it, what we need is always close by. When I feel myself giving in, I remember Mrs. Brown, and I look all around me for what I need. I've always found it.

I spoke to Mrs. Brown when she stepped down from the stage. Before I had the chance to explain who I was, the tears were flowing freely from my eyes, and she put her arms around me. She remembered me. She remembered the day I walked through the doors of the school and the conversations we had; she remembered where I went to college and where I got my first job as a nurse. She even remembered how hard I tried not to be noticed. I felt such joy and complete satisfaction to stand before her and thank her for finding in me that which I could not find alone.

By Mrs. Brown's example I was there when someone needed me to point out her gifts. By her example I have never become complacent when my energy would move someone forward on his voyage. I have always remembered how a single person, a stranger, set me on the path of my journey and gave me the greatest gift I've ever received: self-esteem.

Chris Vitale *is a registered nurse with twenty-three years of experience working with children and teens. She has a master's degree in nursing education, with a focus on community education and outreach, and is the injury prevention coordinator at Children's Hospital of Pittsburgh. Chris has worked in the clinical, administrative, and education areas of nursing, but has found her utmost satisfaction working in the community. She has experience in school systems from grades K-12 and as a prevention specialist, providing education and intervention in drugs and alcohol, violence, grief and loss, and family transitions. Her greatest joy has been as wife to Tony and mom to her three children, Mandi, Chelsea, and Colin. With three beautiful grandchildren to keep her young, she loves hearing people say, "You don't look old enough to be a grandma!"*

D o n n a   D a h l q u i s t

Welcome to Motherhood

When I gathered up all my naive pluck and went to Planned Parenthood, before she would do the pregnancy test the woman made me promise that I would not freak out. I hadn't thought about freaking out till then. After she drew the blood from my chilled arm, I sat at a school desk in the hallway and listened to her loudly tell a couple who obviously were just learning English all about how easy and good the abortion would be. The man and woman sat leaning into each other and away from the counselor, as she repeated in ever-louder-and-simpler terms what lay ahead. I wasn't sure if they were having a hard time understanding the language or knowing what they wanted to do with their pregnancy.

When my turn came, I was humiliated to have tears drip down my inflamed cheeks as she told me the test was positive. She reminded me in a schoolteacher's voice that I had promised not to freak out. Much of what she said is a blur punctuated by my compliant nods and escalating desire to bolt from that cinderblock and linoleum room. I do remember her telling me she was so nauseous during her pregnancy that she had to be hospitalized and couldn't stand the sight of a penis for a very long time. I was less reassured by this welcome to motherhood than determined to be positive about being pregnant and to keep any complaints I might have to myself.

I remember that my girlfriends' reactions were all the same. They would go blank for a moment, then quickly offer to hold my hand and drive me to the clinic. More often than not that was the last I saw of them until it was time to come see the baby. Some I have never seen since.

I also very clearly remember calling my mom. Although I was only seventeen, I had been living on my own for a long time. I tried to make small talk by asking what she was doing. When she told me she was crocheting a tablecloth for my grandma, I told her to forget about that and start making baby booties. She said, "Oh, shit."

Many years ago I read a "Dear Abby" column in which someone asked what she should say to an acquaintance who had announced her engagement to a man who she thought was a bad marriage prospect. Abby responded that the only appropriate response was to say, "Congratulations." I feel the same is true when someone tells you they are pregnant, no matter how young she is or how rough you think it is going to be for her. Look her in the eye, smile, and say, "Congratulations." And, if at all possible, you should mean it.

Donna Dahlquist *is the youngest in a long line of independent women who have deep roots in a small town in western Washington, as well as the delighted parent of three diversely talented sons—Chad, 21; Gerrit, 17; and Colin, 12— who have been glad to have "a young mom." As a truly reluctant writer, she is surprised and pleased to find her words being published and hopes this book will contribute to a much-needed paradigm shift about teen motherhood.*

Donna graduated from the University of Washington School of Social Work in 1997 and now works at a multifaceted nonprofit agency providing community access services to adults with developmental disabilities. She enjoys tending her animals and garden, creating mixed-media art, and celebrating life with good food, friends, family, and song.

Pat Beresford

Revelation

I should have been more anxious, given the day. In twenty minutes I would be standing on the stage of Carnegie Hall to deliver the 150th Psalm. I was president of Walton High School, Class of 1962, accepted to a college that had filled my milliner mother and my union-organizing father with pride, and now was to speak in front of almost a thousand people. But what South Bronx girl could be anxious at the thought of speaking at Carnegie Hall when she'd had morning sickness just a few hours before?

What should have been the happiest day of my young life had curdled into a mix of fear, shame, and misery that I could not shake, especially at 7 A.M. I was a *good girl*. My boyfriend and I had practiced what we had been convinced would be the safest form of birth control—the rhythm method, withdrawal—and only once. Once! Maybe it wasn't pregnancy at all. I'd read a lot of anthropology in my senior year; perhaps I was in the grip of a mysterious Amazonian jungle illness that attacked South Bronx Jewish near-virgins, leaving them nauseous every day and missing their period each month until they went off to college.

Forty years have passed since that day, and I've told my story many times. Sometimes I begin with humor, sometimes with sadness, once in a while with fortitude. Whatever the initial

tone, it never lasts long, for where the story eventual~~ly~~
at shame. My shame—over the hurt I knew I gave my p~~a~~
those friends who turned away, the reproaches I felt from fam~~il~~y
members (soon extended to in-laws), the disappointment in the
eyes of teachers who had written those letters of reference and
believed so much in what I would become.

Today, when I think of the pain I caused and that others cast
upon me, shame's red, jagged edges can still kindle hurt that I
am careful to reveal. Never is this care greater than when I'm
talking with the girls with whom I now work, for they too are
pregnant. My story has taken me from the steps of Carnegie
Hall to the halls of Inwood House, a home for pregnant young
women in New York City's foster care system, where I am the
assistant executive director for programs.

When people compare my story to theirs, some have made a
simple morality tale of judgment: Pat, it's because you had shame
that you've done so well. As if I were some latter-day Hester
Prynne with a scarlet "A" on my still-developing seventeen-year-
old chest, to them the shame I'd felt had served as moral fiber to
help me overcome my obstacles of ten years of night school,
eventual single parenting of two girls, and owning and keeping
my own home. Many of today's young women live in a society
indifferent to marriage and filled with celebrity-soaked divorces
and couplings bordering on cliché; they have less reason for
shame and little for remorse at their swelling bellies. No remorse,
no redemption. I know better.

Following my high school graduation, some friends dropped
away, others went off to college. After my proverbial "shotgun
wedding," living with my eighteen-year-old husband, his parents,
and his identical twin brother off Grand Street on the Lower East
Side would have fit comfortably inside one of Dante's outer
circles of hell if it hadn't been so Jewish. Whether the dark mut-
terings of reproach, the discomfort of so many strangers living in

the same apartment, or the fact that my new husband and I, having dated for a little more than a year, barely knew each other, the days dragged by with the weight that chronic unhappiness demands. If it hadn't been for what I imagined was the beautiful little butterfly fluttering its wings within me, it would have been an even more lonely and desolate time.

Then December 31st arrived, complete with plans for a gala New Year's Eve including prime ribs at the famous Old Homestead Restaurant. Waking that morning, the thought of food made me sick all over again. I stayed nauseous throughout the day and into the evening. At six A.M., January 1, 1963, my water broke and I was off to the hospital. As my husband Moe and I tried quietly to leave the apartment, there at the front door stood my beaming father-in-law, freshly squeezed orange juice in hand. That the juice came up three hours later in the midst of labor could not blot out the loving gift proffered that New Year's Day. For some I may have been a cheap whore for nine months, but with the birth of my lovely Lisa, on the first day of 1963 I became, while not a Madonna, a sweet, young mother.

Downstairs at the hospital sat our friends Danny and Bob, the latter having thrown his jeans over his pajamas to be there. Next to them sat my mother and father, each more anxious than the other. Moe's sisters, brother, and parents arrived soon after. Smiling proudly, my mother-in-law informed me the next day that Lisa had been placed in the front row of the nursery "where all the beautiful babies are placed." I was so happy to see her smile that I believed her.

When working with the girls at Inwood House, I rarely tell my story as completely as this. Moments with a girl may activate a snatch of memory, whether the shared fear of morning sickness or the resonant shock on a fifteen-year-old's face at the sight of stretch marks on her still-developing young body. At such times, I keep my memories to myself, for the world of these girls often has little space for the story of my past. For far too many of these young adolescents—often since their early childhood—their world carries so little support that the task of daily living falls only on them. They will soon be caring for their child without benefit of husband or kin, relying on our foster parents or mother-baby group homes and residences to provide the nurture, support, and stability that they and their babies will need. To trot out my life's lessons would both detract from their moments of need and turn abstract and distant my own lived experience.

Nevertheless, there are exceptions where I take the risk of letting my story enter their own. One occurred with Shondelle (not her real name, of course), a beautiful African-American girl of sixteen who arrived at Inwood House three months pregnant. Shondelle's almond eyes were not quite vigilant but always aware, taking in her surroundings, a habit developed from experience with her overly harsh mother. Bright and curious, she would often visit my office on the first floor just to chat as I finished up my paperwork and filing, often well after the Maternity Residence dinner hour. She would ask about my job and what I did, showing an inquisitive mind and interest in the world that was hard to resist. In my position, I take special care not to encourage "therapeutic alliances" with the young women for whom Inwood House is home. Young women in the foster care system are required to tell their story over and over and over again. Each of our young women is assigned a social worker and has access to our psychologist, so while we encourage warm relationships with all staff, we take care to keep appropriate boundaries. Keeping boundaries made me approachable for Shondelle, for whom personal talk and "getting into her business" were off limits, even to her worker.

As we talked, she would relate some of her hopes for her baby: that she'd be the perfect mom; that he'd be her little man; that they'd have a nice apartment and she would have a good job. Such talk was as familiar as it was sadly unrealistic, for Shondelle's world lacked parents or kin. She, by choice, had no contact with her mentally ill mother but tried to keep involved with her very successful and "good" sister. While bright and creative, she was nowhere near to completing high school or getting a GED and often had difficulty in attending her high school program. Our caseworkers pushed her to attend class, but there were few others around to motivate her. She may have experienced less shame from every corner of society, but she faced bitter disapproval from her mother. While her belly was swelling, there was no soft, supportive balm of familial hands to pat the kicking legs of life she began to feel late in her fourth month of pregnancy.

Shondelle's baby boy arrived healthy and alert one fall afternoon, and suddenly she was gone from our residence and into one of our foster homes, cared for by a kind but in the end too-permissive woman. Shondelle, who resisted but was used to structure, did not do as well as we knew she could and was moved to a supportive but somewhat stern West Indian family. Shondelle would appear at our doors every once in a while to visit her former caseworker, never failing to drop in and see how I was. She talked about her good relationship with her new social worker and reminisced about our late night talks. She revealed, rather shyly, that she felt like a teacher's pet when she was, as she saw it, allowed to sit in my office and talk. An attentive mother, she was indeed trying to be a perfect mom to her remarkably beautiful baby.

While those in the field know all about strength and asset-based perspective and practice, Shondelle's comments were a powerful reminder that something as elemental as a little positive attention can make a big difference. The other difference I could not help but notice was that her slender young woman's figure had returned and she had added another inch to her height. What struck me yet again was the profound collision of childhood and adulthood faced by young women who, not even through puberty, see their bodies once again begin to take on yet another form. Like Alice in Wonderland, they find that the changes are unnerving. As Alice put it, "Oh, I'm not particular as to size . . . only one doesn't like changing so often, you know."

Shondelle and I continued to talk about safe topics, she about her efforts in the GED course that now filled a part of her day and I about the new programs we were introducing. Her opinion truly valued, she offered sage advice about what she thought would be "good for the girls at Inwood House." After a while, however, the director of foster care called to tell me that Shondelle, unhappy in her foster home, had gone AWOL. We called her mom, but her sister reported that she was not there. We called some of the young women with whom she was friendly, but they too had no idea (or wouldn't acknowledge) where she had gone. As she was a good mother, I was not worried that Shondelle would expose her child to harm, but I was worried not knowing where they were. Was she with her boyfriend? How long would it take for her to make contact with us? The other concern was that since her unauthorized departure was one our agency is mandated to report, she had put herself at risk of being seen as neglecting her baby by the child welfare system. Indeed, we reported her disappearance to the city's child welfare agency, and of course to the police.

Not long after, I began to get phone calls from Shondelle. While she left messages on my voice mail, she did not leave a return phone number. My job requires me to attend a vast number of meetings, and inevitably she called when I was not at my desk. The receptionist was told to come and get me from whatever meeting I was in, should Shondelle call when I was actually in the building. Two weeks went by like this. The saving grace, if there was one, was that in each and every call she assured me she and the baby were okay and that she would call again. Her affect seemed weary, but her voice was strong, and I thought her continued attempts at contact boded well.

When she appeared the first time, it was as if nothing unusual had happened. There she stood at my office door, looking tired, somewhat thinner, a bit unkempt but smiling. Her high cheekbones and beautifully chiseled chin, more prominent now, seemed to hold that brave smile in place. The dance began: me trying to find out what I needed to assure myself that she and her son were truly physically and mentally safe, without frightening her to the point of flight, and she telling enough to allay my anxiety without revealing too much. She was going "home" that afternoon, after she picked up the baby from "a friend's." She needed money. Wasn't there a stipend check for her from just before she AWOLed? There was, and I got it for her, but it was pitifully small.

Joking a bit about her "high fashion" cheekbones, I went with her to the dining room and got her some food. "I'm in a hurry," she said as she devoured the sandwich, milk, and cake that sat on the table and took the milk I offered for the baby. Before she bolted out the door, I told her I'd call her home to make sure she was okay. Three hours later, she had indeed gotten home but had been refused by her mother. No beseeching, pleading, or toughness on my part got her mother to back down.

"See?" Shondelle said. "This is why I didn't bring my son with me—too much damn screeching, too much like a nuthouse." My attempts to help her formulate a more appropriate plan for her son and herself were not going to happen with the pain of her rejection so raw and immediate. I focused on the immediate problem, and Shondelle told me she had a safe place to stay that night. My only request was that she call me in the morning.

A week afterward, with no reassuring phone calls in between, Shondelle reappeared. Again, her son was not in tow. She was clearly worn, looking dirty and faint from need of food and water. This time she was too tired to keep up her defenses. Her sometimes tough, sometimes "too cool to care" personas were gone, vanished or vanquished by a hunger that was as deeply emotional as it was so palpably physical. This time food was followed by her request to "clean up a bit." Afterward we went for a walk. She told me she'd been staying with a variety of people but saw that though the baby was fed (said in the only boastful tone I ever heard from Shondelle), he was fretful. She recognized that all the moving around, strange beds, and lack of any regularity were making him cry and cling.

Back in my office, we talked about her returning to her foster home. Shondelle acknowledged that this foster mother was not bad or mean. She was strict, but even that didn't bother Shondelle because this woman was reasonable. However, it was not what she'd imagined. Shondelle thought that in a foster home she might find that idealized "good mother" who offers unconditional love. For the first time since I had met her, Shondelle began to talk about what was actually going on. We went back and forth between her feelings and concrete problem solving. At the end of the conversation she promised to come in with her son the next day and I promised to try to find another foster home.

As she got up to leave, she talked about the limits she now saw for the rest of her life—the truncated dreams for college, a career, a real boyfriend. She looked up and exclaimed, "You know, I know you're a social worker and listen to this stuff all the time, but you can't really understand, not really."

And so I told her. I told her that I did indeed understand. And then I told her why. Pointing to the picture of my family, which has always been in my office, she started to laugh, first from nervousness and then from relief. We sat and exchanged the *what did your family do/say* horror stories until we were both laughing and crying. She wanted to know how I had managed to get through school and, with no intent at irony, why I had married my daughter's father if I was so young. We talked and talked till we were both exhausted.

Being a hard-core pragmatist and at best an optimistic cynic, I do not believe in "presto-change-o" transformations. One woman's personal revelations carry little power for others. Certainly, in my adolescence and young adulthood, my own stubborn nature demanded that I make my own mistakes, sometimes repeatedly. So what followed astonished me. The next day dawned and I found myself in my office, trying to design a new program and beginning to wonder if Shondelle would keep her word, when I heard a baby's squeaks and Shondelle's voice. She kept her word, and I did mine.

Shondelle went to live with Ms. Dudley, a warm and intelligent woman whose foster daughter had just left care. Her gracious and welcoming home provided warmth and a picture of what life could be. Her standards were high, her rules clear and consistent. Shondelle tried it out. She reestablished her relationship with her social worker but continued to check in with me from time to time, always making a point to ask about my family.

Shondelle is now in college and her son is thriving. She would tell you that my story helped her truly believe that she could have the life she dreamed about before she became a mother. She says meeting people who are "real" and have struggled and succeeded makes an enormous difference because it turns the idea of accomplishment into a reality. Shondelle says that the best role models are people not so far away from you that they become superheroes. So, the convergence of emotional readiness, good timing, a good family fit, and perhaps a soupçon of encouragement from an older woman who had gone on to thrive after too-early parenting was the recipe for Shondelle's success. Stories like mine become the emotional power bars for young women who need hope based on reality and reality based on hope. The ten years of college at night, the variety of interesting roommates we had to live with in order to make ends meet, made an interesting tale. My story, so much like those of countless other young women who have experienced people's shock or outrage at young faces atop pregnant bodies, helped Shondelle borrow persistence, determination, and perspective. The power of these stories cannot be underestimated. One day, I am certain that Shondelle will pass along the lesson she learned and will tell her real story to another young woman just like herself.

When not keeping track of Inwood House's fifteen school-based teen pregnancy prevention sites, South Bronx after-school youth development program, mother-baby foster boarding homes, child care and family support programs, and fifty staff members, where can Pat Beresford *be found? She might be engrossed in deep conversation with her friends or children, at the ballet, or reading a feminist mystery deep into the night. Then again, she could be found hiking in the hills of upstate New York or sipping a glass of wine with her sweetheart as they debate the pros and cons of moving to Newfoundland if things continue to devolve politically.*

Speak Out!

What's best about becoming a mother at a relatively young age?

Having my daughter's friends ask if I'm her older sister.

Having the energy to chase an energetic kid.

With only half a generation gap between us, I know what kinds of drugs are circulating on the playground.

My body is designed to handle pregnancy and birth at this age.

I have not forgotten what it is like to be a kid myself, so I think I can reason and negotiate much better with my daughter; I can step back and look at things from her perspective.

My son's grandparents are still relatively young too, so they have lots of energy to play and be active with him.

I can't say that there is a best thing. I think just being a mother is great in and of itself.

Sharing pop culture—such as rap music—with my grown daughter.

When I was around other girls who had no children, their lives seemed frivolous and empty. I felt like I had so much more fulfillment in my life than they did, not to mention a real lesson in adulthood.

It has brought my family closer.

During their teen years, I was wise to their antics.

I'll have an empty home by forty-something, unlike my mother, who at fifty still has her youngest in high school.

Freedom from routine, open-mindedness, and a fuck-you attitude toward society.

It made me grow up.

My kids think it is awesome that they have such a hip mama who looks good, acts pretty cool, and was a kid more recently than a lot of their friends' 'rents!

Two Pink Lines

ON PREGNANCY, BIRTH, AND
LEARNING TO MOTHER

"He flew right out of you," the nurse said as she handed me my baby. And there he was, screaming his poor little heart out, looking like a wrinkly little potato with a head of jet-black hair. How crazy it seemed, that someone so precious could be mine. I saw things differently, like I was zapped into another person's life.

—Debra Sarmiento,
19, mother, student, Tucson, Arizona

One of my teenage doula clients—I'll call her Gina—phoned me two weeks before her due date. Her obstetrician had just informed her that, for medical reasons, she could not get an epidural, a type of regional anesthesia often used in childbirth to relieve pain. She was furious with him—*"He's the one who told me I should have an epidural in the first place!"*—and frightened about having to feel the pain of giving birth.

I reminded her that there were other options for pain relief, including injections of painkillers. She paused. "I *hate* getting shots," she said. Her vehemence startled me. To treat a medical condition discovered mid-pregnancy, Gina had to give herself a daily injection of medication. I'd seen her inject the drug calmly and competently on several occasions.

On my next couple of visits with Gina, we watched films of women giving birth without the use of any painkillers, and their relatively calm demeanor encouraged her. Previously withdrawn, Gina now began asking many questions that revealed her thoughtfulness, intelligence, and willingness to learn. She inquired often about pain. "Labor usually hurts a lot," I acknowledged. "But you can do it."

Early in Gina's labor, a nurse offered her a shot of Demerol, a synthetic narcotic painkiller and sedative commonly given to laboring women. Gina turned it down. A while later, as her labor intensified and her moans grew louder, Gina refused the nurse's second offer of Demerol. The pain she was experiencing had to be many times worse than that which a quick injection would cause her. Her determination to labor without medication astounded me.

After three hours in the hospital, Gina became discouraged when an exam revealed that she'd dilated only from three to four centimeters. The nurse leaned in close and urged her to accept the shot of Demerol now. "It'll take the edge off the pain and make your labor fly," the nurse promised.

"Okay," Gina assented unhappily.

The narcotic slowed her labor, and Gina slept. As the drug wore off, she resumed her hard work. She gripped her boyfriend's or my hands and panted. She moaned and ordered us to rub her aching back. In just a few hours, she delivered a healthy baby boy.

During a postpartum visit four months later, I was struck by Gina's transformation. First, her appearance was remarkably different. The dark circles she'd had under her eyes at the end of her pregnancy were gone. Her face was more animated, and her whole being seemed lighter, as if a huge burden had been lifted.

Second, she seemed significantly more self-assured. Previously almost dour, she now smiled a lot. She also revealed a new feisty side: As we talked about the birth, Gina bouncing her plump, bright-eyed baby on her knee, she said, "I didn't want that shot of Demerol. I didn't need it. That nurse was really pushy. And it didn't help at all with the pain. It just made it hard for me to concentrate. I wish I hadn't taken it." She then talked about her dreams for the future. I'd never heard her talk about the future at all, beyond her short-term plans for caring for her child.

Gina had entered into pregnancy full of fear. She'd taken along concerns about money, sadness over her mother's inability to guide and comfort her, and confused feelings about her changed body. The birth itself—which she'd anticipated with a great deal of anxiety—had helped her to transform. Maybe I shouldn't have been so surprised by the changes in her; I'd seen her frightened but also courageously coping during the intensity of labor. She'd had no idea she was so strong; now she knew.

Each of the writers in this chapter attests to her own transformation, though not all of them felt so spectacular right after giving birth. Rebecca Angel flounders and flourishes through her first tumultuous mothering year. West Coast literary hippie chick Mollie Elizabeth Wood shows how a birth is so much more than just a birth. Karen Landrum takes us along on her careful deliberation over whether or not to keep her child. Erica Wells gives her version of what to do with a life spinning out of control. And Rosie Allain offers up the delightful discovery of her amazing lactating breasts.

Rebecca Angel

Gift

Nineteen and pregnant—we just found out that morning. He asks if I still want to go on the picnic and see the new *Star Trek* movie that we had planned for today. I do. As I take the pickles out of the bag, I think, *How fitting.*

It is finals week. Aside from having to run out of the Spanish final to throw up, I do surprisingly well. I accept my choices, but I cry and cry and cry. My life is changing forever, forever; there is a life, a life in my belly. Yet I am with someone whose reaction to the extra blue line was "Well, we wanted to have children one day. . ." What about all the girls who go through this alone?

I am the first in my group of friends here at college or back home to get pregnant. Why couldn't it have been someone else, and then I could say, "Wow, glad that's not me." A "friend" tells me that now I'm just a statistic. What a stupid thing to say; we're all statistics, somehow, someway.

We tell my mother together and she is surprised, but just gives the hugs I need. My father is even more shocked: "My baby's going to have a baby!" We tell my boyfriend's mother while she's driving, probably not the best place. None of them offers harsh or condescending words to our faces. I don't want to know what's said behind our backs.

I search for another pregnant girl on campus while walking between classes but never see one. I just want to meet someone's eyes and, without saying a word, give an *I know what you're going through* look. People hold doors open for me, smiling, but I know their thoughts. I'm the one who helps the other girls to remember to take their little pills.

My uncle says I glow, and he means it. When I am with my family, I snuggle into their nest, lean on the father of my child, and feel my baby tumble around. Three P.M. is when the baby's most active, just in time for social psychology class. I'm constantly grabbing the hand of the boy who sits next to me to feel her kicks.

"It's like *Alien,*" he says.

I do better that semester than any other. I watch other students fret about tests, and I think, *Like that's really important? I've got a life in me!* I study for the birth, reading everything I think I need to know. I'm a good little student and somehow find out about natural birth and attachment parenting. That sings in me. I came to college in the country to get away from the city. Of course I'll be a country mama, all gentle and calm. Every day I play the piano in a practice room on campus. I wonder if, when my baby is grown up, the sound of Rachmaninoff will bring back feelings of warmth, security, and love. That would be cool.

Sixteen hours, natural childbirth—a feat I will talk about afterward like men talk about war. My stretch marks are my battle scars, all the more worthy because I must constantly fight the people around me: "No, I don't want any drugs." I thought they were supposed to *support* me. A sixteen-year-old girl is in the next room, just starting labor; the midwife hopes I don't yell too loud and scare her. The last hour, I sleep between contractions, thirty seconds or less. Then I wake up screaming. Finally I cannot take any more and start pushing. I don't care if I don't feel the urge; I'm done with this.

My midwife jumps up from the chair. "You're pushing?"

Suddenly lights jump on, I am checked to see if I am dilated enough, and am given the okay. Whatever. I would push anyway. I vaguely hear someone say to push between the contractions, so I push between *and* during. Fifteen minutes later the baby comes out, "all contracted, and then puffs out, like a balloon," as my fiancé says. At least I didn't get an episiotomy.[2] The midwife said she had the scissors in hand but remembered that I had said *absolutely* not. Scary.

I hear the cry and sink down, not caring when they take her away. I'm too overwhelmed.

A nurse comes up to me, "Don't you want to know?"

"Know what? Oh, yeah!"

"It's a girl."

I smile and wonder why they are not bringing her to me. We think our daughter will die from all the "emergency procedures" they put her through. She has no color when born, gets it within seconds—"Quick, give her oxygen." She gurgled a little— "Quick, give her an X ray." An X ray? We sit alone in the birthing room and wonder if God just wanted us to go through the pregnancy but not be parents yet. At that point I'm not even sad; I just want to sleep.

But she is fine. The doctor was worried about being sued later, I suppose, so ran fifty million tests on my poor baby. *You jerk. Don't you know that the first two hours after birth are critical for successful breastfeeding?* After twelve hours, we get to hold her. Eyes like a fawn and cheeks made for kissing, that's what my little girl is made of.

We struggle. It takes two weeks for my daughter to learn to open her mouth wide enough for breastfeeding; the nurses gave her a pacifier in the hospital. My bleeding doesn't stop until eight weeks after giving birth. Why didn't anyone think there was something wrong with that? Plus, my eyes hurt from staring at my daughter so much. Not that I'll stop—she's just so

---

[2] Surgical incision of the perineum at the end of the pushing phase of labor to facilitate birth.

cute. I mean *really* cute. Yeah, I know you think your baby's cute, but mine really is! We are alone in a one-bedroom apartment. She is born in January, so I don't want to go out much. Our antenna doesn't pick up local networks; we become regulars at Blockbuster. In the five months that I am in that apartment after the birth, each of my friends from college visits once. I have a nurse who visits me once a week for the first month because I am "at risk," aka a teenage mother. I don't mind; she's someone to talk to.

My boyfriend and I struggle. I think it's because we are so young. My heart needs time to expand. She has taken over all of it. I have baby-vision glasses. I look at my now-fiancé and can find no love for him. This worries me somewhere in the back of my mind, but the baby's crying. This, of course, means that I'm crying. Some days I manage to fold clothes, but not much else. My fiancé takes classes, goes to work, and comes home to do everything else. He says he wishes I weren't even there, that way he wouldn't expect any help. I feel helpless and wonder if we are hopeless. I don't tell anyone we are in trouble—they would probably think it's because we're immature. We can't even work it out now, but we'll be moving in a few months to where he starts his Ph.D. program; we'll talk then. I'm holding out for the summer. If we can just get to the summer, everything will be okay.

My mother is planning the wedding. She calls for my input, but I don't care—my baby is crying. One day a miracle happens. I have to take a shower, I *have* to, so I get the car seat and put her in it, praying for five minutes. Instead, she falls asleep and I am in a water cocoon for twenty minutes. The only prayer I have is that no matter what, my daughter knows that she is loved. If I can accomplish that, I'm a good mommy. I have no instrument here, so I sing to her. When I think I have run out, I reach deep into me and find more. I am amazed at the number of songs I can remember and the memories that are attached to them. Somewhere in my daughter's unconscious is the soundtrack of my life.

Six months after her birth, my eyes are fully open. Looking back, I realize I had postpartum depression. I have been slowly awakening to the world beyond my daughter. I am married to a wonderful guy. Before this I could only vaguely recall our love for each other. I had those memories, and they couldn't all have been false. That summer my husband and I talk and talk and talk. Not small talk or silly talk or world affairs talk, just working-on-our-relationship talk. Is this what marriage is like? Ugh, it's hard.

I embrace my mothering and nurturing side. I wear long dresses, take my daughter to the library's story time, and cross-stitch. Now that I'm out and about, people seem friendlier, smiling and talking to my daughter and me. I've found that being a mother is all that's needed for starting conversations at grocery store checkouts. There's the usual "What big eyes!" and "Look at those cheeks!" and the annoying "I bet she gets those long eyelashes from her father." Although I'm an "expert" now, it feels weird to give pregnant women almost twice my age advice on birth or infant care, but they ask.

Older women love to tell me about when they were young mothers, back when most women had babies right after high school. I think people are friendly now because my daughter is a beautiful baby. That's at least partly right; before becoming a mother, I was someone an older person might avoid. With freaky clothes and a loud laugh, I enjoyed being with the crowd that made people move to the other side of the street. Despite my outer transformation into what I think a mother should look like, at the grocery store I am still asked, "What are you, like, sixteen?" I start getting annoyed at people asking if I'm available to watch their children, I look like I'm such a sweet baby-sitter. Still, I won't be throwing out the blue hair dye and fishnet stockings just yet.

I make friends who are other first-time mothers. We have endless conversations about our children, but inevitably age comes up.

"Oh my God, you're young enough to be my daughter!"

Yeah, well when my daughter's eighteen, I'll only be thirty-seven. Besides, I want to play with my grandkids.

Still, I am glad for friends who are parents. Talking about parenthood opens my eyes to my own prejudices about age. I tell about feeling immature and helpless with all the responsibility of raising my daughter, contributing it to my young age. Laughter ripples through the room. None of them were ready for a child, though they had planned it out, maybe needed fertility treatments, saving money to take time off or picking the best year to leave their careers. In comparison, I am empowered by my young body. As a group we discover the equation: More energy equals more patience. My supply of energy is constantly commented on. How can an older body possibly compete with a young one when it comes to sleepless nights with an infant and running after a toddler?

My mother finds the old guitar that my grandfather gave me in high school. Since I have no piano in this apartment, I decide to learn something new. The first song I write is a good-bye to my friends in college. The second one is a love song for my daughter, and the third is a love song for my husband.

I'm twenty-five years old now, with a son running after my daughter. His birth mirrored my daughter's, but I chose my attendants more carefully this time; no emergencies. When I come back from open mikes, my husband asks, "How many numbers did you get?" After extended breastfeeding—burning calories while snuggling—my body is back. My mother takes me shopping for some tight pants, a new experience. I will only get the stretch ones for comfort. I chop my hair short and cute. I like the expressions on young men's faces when they ask if I have a boyfriend.

"No, actually, I'm married with two children."

"But you look so young!"

I smile. "I *am* young."

My children have opened my soul. I have discovered what is

truly important to me: family, music, and writing. Others wait fifteen years to grow up and "find themselves"; I have already been to my core and back, twice now. Thank God I didn't have to wait for my blossoming.

I just wrote a new song. The chorus goes, "And the life I never knew is just screaming at me to wake/to get started on my dreams/you know it's never, never too late."

Rebecca Angel *is a singer-songwriter in Albany, New York. Although music is her first love, doing this essay has rekindled her childhood dreams to write. She is currently getting her undergraduate degree from SUNY Albany, home-schooling her children, and playing with her cute, microbiologist husband. Rebecca is also addicted to E-mail, so write her at fw5blue@hotmail.com.*

Mollie Elizabeth Wood

The Birth Planet

My daughter Chloe was conceived on Beltaine, the first day of May, and born on lunar Imbolc, a perfect Pagan baby, and we didn't even plan it. Three weeks after I became pregnant, just days after my nineteenth birthday, I bought a Volkswagen bus, finished up spring quarter of school, and left to travel across the country with friends, to climb through the Grand Tetons, to explore Anasazi ruins, and to dive into hot spring–fed rivers in the June Yellowstone snow.

All that summer, with Chloe growing inside me, I grew stronger, leaner, browner, hiking through the national forests and dancing at drum circles. I would see Chloe as a fire, and we'd talk. She was right there inside my head. I'd started to plan an open adoption, but by the time I returned to my second year of college in the fall, Chloe had become too real. Even as I maintained the option of adoption in my mind, I was preparing for Chloe's arrival in our lives.

I went to a new school, one with self-evaluations instead of grades, where we designed our own majors, outside the craziness of the city. I could stare out the windows at the slanted yellow-white autumn light and walk under the cedars dripping with rain. I knew if I could do this, if I could pull off raising a strong-willed, magical baby on overdoses of love and very little cash, then I could do anything. I felt calm. I felt ready.

One time, when I was fifteen, I sneaked out of my parents' house to go see my boyfriend. I left home as soon as I heard my parents snoring. It was about 11 P.M. by the time I was walking along the road debating whether I would take the long way around on the paved streets or cut through the woods on the nature trail that led to my boyfriend's neighborhood.

My boyfriend and I were really into sex. Most of our relationship was spent scheming about where we could have it. We felt like revolutionaries, friends plotting an overthrow of the adult world that would keep us virgins if it could.

I took the nature trail. I was scared I might run into someone in the woods—maybe the rapist who'd been released from jail and had taken up his abode in our neighborhood; I'd seen his glower on the notices at school. But the trail was faster and I wanted to go that way.

As soon as I'd gone far enough into the woods that the light from the street lamps no longer reached me through the leaves, I turned off my flashlight and made my footsteps soft. It was quiet, and I began to relax and feel the cold, wet air on my face and hands.

The arms of the birch trees overlapping in the distance caught my attention and told me the air was open wide with possibility. I walked farther, slowly now, feeling the sharp rocks that poked into my thin soles as well as the round ones wedged in the dirt. I felt like part of the air, part of the woods, friend of the rocks, bad-ass girl in the night. I reached a ravine and climbed down one side, hopping over the skinny stream at the bottom. I shimmied up the other side of the ravine through the ferns and cut through someone's yard, just blocks from my boyfriend's house.

On the way home that night, warmed up from his bed, I took the nature trail again but ran all the way this time, jumping over roots with determination and leaping sideways deftly when the trail turned. I shot glances through the forest, away from the trail, while I ducked low-hanging pine branches, watching shadows that looked like they were running fast alongside me.

I felt radiant by the time I got home. I was so proud of myself for traveling through those woods alone at night. I was learning that everyone who had told me to be afraid of the world was wrong—not about the world, which was most certainly fucked, but about me, who could survive and flourish.

The choices seemed clear: I could stay at home, safe in my own bed, or I could go get what I wanted.

I remember the physical details of my two-hour home birth in a series of flashes. I have a vivid image of the upper left corner of the wooden frame around our bedroom door, with our tall cast-iron candleholder next to it, and the slow, wobbly tracers of the track lighting on the ceiling. I remember opening my eyes once and wondering where Jason, Chloe's father, was; I located him in the corner by the apartment window, crying. "It's okay," I said to him. "It's not that bad," but a contraction set all my muscles straining and I screamed out the end of the sentence.

Once the contractions started, they came one right after another. When my muscles contracted, my whole body wrenched forward, and when they relaxed, I lurched backward in an arch. I honestly had no idea my body could get that out of control. The nonstop mechanistic rhythm of my muscles seemed horrifying in its efficiency. Over and over, each contraction showed me I had no power and my conscious presence was really not even necessary. I drifted off, not asleep, just settled safely out of my delinquent body, floating and detached.

Out there, adrift in my spirit mind, it felt like a desert at night. There was darkness and a deep black space. I was aware of cold but not uncomfortable because of it. When I looked back at my body, I saw a churning black and red sea with no distinction between the land and the sky. The physical world that I had left located itself in this body, my body, which seemed to have expanded to a diameter of six feet, with an aura that filled the room. This body was made of tectonic plates—a long one from my shoulders to my belly button over a shorter, thicker one from my perineum to the small of my back—that were shifting back and forth over one another with all the grace and destruction of an earthquake.

Sooner than I'd expected, I hazily returned to the apartment scene. It was a long walk back to my body and the tension there was tight, almost to breaking. With half my mind still out on the Birth Planet, I heard the midwife tell me to slow down: I was going to rip. But I recognized my opportunity, and I was not letting go.

"Do you want to catch your baby?" she asked.

"I'm not ready!" I shouted, but I put my arms out anyway. I pushed, hard, and Chloe came out in one *swoosh*—head, shoulders, and all. Ecstatically, all the intensity that was coiled up in my muscles exploded and I slammed fully back into my body. I discovered Jason sitting behind me; we were crying and laughing all at once when the midwife helped lay Chloe on my chest. Jason and I stared down at her and Chloe looked up at us with her blue eyes huge and full of wonder, looked up at us . . . and breathed.

I was not the same person. I wanted to stop crying and laughing so hard but I couldn't. My confusion and my sorrow ran so deep, through the very center of my bones, and my joy hit me hard. I saw tracers of light so white it hurt my eyes. I saw Chloe.

Life, it was. This was life.

About a month after Chloe's birth, I stood in the shower, running my hands along my arms. It was the first time I'd broken through my haze of bliss and exhaustion and noticed what was happening with my body. I marveled at how thin and sleek my arms had become. Had I been this thin before Chloe's birth? I couldn't tell for sure, but at the same time I felt somewhat alarmed at my dwindling.

When Chloe was two months old I went back to college, spring quarter. By summertime, Chloe would take precisely thirty-minute naps, so while my hands were busy wrapping her tiny six-month-old fingers around a paintbrush dipped in green tempera and guiding her strokes across the paper, my mind was at work planning what I would do while she slept.

I was working on a painting of my own, a desert woman giving birth in a dark landscape that captured my feelings during Chloe's birth. After Chloe was through with her turn to paint, I'd add a few touches to my painting and make a plan, something like this: When Chloe goes to sleep, I'll do the laundry, type the British-Irish lit paper I scribbled out on the bus, water my basil, pay the bills, make food, and eat, all in twenty-nine minutes, so that will give me one minute to rest before she wakes up.

What really happened was that I would put her in bed and collapse on the couch and stare at the wall for half an hour. Eventually, after months of staring at the wall, I finally had a few calories of energy that I could use to think. I'd moved into an apartment in the suburbs where I could walk to Larry's Market and the botanical garden, but I would have had to walk a really long way to find another young, intelligent, tattooed, artist mom. I wanted to move to the city and be closer to my friends, but in stark contrast to my previous adventurous spirit, I now felt powerless to make such a change.

Occasionally, I would look around at the mess my home had become and think, *I would never start the flames, but if the whole place caught on fire, I wouldn't put it out. I would hold Chloe and stand outside and watch it burn. Then, when it was ashes, I would calmly and gladly walk away.*

I remember trying to have sex at this time, wanting to have good sex, soul-stretching, reeling sex, but I had to be careful because when my body started moving similarly to the way it had at Chloe's birth, I'd tense up and panic. One night, we celebrated my birthday with a party. After almost everyone had gone home, I lay down to nurse Chloe. One of my best friends stayed late and sat up in bed next to me while Chloe fell asleep. Once Chloe was sleeping my friend curled her body around mine and rested there with me. As she got up to go, she kissed me, and I was blissful over the fact that she kissed me, but also I was despairing. This was a girl I had loved with all my soul for as far back as I could remember. I wanted to be kissed, and I tried so hard to get myself to respond to her physically, but my guilty secret was that I didn't feel like a person anymore. I didn't have any idea who I was, and I couldn't kiss her back when I didn't know what I had to offer.

I felt it was impossible to have such a consuming experience like birth and just go on with life. It made me angry, frustrated, and tearful to keep it inside. As time went on I became amazed by how strong the feeling was. I felt like screaming. But life just went on and I wasn't left behind. I was still in the stream of it, looking around bewildered. I felt like I hadn't taken a step in any direction since the day of Chloe's birth, but the world had pushed me along and who was moving me? Not me.

I started talking with other moms about birth—it took years before I found anybody with a birth story similar to mine. But eventually I discovered I'd had what is called a precipitous birth, which basically means a birth that happens really, really fast. Biologically, your cervix still has to dilate to ten centimeters and your uterus still has to push the baby through your pelvic bones. The difference is, when your body intends to get all this done in an hour or two, it makes every contraction unreal and unbearable in its intensity.

Linguistically, "precipitous" means you're on a precipice, you're on the edge of a cliff and you're about to fall. My doula friend says women with precipitous births often start to scream uncontrollably for minutes on end because their minds simply can't keep up with what is happening to their bodies.

Consciously, learning all this made me proud of Chloe's birth; leave it to me to have the most extreme natural birth there is. However, that didn't change the fact that my body, nature, and reality now scared me shitless. There were parts of my groin that I pulled my soul so far up and out of, it felt like I was constantly holding my breath.

As Chloe grew, I needed some time just to be with her in awe and marvel over what I'd created and languish in my own nothingness. For a long time I saw it as negative, the way I'd felt my identity being scattered at Chloe's birth, but after I gave up fighting it, I was there on the verge of, well, anything. Precipitous, except maybe falling wasn't the only option. I changed the words of "Rock-a-Bye Baby" so that when the bough breaks the baby flies up through moonbeams into the sky.

Throughout the summer when I was twenty-three and Chloe was four, I would take her to the lake in the evenings and watch her swim when the sun was setting behind her and she became a silhouette among the flashes of light in the water. I went in the water with her sometimes, and we would play that we were fishies, chasing each other through the light, rippling waves on the lake. But then, after a while of fishy, I would tell her I needed some time to feel the water around me. I would spin and secretly smile at having a body that was mine, that I lived in, that nothing but the water could touch.

I decided that summer to let myself be asexual for a while, which was a label I used to assert that I wasn't going to have any sort of sexual contact with anyone. Metaphorically, it was also a way to say no to the world: *I have enough to deal with and just let me handle this before you throw another experience at me.* The air changed around me when I made that decision. This body was mine and only mine, and I was going to use that space to feel the echoes that still coursed through me from Chloe's birth until I could figure out what I wanted to grow into, what I wanted to be.

By one of those lovely ironies, I became flooded with memories of past sensual experiences: warm skin on long green grass in the hills of Marin County, the slapping cold ocean air of the

Oregon coast, the drumming tension of Seattle in early summer. All my favorite memories were caught up with place, inseparable from the land where they had happened. Recalling running through dark woods at night when I was fifteen, I realized that what made me feel empowered was going to uncharted territory with full faith that something good awaited me in the places—and in the parts of myself—where I'd never been before.

I wanted to travel again. As I researched where to go, I knew it had to be someplace away from cities, with cheap lodging, strong community, land unlike the places I'd lived, and it must be far, far away. Consulting the Internet, books, maps, and friends, I looked all over the world and set my mind on Bolivia. Several months later, as Chloe and I floated through Bolivian customs and ate Humahuaqueña potatoes with an Argentinian curandero, I felt welcome and good, like the world was taking care of me, not threatened like I was supposed to feel, a woman traveling with only a backpack and a four-year-old child.

One night in South America, Chloe and I were on a bus ride between Tarija and Tupiza, two cities in the Bolivian Andes. The ride took all night, and Chloe was sleeping next to me, wrapped in the pink and blue sleeping bag that kept her warm the whole trip.

I was up late, watching the landscape through the window in the dark. It looked like the moon. You can't imagine how beautiful South America is, and how raw. People stay up all night and play music and I would stay awake, sick from the altitude and starving from lack of vegetables, my lips aching from the dryness and the sun. I would wish I could forget the illusion of distance and my own loneliness and talk late into the night like them. It was the very beginning of spring there, which is the end of the dry season, and the ground was whitish gray and cracked with empty rivulets carved in the earth. That night the bus wound around the sides of the mountains, terrifying me as it leaned over drop-offs, while all around us hills rose up into the sky.

It happened in an instant. I felt myself fill up. There wasn't even a moon. I don't know why it happened then except that I was on my own and proud of myself and unbelievably lonely in a land so passionate I had a hard time believing it was real. And the desert resembled precisely the desert-at-night feeling I'd had at Chloe's birth and had been chasing through paintings ever since. The part of me that had been hiding out in those desert mountains rose in through the window, entered at my feet, moved up through my spirit, and stayed.

Later, the bus stopped at a tiny mountain village for the driver and his assistant to have their midnight dinner. Chloe remained sleeping on the bus with the other children while I ventured outside. The women from the bus stayed close to the building, where they gathered their skirts around their calves and squatted against the mud wall, talking quietly and pulling their fingertips through the dirt in circular patterns in front of them. I contemplated joining them but instead, like the men, wandered toward the cliff, where the echoes of cicada calls bounced from valley to valley.

Looking up at the stars and knowing none of them but thinking that maybe they smiled on me just the same, I turned and looked out into a dark abyss off the side of the mountain. For months I had been smoothing out the air around me like a sculptor, defining where my body would move. Now, as I stared across the valleys to other mountains, I could feel the empty, foreign space at the base of my spine—the part of my body I'd been afraid of since Chloe's birth—becoming whole, becoming something I owned again.

Mollie Elizabeth Wood *holds a BA in creative writing from the University of Washington. Her essays have appeared in zines such as* Soul Notes *and* Patchouli. *She lives with her daughter in Seattle, where she swims, dances, plays the piano, grows a garden, works at the neighborhood bakery, teaches Reiki, and pines for travel to India and Europe. All the neighborhood cats hang out at her house, and there is a bird's nest in her roof.*

Karen Landrum

A Leap of Faith

was midway into my senior year of high school in 1981. I had just arrived at school one cold, January morning when I received a message that the principal wanted to see me. I had a hunch about what was coming, and I felt an overwhelming sense of dread. Morning sickness and fatigue had kept me out of school a few days prior. As I walked down the empty hall toward his office, the fear in my belly grew.

I stepped inside. "You wanted to see me?"

My dread and fear suddenly turned into nausea. I didn't know if it was because of my pregnancy, the stale school air in his office, or his balding "Herman Munster" appearance. I confirmed his suspicions, and he began to give me my "choices." With every word he spoke, my queasiness turned more and more into anger.

In order to finish high school, he informed me, I needed to withdraw from my regular classes, come to school through the back doors after school hours, and complete the year by correspondence course. He strictly forbade me to communicate with other classmates; talking to them would be cause to terminate the course and I would not get my diploma. If I completed the course, I would receive my diploma through the mail. He would not allow me to participate in the graduation ceremony.

My other choice, he told me, was to drop out and get my

GED. I was filled with bitterness as I sat on the edge of my seat, listening to him state my "choices" in his stern, matter-of-fact tone. I hated him—his authoritarianism—as well as the rigid school structure. However, we did see eye to eye on one thing: I didn't want to be there and he didn't want me there. Although I was only a few months from graduating, I didn't accept his offer to stay in school. I couldn't wait to leave his office. I gathered my belongings from my locker and walked home feeling angry, relieved, and scared.

Later that day as I talked with Jeff, my boyfriend and future husband, I wondered why the same conversation didn't take place for him. He was a student at the very same high school and yet would continue his regular classes and go on to graduate with all ceremonial privileges, as if he hadn't fathered a child. The discrimination was crystal clear, and the unfairness of the situation made me increasingly resentful.

As a child, I couldn't wait to grow up and be a mom, so on a maternal level, I was very happy to be carrying a baby. Yet I also carried with me the shame of being so young and conceiving out of wedlock. As my belly grew bigger, I could no longer hide from the world the fact that I'd had sex! And having sex was against the rules. My fear and shame eventually turned into animosity toward anyone who delivered unsolicited advice. It seemed that everyone had opinions to offer. They informed me of the many difficulties that would inevitably come my way from keeping my baby and working to provide financially for her. I was often told that I was cutting my life short by taking on such a huge responsibility; I wasn't being fair to the baby or myself. All the well-intended advice just pissed me off. I daydreamed of running away to a far-off place where no one could tell me what to do, how to do it, or how to feel about it.

A few weeks after leaving school, I began to see a counselor from Catholic Social Services. I felt a rapport with her and a reasonable level of trust. Sometimes, I saw her alone. Other times, Jeff came with me. In one session, she suggested that I move into a maternity home. She thought it best for me to be with other young women around my age facing a similar life experience. I believe she also hoped I would be persuaded to put my baby up for adoption.

I decided to take her advice to make the move, partially because of her reasons, but also because I wanted to get away from my mom. I'm certain Mom felt the same. The tension was thick every time we were in the same room. Part of me felt ashamed for bringing this ordeal to my mom. Mom tried her best to help me, to be there for me, but I wouldn't allow it. I resisted every suggestion or offer for help. I wanted to grow up, and from my perspective, Mom was in my way. I did not want to be treated like a child or told what to do. I had too much respect, intermingled with fear, to truly argue with Mom. I mostly tried to stay away from her, but whenever we encountered each other, my behavior was limited to sarcastic answers to her questions. I carried an attitude that screamed out, *"Shut up!"* If she didn't, I would walk out, slamming the door behind me. I believed that by moving away, I could make decisions on my own.

On a beautiful, warm summer day, I moved into St. Joseph Maternity and Infant Home in Cincinnati. The home was nestled amid acres of rolling hills and wooded terrain and perched high atop a country hillside overlooking the city. At a time when I felt so vulnerable, the serene landscape was comforting to me and I spent a lot of time alone. I completed my high school education. I came to know other young women and listened to their stories. Discussion groups were set up with recent "alumnae" for those of us who lived in the home. Some women had kept their children; they talked of the challenges as well as the joys of having a new baby. Others had given their babies up for adoption and talked of the dilemma in making that choice and how it affected each of their lives.

I compared, I listened, and I watched for a sign to guide me in the right direction. I recalled the voices of my parents, my counselor, and my teachers telling me what my life would be like raising a baby at such a young age. Each had given me good reasons for giving my baby up for adoption to two mature, financially stable parents who could give her a better life than I could provide for her. I didn't want to hear their voices, but they came anyway. What if they were right? On the other hand, if I gave her away, what guarantee was there that she would have a better life? If I kept her, would it be in her best interest or mine? Was I really so selfish to want my baby?

On weeknights I called Jeff on the one pay phone in my section of the dorm. I had very little money to make phone calls, so when he came to visit on the weekends he always brought me a roll of quarters. Our dates consisted of going out to eat, seeing a movie, and spending time driving around and talking about what we thought we were going to do with our future. Jeff talked of feeling too young to be a dad, but he was also committed to seeing me through this.

My favorite song then was "The Voice" by the Moody Blues. As I listened to the song, I heard a message in it that spoke of honoring the voice within. I prayed every day that God would give me answers and hoped I would hear that voice. I wrote letters to my baby in hopes that she would know my reasons for giving her away, if I were to make that choice. As she grew bigger and stronger with each passing day and I felt her move inside of me, I also felt an ache in my heart, knowing I might need to give her to another mother and father to raise once she was born. Many nights, I cried myself to sleep. I cherished every moment she was with me, growing inside my womb. I did not want to let her go, but I also knew that once she was here, I would make the best decision possible.

On September 7, labor contractions began, and they continued into September 8, 9, and 10. Jeff and Mom became my constant companions. By the third day the contractions came every two minutes and were increasingly painful. It was impossible to sleep. With each contraction, I paced the room and tried to remember the breathing exercises taught in the prenatal classes provided at the maternity home. I recorded the duration of each contraction, trying to keep my mind off the pain.

The next morning, two of the nun-nurses checked me and decided that I was not in true labor. Though the nuns I encountered at the maternity home were generally very kind and compassionate women, there was one who had a masculine, drill sergeant personality. She told me that the reason I was not dilating was because I was not walking around enough to push the baby down into the birth canal, so she had me walk around the building several times with her. When I literally could not take another step, I crouched over and broke into tears, insisting that I be taken to the hospital.

She was not pleased, but she took me. At the hospital, the doctor seemed surprised when I told him the date the contractions began. He thought that my small pelvis was not wide enough to allow the baby to pass through. Because of the amount of time I had already been in labor, he was concerned.

I received an epidural and wanted to collapse into a deep rest, but that was not the plan. Within minutes, I was told that the baby was in distress and her heart rate was dropping rapidly. There was no more time to wait for a vaginal birth. Ten minutes after entering the operating room, I had a baby girl, weighing an even seven pounds. While the doctors stitched up my abdomen, a nurse brought Christin to me and asked if I wanted to kiss her. As I placed my lips on her forehead, I had a feeling of shock and wonder, of deep connection, and of letting go.

Christin was taken to the intensive care unit, and I was sent to recovery and given morphine injections. I remember Jeff being at my bedside in the recovery room. He stood next to me holding my hand, his tears dripping onto my arm. I felt like I had gone through the wringer, shivering from the effects of the epidural. I couldn't open my eyes much, but I heard Jeff say, "If I could do anything to take this pain from you, I would. I wish it were me lying there, not you." I drifted off and remained asleep until the next morning.

During my weeklong stay at the hospital, I kept Christin in my room as much as possible. My love for her was growing stronger every day. With every kiss, I hoped to remember her newborn smell. As she looked into my eyes, I wondered if she would remember me. I imagined what she would look like at age two . . . at six . . . ten . . . fifteen . . . twenty-one. I wondered what kind of life was ahead for her. I wanted to give her a good life. I wanted to be her mom . . . then, now, and for the rest of her life.

My counselor made several visits to me during my hospital stay. She persuaded me to put Christin in foster care while I went home, gave myself some time to heal, and made a clearer decision. The day I left the hospital, I signed a paper to place Christin in foster care, and went back to the maternity home feeling alone and empty. I sat on my bed. A song from Michael Jackson played on the radio, "She's Out of My Life." I had one wallet-sized picture of newborn Christin, and I held it close to my heart and cried.

I went home to my parents' house a few days later. During the two weeks without Christin, I prayed even more that I would make the best decision. One evening after a prayer meeting, a woman came to me and said she had a vision. She envisioned me standing before Jesus. He gently took my pain, placed it in his heart, and said he would carry it no matter what decision I made. That was my sign! I knew what I needed to do. I called my counselor the next morning and told her of my decision. It was not the decision for which she had hoped. She asked if she could come over and talk with me. I said yes, but I knew she was not going to change my mind.

When she arrived, I could tell by the somber look on her face that she did not approve of my decision. I invited her in, full of excitement but trying to keep a lid on it. She sat on the sofa in silence for a time, possibly not knowing what to say or even how to start. I looked around the room, waiting for her comments. She wanted to know my plans for taking on such a big responsibility, my plans for making an income, and my plans for marriage. "How on earth are you going to accomplish all of this?" she asked. "How could you possibly give Christin a life in which she could thrive?"

For every question she asked, I said, "I don't know, but I know I can do it. And I know that I have enough love to be the best mom for her." That answer did not map out a specific plan and was way too dreamy for her liking, but I didn't care. It was not her life—it was mine, and I knew I would do whatever it took to be the very best mother I could for Christin. My counselor had no choice but to give Christin back to me. On September 30, 1981, my eighteenth birthday, Jeff and I received Christin—a birthday gift I'll never forget, and one I will always love.

I no longer have to wonder what kind of young woman Christin has turned out to be, or what she looks like. I know. I know the good and bad, the happy and sad. I know I did the very best job to be the mom she deserves. No matter how many mistakes I have made along the way, I know that someone else would have made some too. When Christin struggles in her own life, even if she lashes out in the midst of pain, I understand how she feels. I've been there. I give her space to live her own life and discover her own mystery. I love her enough to give her the support of good conversation and a good hug, and I love her enough to let her go.

Throughout my pregnancy, I continually had to make tough decisions—decisions I didn't feel ready to make but that, even then, I knew I could. I resisted listening to the collective belief of my community and began developing my own intuition. Although my intuition takes me away from the security of familiar structure, it has proven time and again to be a wise voice that guides me deeper into my true self. There are never guarantees that life or love will not betray me, yet discovering my own courage has never betrayed me.

Karen Landrum *is a certified Atma Yoga instructor and member of the Cincinnati Yoga Teachers Association, teaching yoga in the Greater Cincinnati / Northern Kentucky area. She has recently joined Temenos, a holistic psychotherapy group in Cincinnati, as a yoga therapist. She is also a writer, dedicated to writing inspirational memoirs and profiles of courageous women. She is a mother of three—Christin, now twenty-two and attending the University of Kentucky in Lexington; Adam, twenty, a student at Northern Kentucky University and a specialist in the Army National Guard; and Taylor, eleven, still living and growing at home and a student at St. Paul Elementary School in Florence, Kentucky.*

Erica Wells

Mrs. Clean

At nearly four months along, when I physically could no longer hide my secret, I told my mother I was going to have a baby. The look on her face made my stomach feel sick and my heart feel empty. In a few short moments, her expression moved from confusion to worry to anger. "You won't be able to go to school," she said. "You'll be too tired. Are you really planning on keeping it?"

In my endeavors to win back my mother's approval, I tried many things. One of the strangest was to clean her kitchen ceiling. People call my mother Mrs. Clean. Not only did she value a clean house, cleaning was what she did when she was upset or unhappy. If I found her pondering how her cleaning job was looking or how her new arrangement of furniture was working, I knew she was happy. If, however, she moved rapidly about the room spending little time looking at things or paced back and forth, I could tell she was upset and working through her feelings rather than discussing or yelling about them. I'd heard her complain about the dust from the heat vent accumulating on the ceiling and how she needed to take care of it. She said it dulled the color. While she was at work one day, I got up on the kitchen table and scrubbed the ceiling. Without thinking, I used cleaners that were too strong and scoured off a great deal of paint. When she got home my mom seemed surprised that I was trying to reach her in the way she communicated—by cleaning. She also really appreciated the effort. Unfortunately, her ceiling now needed a paint job.

I found that having a baby and managing school and work were much harder than I'd expected. I was exhausted when I got up in the morning. I had to walk to work, and I usually completed my homework late at night. Sometimes the baby cried endlessly into the night. I was so tired that one day I fell asleep in the Laundromat.

One night when Ken was about two weeks old, he wouldn't stop crying. His father and I tried to comfort him in many ways, but no matter what we did, he cried. The next day he was quiet and sleepy. I put him in his car seat and took him in the bathroom with me so I could take a shower. (There weren't any of those cool bouncy seats they have out now.) *Poor little thing must have tuckered himself out with all that crying last night,* I thought. As the day went on, he remained sleepy and never really perked up to eat. Then, I felt him. He was hot, and I took him to the doctor. Luckily, I had enough sense to do it that day.

When we arrived at the doctor's office, he took one look at the baby and looked at me. "Don't you see the crane on his head?"

I wondered, *What crane? What is he talking about?* I thought of a crane as a bird. I didn't know it had another meaning.

The doctor was red-faced and angry with me. He pointed to the top of baby Ken's head. "Right here."

Now that he was pointing, I could see a large lump on the top of Ken's head the size of a golf ball. How could I have missed it?

The doctor said, "This means he has meningitis, an infection affecting the fluid around the brain. It is very serious and can be contagious." Later I would learn that "crane" is short for craniosynostosis, the swelling on a baby's head caused by meningitis.

A spinal tap confirmed the doctor's diagnosis. It turned out to be the bacterial form of meningitis and was not contagious, but Ken had to stay in the hospital.

This was a pivotal time for me as a mother. I felt as though God was giving me an out. Baby Ken had been sent to help me along, and I had seen the light in some areas. Now, he would leave me and go back.

I thought about how my life had changed since Ken came into my life—for the better. I thought about the choices I had been making since I'd become pregnant, and how they were good. Yes, my life was more challenging now, and sometimes I felt trapped. But before my pregnancy, I had done nothing with the freedom that I had. I had wasted my time and my intelligence. It was having the baby that had awakened me and helped me to live. It was the baby who had helped me to understand my mother's desire for me to do well. Although still mending, my relationship with my mother was better than it had been in a long time. My grades in school had improved. I had started to play with the idea of going on in school, to a trade school or even college. I had always wanted to become a teacher, but I'd never before thought it was a realistic goal. Now I wanted to make something out of my life.

I had similar desires for this new small being. Ken looked so small and helpless, and yet he had taught me some of the most important lessons I had ever learned. I wanted Ken to be healthy and happy. I felt so thankful to him for helping me to change. I felt great appreciation for my life. As I looked down into the bassinet at his listless body, I prayed to God and asked if Ken could stay with me. I promised I would go all the way as his mother.

Ken's treatment included injections in his legs that must have burned, because he screamed for ten minutes after getting a shot. He needed to be fed half an ounce of Pedialyte every fifteen minutes, twenty-four hours a day. I borrowed a nurse's watch and timed the fifteen-minute intervals on the nose so I could give him the Pedialyte. I picked him up carefully to give it to him. He was so parched, he'd slug it down and want more.

A number of doctors came to see him during the first few

days. They warned me that a two-week-old baby is a very delicate creature and that it would be hard for him to pull through. If he did get through this ordeal, they said, he could have numerous side effects, like brain erosion, paralysis, or deafness, to name a few.

I would look down into Ken's little bed and he'd stare back at me intently with his sparkly blue eyes and smile. One day the nurse saw him smiling at me and said, "I can't believe he is smiling at you like that already. Do you know about bonding?"

I replied, "I know about it, and we've bonded."

I stayed with him every day while he was in the hospital. I had friends who said it wasn't necessary to stay with such a young baby the whole time, that he wouldn't know the difference, but I knew. I think he would have too. When those horrible shots were injected into his little wrinkly legs, he screamed and howled. I made sure to be by his side each time they were administered. I would hold him and talk with him, and he'd let me soothe him.

Ken is a teenager now, and I still have a special bond with him. I can still see him as a young boy. He was an army guy in the field and a pirate digging in the sand for buried treasures. He was a magical child. His light filled me and made me love being a mother.

Sometimes, I'm still not certain about all that I am meant to do with my life. I did become a teacher, and I did become a mother again. I'm sure there will be a few other things I want to try when I grow up. I guess I have to give up on that ballerina thing that I, like many young girls, fantasized about as a child, but writing about a ballerina or other characters may not be too far off the mark.

These days, I think I finally understand my mother's affinity for cleaning. When you can't control all that happens in the world, you can maintain the smaller area of your home, at least sometimes. Like my mother before me, when the turbulence of my son's teen years bears down on me, when I look at my bill pile, or when I watch the news, I can frequently be found straightening up the house.

Erica Wells *lives in upstate New York with her husband, two children, two dogs, and a cat. She teaches in a specialized fourth-grade classroom for students who have emotional and/or behavioral problems. Writing, spending time with her family, and playing with her animals are her favorite hobbies. Erica's mother and her dog, Max, will soon be joining the household.*

Rosie Allain

My Amazing Breasts

My mother is a very supportive woman. She nursed me for fourteen months in a time when nursing was not widely accepted, around people who weren't comfortable with it. She let me end our breastfeeding relationship when I was ready. She practiced attachment parenting, a style of parenting that focuses on following your natural instincts, connecting with your child, being responsive to your child's cues, and respecting your child as an individual, among many other things.

So why, when I found out I was pregnant at fifteen, did I doubt my ability to nurse? Why did I say I would *try* to breastfeed my daughter, not that I *would*? Why did I think for even a moment that I, a healthy, strong, caring, and informed individual, would not be able to carry out a task that women have been doing for thousands of years?

Because I was scared. I felt weak and unsure. I was in territory that I hadn't planned to be in for at least another ten years. I was uncomfortable with the notion of a child suckling at my breast. My breasts were mine, and I wasn't sure if I'd be comfortable sharing them. And wouldn't it hurt to have a child sucking them?

I was afraid that breastfeeding would make it hard to leave my house. The thought of breastfeeding in public embarrassed me. Wouldn't everyone see my breasts? How could I expose one of my most private areas for the world to see?

My family and friends doubted my ability to be a good mother, and along with them I wondered if I really had what it would take. I had heard from various people that pregnancy, childbirth, and breastfeeding were especially hard for teenagers, and this made me further doubt myself. I'd also heard that the number of teenage moms who nurse is very low, and I was afraid I would join those statistics, proving how inadequate teenage mothers are.

I wanted to do whatever I could to make others see that age is just a number, that I could be a great parent regardless of how many years I had been alive. I wanted so much to do the right things and make the right choices.

For my sixteenth birthday my mother bought me books. Lots of books. Books on breastfeeding and other natural parenting subjects. I zoomed through the first book on breastfeeding, amazed at all the stuff I learned. My body could support another human being, not only while she was living inside of me, but also after she had come into the world. That was incredible. I learned about different nursing positions, what challenges I might expect, and why breast milk was so good for my baby's health and well-being. I also learned that breastfeeding could help my body get back to normal much quicker, that breastfeeding not only burns calories, but also tends to make a mother's weight loss after pregnancy quicker and easier. That sounded great. I was anxious about my body changing and wanted to do whatever possible to get back to normal.

Then I read something that really hooked me: By nursing for one year, I could reduce my chance of getting breast cancer by as much as 50 percent. Since breast cancer is prevalent in my family, I was very excited about that possibility.

You might say I became a breastfeeding fanatic. I talked to every pregnant girl-mom I met about breastfeeding. I filled their heads with all the facts I had learned: "Did you know that when you kiss your baby, you pick up his germs and create antibodies for him?" "Did you know that your milk can change temperature, depending on your child's needs?" I printed out information on formula recalls and on breastfeeding facts and myths. I told the other teen moms at my high school I had books on breastfeeding, that if they had any questions, I would find out the answers for them.

It seemed that the girls appreciated the information I was telling them. One girl called me from the hospital to assist her with her newborn son. I showed up at the hospital with information and words of encouragement. The nurses, as well as her family, were not supportive of her choice to breastfeed. A few days later my mom and I even went to her home with teas and herbs to help her produce more milk. She is now one of the biggest breastfeeding advocates I know.

At the same time that I was informing all the girls at my school about breastfeeding, I was also working on my boyfriend. He was very uneducated about breastfeeding and didn't understand why I was becoming so passionate about the issue. He isn't much of a reader, so every once in a while I would say, "Hey, Jake, listen to this." I told him how inspections have found salmonella and pieces of glass in formula, for example. He listened intently and pretty soon became really supportive. His child would have nothing less than breast milk, he would say.

Although he was beginning to see how amazing breast milk is, he was still uncomfortable with breastfeeding. His biggest issue was about other people—men in particular—seeing my breasts. I told him he would just have to get over it, that I knew it would be strange at first to see me breastfeeding in public, but it was for the best. He also wanted to help feed her. He didn't live with me, though, and it seemed silly to me to formula-feed our daughter just because he wanted to help once or twice a week. I knew that when she needed to feed at nighttime, he wouldn't be the one making her bottle or cleaning the supplies. If I breastfed her, all I would have to do is latch her on while lying down and fall back to sleep.

As my pregnancy progressed, I thought about how long I would breastfeed. I had originally planned on nursing for six months, then I expanded that to a year. Near the end of my pregnancy I found a wonderful online support site for breastfeeding. The women's stories about extended nursing experiences interested me. Reading about the silly names toddlers call nursing and the cute things they say, as well as the benefits, like being able to comfort a tantrum-throwing child, I became eager to nurse my daughter longer, changing my plan to nurse from one year to two, and maybe longer.

The changes my body as well as my breasts went through astounded me. Throughout my whole teenage life my breasts had been a size A, but during pregnancy they grew to size B. I was thrilled to finally be able to fill out my shirts. My body stretched to support the child growing inside. The physical changes were scary, but mostly I found them empowering. For once in my life, I didn't worry about how I looked. No one looked at me funny when I was eating meals made for three. I was nourishing my child, and nothing else mattered much to me.

My labor finally started the morning of December 9, ten days after my due date. I ended up having a perfect, natural, drug-free birth—the kind of birth I'd dreamed about. I was seven centimeters dilated when I got checked at the birthing center and my contractions were getting more and more intense. Less than two hours later, I felt an uncontrollable urge to push. Just three pushes later, my daughter Cheyenne was born!

As soon as Cheyenne took her first breath in that birthing room, the nurse wiped her off a little and handed her to me. I was so excited and on such a birthing high, calling out, "My baby, my baby, oh, my, look how pretty she is!" Instinctively knowing what to do, she suckled at my swollen breast. Throughout that first night she nursed often, lying next to me in the hospital bed as I watched her sleep and tried to get some rest.

At first I needed assistance getting her mouth to latch onto my breast properly. I remember feeling her strong suckling mouth and thinking how incredibly powerful her grip was. It was a little difficult in the beginning, and at a few points I had little hickey marks on my nipple. But my mom and my books reassured me that I was doing fine.

When Cheyenne was two months old I had a breast infection, which I took as a sign that I needed to rest more and slow down. It was very painful. I managed it by massaging my breasts, nursing Cheyenne frequently, using warm compresses, and drinking lots of water.

In the beginning of our nursing relationship, I was very nervous when we were away from home. I tried to be as discreet as possible, using a blanket made especially for nursing in public, trying to make it look as if she was just sleeping in my arms. When my daughter was a few months old, she forced me to overcome my feelings about breastfeeding in public. She did not like having a blanket covering her face; she wanted to look around while she nursed. She would kick or pull at the blanket, which just made nursing harder. I finally decided it was more of a hassle to bother with covering up while we were nursing, and I put the blankets away. I didn't get many comments or dirty looks about breastfeeding her, and the times I did, I didn't let them get to me.

My concern that nursing would tie me down didn't pan out. I found that for me breastfeeding does quite the opposite. It not only makes outings ten times easier than if I were burdened with carrying around bottles and formula, it also saves time and allows me to feed my daughter the moment she cues me of her hunger.

I'd heard that if my breasts were too small, they wouldn't be able to supply all the milk necessary to exclusively nurse a child. I learned quickly that was a myth. The size or shape of my breasts has nothing to do with the quality or quantity of the breast milk my body produces. The amount of fat in one's breasts determines only the overall size and shape of breasts. The glands are what produce milk, and they expand or shrink as needed.

Jake, Cheyenne's dad, acted differently around my bare breasts than he had before our daughter was born. I think he thought of Cheyenne when he saw my breasts, as if their sole purpose was to nourish Cheyenne, and they were now left out of our intimate moments. That wasn't such a bad thing, since after having her nurse throughout the day I just could not stand to have them touched anymore.

I have since been through the first tooth and many more challenges: the times when her latch was painful because of all her newly sprouted teeth, when her gums were bothering her and she just couldn't help but bite down on my breast, trying to relieve some of the pain. We have gone through the nursing acrobatics stage as well as the "I can't decide which breast I want" phase. Recently I was thrown another breast infection. I went to the doctor and she told me I had to wean Cheyenne because the antibiotics I needed to take would be too strong for her to ingest.

My daughter isn't a very good solid food eater yet, so I was worried about how weaning would affect her nutrition. Plus, she is used to nursing before she goes to sleep, and I was concerned about how weaning would affect our sleep patterns. I didn't think abrupt weaning would do anything positive for us, and I told the doctor that it simply wasn't an option. I wasn't about to rip away what my daughter depended on and found incredible comfort in, just because my breast was sore and I had an infection.

The doctor went into her office and, lo and behold, found another antibiotic for me, one that I could safely take while nursing. I was very proud of myself for speaking up and questioning the doctor, and I suspected that she was attempting to push her own personal feelings about when a child should be weaned onto me. I took the medication and continued nursing Cheyenne. My infection disappeared in about a day and a half.

My daughter is two and a half now. Nursing comforts her when she's sick, hurt, upset, or tired—you name it and nursing can make it better. I have to wonder why people ask when I'm going to wean her. Why do they even care? They're not the ones getting up with my daughter in the middle of the night or comforting her when she bumps her head. I'm really confused as to why everyone seems to rush babies to grow up so fast, and then, when they're teenagers, people wish they wouldn't act so grown up! It's silly. We need to let our children be babies for as long as they want, enjoy them, and comfort them while they still think we are the world.

Rosie Allain *is a nineteen-year-old college student with plans to transfer to a university in the fall of 2004. She intends to major in sociology with a minor in women's studies. She lives with her daughter Cheyenne in San Diego. Rosie wants high school–based teen parent centers to empower teen moms, to respect their parental authority, and to not treat them as sexual criminals. She plans to work as an advocate for teen mothers who are still in high school.*

Speak Out!

What quality in you has contributed most to your success as a mother?

My belief that I can figure it out—whatever "it" is.

I know when to be strong and when to be gentle.

Determination.

Patience, acceptance, and the fact that I try not to let myself regret ("So-and-so can go out and not worry about a baby-sitter"; "Damn these stretch marks"; "My boobs look like they belong to a middle-aged woman"; and so on).

My ability to smile, relax, and say, "Doesn't matter. Let's go blow bubbles."

Compassionate courage.

Sheer stubbornness! No way was I going to prove the people right who had said I wouldn't be able to handle it.

Believing in myself.

My desire to learn: I spent my whole pregnancy researching pregnancy, birth, and parenting.

Tenacity.

My sense of humor.

Respecting my kids.

Open-mindedness and flexibility.

Spirituality. Praying for peace when I'm stressed. Asking for strength when I feel helpless. When I'm happy, I thank God.

Perseverance.

Gaining an education and developing a sense of self-worth.

Understanding.

My tendency to think outside the box.

PART 3

Growing Up Together

ON SEXUALITY, RESPONSIBILITY, AND PARENTING

In Alex's first days at home, Nick and I realized we would have to bathe this little being. How do you bathe someone who is so tiny? My mom showed us—or rather, told us—what to do, and I believe that was the longest bath that Alex has ever had. I remember washing his ten little fingers and his ten little toes and being scared of hurting this delicate little boy and at the same time being amazed at how soft he felt, like silk, and then being scared of not knowing what to do next. But looking to my left and seeing my mom standing there smiling put my mind at ease. Though nervous, I knew I had no reason to be scared, because my mom would always be close enough to help but a step back so I could learn on my own. And she has.

Nothing is better than the smell of a freshly oiled and powdered baby, though I think we overdid it those first times, considering all the excess oil we had on our hands and how white our baby was.

—Stacey Shackel,

24, mother, Killarney, Manitoba

Virtually every essay I received spoke of growth and change—emotional, intellectual, spiritual. Though many women described maturing over months or years, their stories also revealed how the changes of pregnancy and the sudden responsibility of caring for another person combined to hurtle them into rapid growth that under other circumstances might have been significantly delayed. Like anyone who is forced by circumstances to mature, some women embraced the challenge, others dragged their feet, but most experienced a combination of reluctance and readiness.

A number of women wrestled with one aspect of their maturing selves—their sexuality—long before they found themselves carrying a child. A woman who conceived at nineteen wrote, "Why did my culture push me to be sexy, to obsess about my weight, my hair, my skin, my breast and ass size and shape, taunt me to be beautiful, skinnier, sexier—and then not expect me to act on my body's hormonal imperative? It is so confusing to live in a culture that values women's sexiness and chastity but not women's sexuality. It is so confusing for me to live with a popular culture that expects me to look like a teen forever, a culture that plasters pictures of half-naked, teenage-looking women everywhere and then punishes me for acting on my sensuality, for having sex and no longer being chaste."

Getting pregnant was certainly no cure-all to the discomfort and confusion these writers experienced regarding their sexuality. One woman who got pregnant at eighteen enrolled in a program for adolescent mothers-to-be and was dismayed to learn that the first session was on pregnancy prevention. "I didn't think at the time I needed to be hearing it—or putting a condom on a banana, for that matter—but I did need to hear it, and so did my boyfriend. I remember feeling so uncomfortable during those forty-five minutes, which seems silly to me now, but it was the beginning of the journey."

Women of any age—and a number of men, too—are likely to identify with each of the journeys of growth in this chapter. Like

Samantha Lucas, what new parent hasn't felt hopelessly inept and frightened over her awesome responsibility? Like Trina Willard, what mother hasn't bristled at a stranger's overheard criticism? K. J. Steele evolves through the challenge of teaching her own girls about self-esteem and sexuality. Allison Crews is bold and fearless—if also uncertain at times—in assessing why her child alternates between acting delightfully charming and infuriatingly wild. And Alice Campbell tells the moving story of losing her voice as a child and attempting to find it again as a woman.

Samantha Lucas

Bewildered but Blessed

Before Emily, I hadn't ever held a newborn. For the first few days after the delivery I was in pain and exhausted and terrified of her. When I did hold her, it was never for long; I was quick to pass her back to the plastic bassinet or to anyone close. I know now that mine was a common reaction among young mothers, but I still feel the sharp pinch of guilt at my reluctance to hold and greet her during the first few days.

After about a week I was sent home with my daughter, and she was screaming before I even made it out of the hospital. Kevin was waiting with our beat-up Hyundai when I was wheelchair-delivered to the double doors of the lobby. I juggled Emily, a diaper bag, and whatever other junk I was schlepping home to meet Kevin at the car door. A secondhand infant carrier resided awkwardly in the backseat of our two-door car, and as Kevin loaded our entourage of hospital souvenirs in the trunk, I struggled to strap Emily into her car seat, fumbling with the seat belt and her red-faced frustration. Looking back now, I think Emily was cranky because she knew that she was in the presence of absolute incompetence.

Thankfully, my arrival home was peaceful and uneventful. My father and stepmother gave us one of the best baby gifts I could have asked for: a clean house and folded laundry. There was food in the refrigerator, too, and they cooked a few meals for us.

I hardly slept that first night home. Still reluctant to hold Emily, I kept her in a bassinet next to me on the couch and spent most of the night staring at her glowing face and listening to her breathe. She reminded me of strawberries, and I felt insignificant next to this awesome life that had somehow managed to arrive through my self-doubt, self-pity, and overall cluelessness. Despite my difficulties adjusting to motherhood, loving Emily was never a struggle.

Early the next morning my mother arrived at my door, having flown overnight to reach us. I promptly handed her an extremely fussy baby, opting instead to carry her huge suitcase. My mother knew I was unprepared for motherhood, but I don't think that she realized exactly how unprepared until I handed her a bottle of Enfamil the consistency of liquid cottage cheese. She looked at me like I was joking. My mother then instructed me, very patiently I might add, in the art of formula mixing. Luckily for Emily, we had gotten through the first night at home with the premixed formula the hospital gave me. My mother even drove my nasty car to the store to buy different brands of formula, because she suspected Emily's crankiness was due to a milk allergy. I wouldn't have spotted a milk allergy if the cow had smacked me in the face.

As I undertook intense baby lessons that first official week as Emily's mommy, I expected many "I told you so" and "You should have listened to me" comments from my mother, but she did not offer many. She was gracious, and I was grateful, because I don't think I could have handled another inadequacy lecture. By then, I was really starting to see myself for what I was—a child—and I knew that I had to change if I wanted to be a part of this little person's life.

I relied on my mother to get up at night with Emily and to jump first whenever she needed anything. I watched her wake with Emily two or three times a night, changing diapers, feeding her, and rocking her. The sharp edges between my mother and me softened, and I learned to respect her.

Then she went home. And I seriously considered packing Emily into her suitcase!

I spent the next few weeks feeling completely frayed. I cried a lot as I struggled to interpret the different wails of hunger and wet diapers, but eventually I learned Emily. I spent many hours rocking her, watching her chest steadily rise and fall, and studying her face. As I became more comfortable with her, I began to relax and feel a more intense connection with her. Sometimes I miss those quiet nights of rocking, when it felt like there was no world outside of the creaking chair and Kevin's steady snoring, nothing outside of my little family safely encased in a sleeping snow globe.

Kevin and I married when Emily was about four weeks old, and we decided that it would be best for me to stay at home with her. It didn't make a lot of sense for me to work if we had to use more than half my earnings to pay for day care. So at nineteen I became an official sweatpants-wearing, stay-at-home mom.

Emily's firsts coincided with a lot of mine. Because we could no longer afford fast food and Pizza Hut, I was learning to cook when Emily was learning to roll over. After many burnt suppers and an equal number of undercooked ones, I did learn how to cook and actually became quite good at it. I accomplished the great feat of grocery shopping with coupons and store flyers, my baby in tow along with a diaper bag, shopping cart, and infant carrier, something that I realize now is a struggle even for the most experienced mothers. Emily was sitting up without help by the time I figured out how to write checks, pay bills, and successfully reconcile a checkbook. I mastered the skill of waiting patiently in lines at the WIC office and doctors' reception areas, but most importantly, I learned how to put someone else first. I was learning that lesson when Emily was learning to crawl.

I think my adjustment into motherhood would have been

much more difficult had I been working forty hours a week on top of learning the baby basics. However, whenever I answered the question of what I did for a living, "stay-at-home mom" seemed to provoke narrow eyes and false smiles, like I was sitting around eating potato chips and watching soap operas every day. Being young on top of being unemployed seemed to make me a virtual Antichrist to a few of the other moms I encountered. No one was afraid to remind me of my incompetence or my youth or my lack of education.

But no one told me how my baby's first giggle would make me shiver with delight. No one told me how wonderful it would feel to have little hands grasping my forefingers as she took her first steps. No one ever mentioned the joy of being called "Mommy" for the first time. I wish I had been told more about the joys of motherhood during my pregnancy, rather than just its chores. I never knew that the best dancing partner I would ever encounter in my life would be a fussy newborn at 3 A.M., and that my dancing shoes would be fuzzy slippers as we swayed to whatever was in the CD player. I don't think it would have made me more optimistic about becoming a mother, or even more prepared, but I do think it would have eased a lot of my anxiety.

At some point, I graduated from a scattered, silly girl into who I am now. I wish I could say that there was one revealing moment that prompted this huge change. Everything from the double blue line up to today has contributed. Things as significant as my stopping smoking—because my little girl asked if she could smoke like me when she grew up—and as insignificant as the sight of a tiny baby shoe.

I still wake up many mornings suffocating from the realization that I am this grown-up, adult person with real responsibilities, that I am not like most twenty-four-year-old kids. What few friends stuck around after high school have now graduated college or are just graduating, while I am just beginning. They have found jobs and their own apartments. They still have the luxury of buying that shirt simply because they want it. They still have the freedom to go out whenever, for whatever. Sometimes it is almost impossible not to be jealous of that, especially when I am adding up the spare change at the bottom of my purse and comparing the prices of spaghetti sauce.

It has been five years since I delivered Emily, and I am not as terrified or as clueless about being her mother as I was. I am continuously amazed as I watch her become a beautiful and intelligent person, and I'm astounded to realize that I am part of the reason for that. When I look at her shining face now, I know I need to make myself better. I want to be strong and self-reliant. Most importantly, I want these things not just for her, but for me. Because of her, I will never stop growing as a person, as a woman, and as a mother. Emily will always be the best thing I have ever done.

Samantha Lucas *is twenty-four years old and lives with her husband Kevin and daughter Emily. Because she stays at home with Emily, she works out of her house for a national company as a medical transcriptionist. She has just completed her first semester at Greenville Tech in South Carolina. When she is not playing with Emily or working, she spends a lot of time reading, writing, and painting.*

Suiting Up to Fly

When I first became a mother, the only parenting books I read were those that validated what my heart was already telling me, the ones that say it is okay to sleep with my kids, okay to hold them when they cry, okay to let them fall down sometimes, okay to nurse them until they tell me they are done nursing. I read La Leche League's books and trained to be a leader. I wanted to support women like me who were struggling to mother from their hearts, despite their own mothers saying, "You're going to make a monster out of him if you hold him so much," or their pediatricians saying, "She'll never learn proper sleeping habits if you nurse her every time she wakes up."

Before the birth of my second baby I studied at Seattle Midwifery School to be a doula, learning how birth can be if we are empowered with support and the confidence to trust our instincts. I studied sociology, examining why mothering isn't valued in our culture. I learned about anthropology and what our bodies, our history, and other primates have to teach us about parenting, diet, schooling, and lifestyle. I have been completely thorough in my self-education, making certain that I am an expert on all things mother, even getting trained to check car seats for proper installation and use.

I regularly fly back to the Midwest from my home in Seattle to visit family. I am good at flying with my kids. I always have diversions—a couple of new toys that will be sure to hold their attention, plenty of food, a change of clothes. I schedule flights for times I know my kids will sleep, at least for some of the flight. I use the kids' car seats on the plane. I am prepared.

One time, just before boarding a plane, my one-year-old was too wound up to sleep. I walked around with him in the sling and nursed him. I even went to the bathroom to nurse where he could have some quiet, but nothing worked. He was past the point of no return. He toddled giddily back and forth between the seats and all the other people waiting to board the plane, laughing that wild, slaphappy laugh that says, "Please help me! I don't know how to stop!" As we boarded, I told his dad, "We're in trouble."

We were all strapped in with the red buckle-up light warning us, "You're stuck now," when the crying started. I couldn't walk around with my son. I couldn't even stand up and bounce him. I knew that there wasn't a trick or treat in my bag that was going to bring him down from the frenzy that he was working himself into. There was no way around the crying fit that he needed to usher him to nap land. I was powerless. He screamed that *I want my bed right now* scream for thirty minutes, tossing and turning in my arms, before settling into the comfort of a cradle hold and, at long last, latching onto my breast. Between sucks and sobs, he jerked fitfully in and out of dreaming. When he finally lay limp in my lap, overtaken by the sleep he so desperately needed, my own body slumped over his with the same undeniable need.

That's when I heard what I thought to be an intentionally loud voice of an older woman a couple of rows back: "It's just so selfish," she said. "It's especially hard when they're teenagers." My mind filled in the blanks, and I heard, "It's just so selfish *when parents bring such small children on airplanes. It's especially hard for them to take care of their kids* when they're teenagers."

95

Too exhausted to be furious, I just felt defeated. After what I had just gone through, I could have used some compassion and a hug! I had done all I could. I was thoroughly equipped and thoroughly educated. I did my best. An old, familiar thought ran through my mind: *I do my best, and it still isn't good enough.*

One ignorant comment from a stranger, and I thought about it through the whole family visit: *Why does it bother me so? She doesn't know anything about me—why I'm flying, how well prepared I am, how many times I've made that trip entertaining two kids for four hours with no incidents, or even that I'm twenty-five now. (I only look eighteen.) But what if I were eighteen? Who the hell is she? What the hell does she know?*

I had thought my armor against criticism was complete, that if I seemed perfect no one would have anything to criticize and I wouldn't have to face how terrified I am, even now, that I won't have what it takes to be a "good mother." If I seem perfect, I'll never have to ask myself, *Is she right? Am I selfishly putting my children and everyone on this plane through this horrible half hour so that I can have my own way?* Or, *Is he right? If I weren't so young would I know how to keep my daughter from having a tantrum in the middle of this grocery store aisle?* Or—here's the kicker—*Were they right? Were we crazy to think that at our age we could give our children what they need?* It is so self-defeating to ask myself, but they are the dragons against which my armor of overpreparedness and competence was meant to protect me.

About a week after that incident on the plane, I replayed in my mind the woman's comment. I began to recall more of it, put the pieces together, and realized she wasn't talking about me at all! I'd heard more than the defensive part of my brain wanted to admit. She'd been talking about *divorce.* She was saying that she thought it was selfish of parents to divorce, and that it is especially hard on teenagers. It was only my own fears of criticism that created my perception that *I* was being criticized. It was my own belief in the idea that young parents aren't good parents that created my reaction on that plane.

The experience of misinterpreting what that woman said helped me to release that belief. I now believe that my mind created that experience in order to give me an opportunity to grow.

We are so much wiser than we give ourselves credit for.

The unpredictability of life with children is the much-needed hole in my suit of armor. The many moments of powerlessness provide opportunities to face my own assumptions, to shed the judgmental filters through which I perceive the world. I have learned from experiences like that half hour of screaming on the airplane to St. Louis that I don't have to be perfect. My best is always good enough.

As I let go of my self-doubts and self-judgments, I find that I don't need books to validate what my heart tells me (I stopped reading all of those books about parenting). I don't need a suit of armor to be immune to criticism (I didn't become a La Leche League leader). I only need faith in the perfect blossoming of my heart as my life unfolds.

When she isn't focused on her kids as a stay-at-home mom, Trina Willard *is a performing songwriter, artist, peace activist, writer, and doula. She lives in a cohousing community in Seattle, with her son and daughter and their many loving neighbors. She loves to laugh, sing, be with loved ones, and commune with the earth in the peaceful wilderness of the Pacific Northwest.*

K . J . S t e e l e

The Great Pretenders

I received my first bra in a brown paper bag, smuggled across the bed to me by my mother as if it contained some risqué contraband.

"Here," she whispered. "I bought you something."

Something. Not a bra. Not a brassiere. Certainly not lingerie. Just something. Some thing.

We stood for a moment soaking in embarrassed silence as her eyes darted around the room, frantic as two birds looking for an escape. Seizing upon the door, she fled, leaving me alone in the turbulence of her emotion. Me and the thing. The first straitjacket of womanhood. Needless to say, sex wasn't a big topic of conversation around the dinner table in our house. We simply pretended it did not exist.

The only problem with this was that it did exist, and when it made its inevitable visit and came knocking at my door, I was wholly unprepared either to greet it or turn it away. I didn't even realize I had a choice. Drowning in a situation beyond my control, I just pretended I could swim and was quickly swept along with the current.

We were so good at pretending in my family that when my period ceased and my belly began to balloon, I pretended they hadn't. Pretending entered a whole new dimension—denial. I was six and a half months pregnant before my subconscious brain let the rest of me in on its little secret. How do you hide six and a half months of expanding baby? You don't. You can't. At least, not on a skinny kid like me. I looked like a toothpick that had swallowed a grape. Yet in my family the physical signs became something that simply could not possibly exist and therefore didn't. Even my mother, who had already borne four children of her own, chose not to see my pregnancy.

But babies don't really care about your reality or your denial thereof. They just keep rising up like bread dough, swelling out your tummy until there is no place left to go except out. And out they come. And being such noisy, tangible little creatures, they are pretty much impossible to ignore. No. Denial will not work here.

My pregnancy was the result of mistakes. Not just one mistake, but many, my own and others'. A great many errors in judgment had been made and covered over, the sands of time eventually blotting them out. I learned far too late that my own mother and paternal grandmother had both had unplanned teenage pregnancies. Because of the shame involved, however, these incidents were hushed up, the knowledge and wisdom gained from them lost rather than passed along to the next generation. In their denying the truth of these mistakes, they were allowed to happen again.

I decided to do it differently, to break that unending chain of denial and shame. I knew my pregnancy was a mistake, but I also knew that my daughter was not. She was as inspired and pure as any newborn child, not a mistake but an opportunity. An opportunity for change. An opportunity for me to do better.

I grew up overnight when I had my daughter. Suddenly I fit nowhere—not in the adult world; even less so in the world of my school friends. I straddled that lonely land in between and determined how I would raise my child. I took my job seriously. I was adamant that what had happened to me would not befall my daughter. Like the birthing of the seasons, however, change is not instantaneous. It is progressive and needs time in which to find its way. I did not immediately become a better, more sensitive mother just because I desired to do so. Mothering is an extremely disciplined job, requiring a vast assortment of ever-changing skills that must be learned and then honed in the tumultuous traffic of everyday life. Few if any of these skills are ever fully perfected.

Looking back on my experiences, I identified things that I believed had played a part in my own unplanned pregnancy. In my first sexual encounter, I had said nothing, when all I wanted to say was "No." So, why didn't I? I couldn't. I thought I would look stupid and naive. I was insecure about the value of my judgment. Instead, I bluffed. I pretended that I was fine with having sex. Bluffing came naturally to me. It was the way I had been raised.

My eldest daughter was the canvas on which I learned to paint. It was not always a pretty picture. I made mistakes, new ones of my own making. As is common with change, I overreacted. One time, when my eldest daughter was about fifteen, she missed her curfew. I knew she had been watching a video at her boyfriend's house and I panicked, jumping into the car and driving over there to get her. Of course, they passed me on my way, and I turned around and followed them back home. I don't think that poor boy made a complete stop at any of the stop signs along the way!

Because of my own experience I became fearful and controlling, hoping to protect her from my perceived dangers of boys and sex. This was wrong. By its very nature fear builds walls and secrecy, not trust and communication. It was about this time that my daughter informed me that I could not control her. She said it not as a challenge, or even in anger, just as a matter of fact. After a good strong moment's irritation, I had to agree. We do not live in a Rapunzel society where fair maidens are locked away for safekeeping. The best we can do as parents is to develop a relationship built on respect and trust. A relationship that encourages our children to ask for and value the wisdom in our advice. As we have grown up together my daughter has taught me this, so that I didn't repeat the same mistake with her sisters.

One thing I did right was to become more comfortable with my own sexuality. When my daughter was little and saw me taking my birth control pills and asked what they were, I told her. I didn't tell her it was "Mommy's medicine"; I told her it was a pill I took so I didn't get pregnant. I told her this when she was five years old so that I could still tell her this when she was fifteen years old. When she became old enough to begin wearing a bra, we had a shopping date and made a great event out of it. When she approached menstruation, we sat down together and went over the tampon instructions in detail.

I have learned that empowering my daughters to make their own wise choices is far more beneficial than attempting to control them. To be sexually active is a choice—*their* choice, not mine. I have tried to teach them that choices and privileges also carry the weight of consequences and responsibilities. I never hid from my daughters the consequences a teenage pregnancy has had on my life. They know the sorrows and regrets I have felt at never having experienced the freedoms of adolescence, the secret whisperings of pajama parties, or the carefree abandon of traveling with no other responsibility than the pack on my back. By far the most important thing I have done in raising my daughters is to encourage them to share their opinions, listen to them, and value what they have to say. As a result, my daughters have strong, healthy self-esteem.

With the help of my mother and correspondence courses, I went on to finish high school and graduate with my class. After graduation my daughter's father and I got married and eventually added two more daughters to our family. I continued working on my own self-esteem and that of our daughters. I raised my girls to believe that they are the center of their own universe. All three of them have grown into strong, confident women, complete in themselves. In the end, I think it is important that we, as teen mothers, understand that the breaking of chains is not so much about what we do as it is about who we are and who we endeavor to become. Ultimately, we will be the mirror that is held up before our daughters' eyes.

K. J. Steele *lives with her husband and three perfect daughters in British Columbia, Canada. With no grandchildren in the foreseeable future, she has decided to pursue a career in writing.*

Allison Crews

I Was a Teen Mom Success Story

When he was two, people thought he was a genius. Child care providers, servers in restaurants, strangers on the bus: "I can't believe how articulate he is. You must be an excellent mother."

I could smile, demurely smug. "Well, we read a lot, so I definitely think that enhances his vocabulary. Some days he just wants to read for hours. And, he is breastfeeding still, of course."

Depending on the context and the identity of the admirer, I could mentally chalk up the points that I was scoring with my son's intellect and ideal demeanor:

One point: teen moms!

Two points: extended breastfeeders!

My son and I could exist forever, I thought, as walking contradictions to the stereotypes used to define us. I could call myself "Teen Mom Extraordinaire" and know that my son in all his brilliant glory was a co-conspirator in my plan to change society's collective attitudes about teen parents by being nothing less than *excellent*. I called my parenting "reproductive activism," and my son was the product of my efforts at social change: *dismantling the patriarchy, one male baby at a time.*

Sometimes I still feel like I'm doing my "job" as a mama to this superintense kid of mine. He's four now, and I am turning twenty in four months. Some days I marvel at my naivete and youth: *How* am I supposed to be a grown-up, again? Most of the time I forget that we're something deviant, my son and I, and my partner and her son—our blended family of teenage, lesbian, student mothers and our illegitimate sons. I spend important periods of time awed by the power and wonder embodied in my boy, proud of this person that I created and somehow helped mold. We go to all-ages punk-rock shows, and he demands that we stand right in front of the stage, adding: "Remember, Mom, I need earplugs." Sometimes he weasels his way onto the stage, standing next to the lead singer, joining the band. Over and over we hear, "This kid is a rock star!"; "Dude, will you join the band?"; "Hey, buddy, wanna play on my drum set?" and I feel validated in my success. I believe, at those times, that I've met my teen mom goals: My kid would be brilliant, and my kid would be cool.

But sometimes I know that I am failing. Is it normal for four-year-olds to seemingly gain superhuman strength the moment they are blatantly disobeying you? Is it normal for you, the parent, to find yourself wounded in a battle waged against you by your preschooler, when all you wanted to do was stop him from running into the street? Cade will scream until he struggles to breathe, then clench his fists and just stop breathing. He picks things up and breaks them and demands, "YOU KNOW WHAT I MEAN! DO IT!" and I sit, holding my fists in my pockets so I won't be tempted to let them fly out and strike him; I literally bite my tongue and force a strained calm when I ask, "No, Cade. I do not know. If you need me to help you, I need you to tell me what it is you are asking." He screams, "I HAAATE YOOOUUU!" and I am afraid he will burst a capillary in his eye. I want to hurt myself, somehow, after those times when I have hissed under my breath, "Shut the fuck up right now" or "What the hell is wrong with you? Why are you like this? This is *not normal.*"

When this happens in public, people stop. They get angry and annoyed. They offer unhelpful critiques of my parenting. They snicker at us as they walk past or refuse to validate the positive, brilliant sides of my son whenever they are around him again. He's either the rock-star cool kid everyone wants to play with or he is the freak-out, untamed, feral child who everyone thinks needs a drug to get him to calm the fuck down. Either way, he's labeled, and I am pretty sure that it is my fault.

Negative two points: teen moms.

Negative one point: attachment parents who "spoil" their kids.

I don't know the reasons that my son may or may not be inclined, on any given day, to throw a glass of soy milk across a restaurant or yell in your baby's face. Or to sing a quiet song to all the adults in the room about why we should love everyone and about how ghosts can be mommies too, or to whisper into your baby's ear, "I love you so much because you are small and sweet." I don't know, so don't ask me, unless you have some new insight to give and can offer me at least, "I know how it is—mine was like that. I was alone too. And all I can tell you is that it ends, someday."

I know it *isn't* because I was only fifteen when I got pregnant. If I allowed myself that thought, I would betray the line of reasoning on which I have worked to build my identity and base my life's activism. But maybe it *was* because of that meth I did before I knew I was pregnant—maybe it's still running through his body, having irrevocably altered the makeup of his brain's chemistry, having poisoned him at a crucial stage in embryonic development.

Maybe it's because I nursed him too much, held him too

close, listened to his nonverbal cues too closely, spent too much time with him immediately next to, if not on, me. Maybe he only learned to demand and didn't learn how to do for himself. Perhaps I developed—or he did, on his own—his ability to communicate articulately and accurately, but not his ability to interact or to cope with frustration and upset.

Then again, it could just be born into his blood, like his blond hair or his slim figure. Just another one of the things his father left with us. Maybe none of them—none of the men who share my son's misgiven last name—actually *can* control their rage; maybe it's inherited, like their alcoholism, and my son is destined to the same fate. No, I'm a sociology major, and I believe that alcoholism is a product of social conditioning and not biological disease. I think back to the two years that Cade spent learning violence and anger and fear—almost three, if you count the months that his fetus-self spent dodging the fists that his father drove into my belly, jostling warmly inside of me whenever I tried to run away. His father yelled, I cried, and it's as if Cade learned to internalize both his father's actions and my reactions, and now he can't decide which one of us to model.

Maybe it's because of all that time I spent fighting to achieve "success," seeking the approval of a society that tried to convince me that I would never have any value or worth. Maybe my kid is wild because of all the hours I spent working in clerical positions, entry-level social services, and making pizzas while he was in day care. Not Montessori, not Waldorf (what teen mom can afford the best?), but just day care. Or maybe it was all that time I spent rotating videos (*Scooby? Blue? Yellow Submarine?*) while frantically trying to write speeches, polish term papers, finish Web site updates, compute algebraic equations, and study for finals. The times when I couldn't decide which was more important: achieving the elusive "success" that society said I would never find or spending time with my single greatest accomplishment?

I don't know why my son is so difficult now. I don't know where or when or how things shifted. I don't know when I started slipping and my "teen mom success story" turned into "failure as a mother." But I have learned, through this shifting of his personality and this morphing of our parent-child relationship, that parenting isn't simply a set of definable accomplishments.

Maybe things just aren't as easy as they are supposed to be. Maybe there isn't a singular trajectory path to success, to a happy family, to overcoming maternal age. Maybe in my attempts to buck societal scripts for teen mothers, I let those same scripts define my happiness. As my contentment in and satisfaction with my progress has become less and less defined by what new milestone of success I have reached, and more and more by the details of everyday moments and newly learned tactics for survival, I am relearning what it means to be a mother and what it means to mother well.

I did everything "right." I gave birth naturally, I breastfed for years, I graduated high school as Student of the Year, I worked to support my son and myself, I went to college and pulled A's. I edited a Web site and wrote essays about being an empowered teen mother. I tried to define my successes by my paper trails, grades, and monetary value. I realized, maybe too late or maybe just in the nick of time, that success isn't a singular goal. You do not "arrive" once you complete the steps assigned by our moral gatekeepers. You do not "achieve" once your success, your choices, your children, your life have attained the proper certification. You do not "succeed" because you finish school, marry your teenage boyfriend, or find a secretarial position in a corporate office. Success is not a tangible, attainable position that you arrive at because of your hard work and dedication. Waking up each morning, getting through each day the best that you can, and finding as much joy as possible in the life you have created and the life that you are living is where we can be successful. Only when we are empowered to make our own choices, meet our own goals, and define our own successes will we ever really feel accomplished.

My son became sick at preschool today, and his teachers called me to pick him up early. They found him shivering, lying on the playground. I brought him home, made him soup (which he refused, demanding in his nasal voice "I WANTED a cheese sammich!"), and gave in to his needs for constant contact and cuddling as best I could. My girlfriend and I had to fight his delusional, feverish self to get him to take the medicine he desperately needed to help him relax enough to sleep. He fought, hit, screamed, bit, and wasted five doses of medicine before the two of us could finally coax him into taking half a dose.

Over an hour later—including almost an hour of cuddling—he was finally calm enough to lie still and try to fall asleep. I watched his eyes fluttering, and I remembered when he was a sick infant, hospitalized for Kawasaki Syndrome when he was ten months old, and how sad and sick he looked, and how I cried with the knowledge that despite my best efforts, he was fragile. I smiled at him now, heartstrings pulled taut, and he opened his eyes and looked back at me long enough to say, "Thank you for always taking care of me." I know that however much I falter, struggle, step off the path to doing a "successful job" as a teen mother, I am doing something, somehow, just right.

Allison Crews *is a twenty-one-year-old mama, dyke, student, worker, and idealist. She lives in Austin, Texas with her partner, Julie, and their sons Cade and Dylan. She is the editor of www.girlmom.com, and her writing has been featured in* Hip Mama, Breeder: Real Life Stories From the New Generation of Mothers, Listen Up! Voices From the Next Feminist Generation, *Greenhaven Press's* Teen Pregnancy, *and elsewhere. You may see Allison in a teen magazine feature or reproductive rights protest near you.*

A l i c e   C a m p b e l l

The Power of No

By the time I got pregnant at age seventeen, I had bought into the idea that women should be quiet and submissive.

No one ever came straight out and told me women should be this way. I saw it in the way my parents interacted, how my dad's voice was always worth more than my mom's, the way my brother was allowed to behave in ways that were out of bounds for my sister and me. The messages from outside my home were just as subtle. Most school administrators were men, while my teachers were women. The men in my community were the heads of their households, leaders in their church and community, while their women stood behind them with their packs of children. Good women didn't work. Their role was to stay at home and serve their families. When I looked at power, I saw men. This unchallenged idea that women should be submissive and passive, that power is in being male, kept me from being able to say "No" the first time my boyfriend laid himself on top of me. The old clock in the camper outside his house slowly marked each passing moment as I tried to distance myself from what was happening. I shoved the fear, confusion, and pain into every single tick of that clock, and with this, what little thread of who I really was ticked away.

When my boyfriend and I discovered I was expecting, he told me how excited he was. We could all live together, be a family. It would be great. During the following months, however, he dropped out of school and quit his job. His main concerns were about not getting enough sex and how he was going to find more cigarettes now that he didn't have any income. I worried about the overwhelming responsibilities of parenthood. I was going to school and doing well, maintaining a part-time job, and growing a child. He sat around and criticized every positive move forward I made. "Don't be so proud," he'd say. "Pride is a sin." When I attempted to disagree with him, he would say angrily, "Why are you always trying to pick a fight?" He'd walk away in disgust and ignore me until I apologized for picking the fight. Desperate for someone to love me and pay attention to me, I silenced my dissent.

My parents hadn't noticed me in years. I slipped in and out of their house, and no one really noticed or cared. It was really all about appearances at my house. "Nobody is going to like you," my mom would say. "You're too shy. And look at you. You're so pale, and your hair is so stringy." In seventh grade, when most girls are begging their moms to let them wear makeup, my mom dragged me to the cosmetics counter and loaded me up. I never wanted to wear so much makeup. She even took me to the tanning salon because my pale legs were such an embarrassment to her.

When I gave birth to my daughter, the pain was overwhelming. The burning sensations as her head moved through the birth canal paralyzed me. I couldn't speak, but I could hear my own silent screams. My family and my boyfriend were all there, the doctors and nurses running around. All this pain and the loneliness blowing through my chest collided as her head crowned. I was drowning in it all, losing all connections to what I was. I felt as if I were dying.

They wrapped my daughter in towels and placed her on my stomach. She gazed up at me, and when we made eye contact, all the pain and loneliness vanished. My body filled with a warmth I hadn't felt since I was a small child, and I could breathe again. I loved her like I had never loved another person. I loved her simply because she had been born. I looked around the room at my boyfriend and my family. Nobody loved me this way, and I couldn't believe what I had thought love was—suppressing my needs and fulfilling the needs of others.

A few days later, I broke up with my boyfriend. I did it over the phone because I was too scared to face him, too worried that the small touch of resolve to do better for my child and myself would slip away. "Okay," he said, and then he called the next morning as if I had not broken up with him. I told him again that I wanted something different for my life and my child. I needed a love he couldn't offer either of us. He called again that night. This time, he finally heard me. He called consistently for a couple of weeks afterward, telling me he loved me and how he couldn't live without me. He began telling me he was going to kill himself if I didn't get back together with him. We didn't get back together, and he didn't kill himself, either.

Over time, the strength of my voice continued to grow. I started on little issues such as choosing the restaurant I preferred instead of deferring to the person I was with. My daughter's pediatrician encouraged me to make my own choices for my child, and knowing he believed in me, I eventually had the confidence to tell my mom I knew what was best for my child. This pediatrician was the first person to tell me I was capable of making good decisions. The confidence that came with the knowledge that one person believed in me was something I hadn't realized I had been missing in my life.

In my senior year of college, I became friends with a man, and during one of our first conversations, I told him that we were not going to be anything more than friends. I was focused on school and my child; there was no room for any relationships beyond friendship. He and I spent hours talking and debating as equals, and I found a new wisdom in being able to say, "No, I disagree with you," knowing that disagreeing would not change our relationship.

Our relationship went on this way until I was accepted to graduate school. It was a good six-hour drive from my home, and from the man who had become my best friend and confidant. While overjoyed to have been accepted, I was deeply saddened that it would mean leaving him behind. He was the second person in my life to believe in me, and I was still learning how to believe in myself.

I told him I was leaving to attend school, and, as I had expected, he was supportive. Later that night, we were sitting in my living room, watching a rented movie. I looked over at him and began studying his face. His eyes were so gentle and caring. A rush of emotion welled up, and all of a sudden, I realized I didn't want to leave him behind. Since I had known him, he'd understood that I didn't want to be passively chosen by any man, like an orphan desperately needing to be "wanted." However, I now found that *I* wanted to choose a man to be a part of *my* life. If I could choose where to eat, which medicine to give my child, and what career I wanted, I certainly could choose whom to invite to participate with me in an intimate relationship. In my excitement at this realization, I reached over and grabbed his shoulders with both hands so he was facing me. He was surprised and a little worried at the urgency with which I had seized him. For a moment I experienced the old powerlessness, where what I felt and wanted was not important. *No, what I'm feeling is important!* I needed words, words that could express all the emotions flowing through me, and then they came. "Will you marry me?"

I have since married, finished graduate school, and had another daughter. I love hearing the voices of my two girls as they run around the house, laughing and yelling in a joyous celebration of life. However, as the oldest is now entering puberty and the youngest is about to turn two, opportunities for disagreements in our house abound. I watch other parents with children at these difficult ages. I see the sting, hurt, and embarrassment in their eyes when their children tell them, "No." These parents react, and in no uncertain terms they teach their girls it's not okay to say *that* word to anyone bigger, especially someone who is powerful.

That's exactly whom I want my girls to be able to say "No" to—anyone who is bigger, and especially those who are more powerful. My children see the glimmer of satisfaction in my eyes when they flex their independence with me. I know my role is to help my girls listen to their needs and practice their voices now, so they will be prepared to use their voices well on their journeys in life. My husband and I have built a home filled with strong voices singing their own songs in harmony, a place where love is about the freedom to share our authentic selves.

Alice Campbell *works for a nonprofit social service agency. She lives with her husband and two daughters, and enjoys gardening in the Northwest drizzle and occasional sun breaks.*

Speak Out!

What's the most important lesson you've learned since becoming a mother?

Patience.

I'm strong enough to handle anything that comes my way.

To be proud of who I am and what I am.

How to love and do my best.

Happiness does not have a price tag, and the best things in life are free.

The serenity to accept the things I cannot change, the courage to change the things I can, and the wisdom to know the difference.

Never-ending patience.

My son has taught me how good people can be.

Nothing is more important than your family, and together we can make it through anything.

To slow down and enjoy our time together.

To love unconditionally, even when their diapers stink and they throw up on you.

I'm capable. Sometimes I'm the *only* one for the job, and I do it well, dammit!

That life is worth living.

How to really gut-bust laugh.

Selflessness.

You can always get up after you've fallen down.

Responsibility, responsibility, responsibility.

Motivation.

Patience, definitely. I had none before.

To see beauty in everything, even bugs, dirt, and melted crayons.

PART 4

Growing Belly, Shrinking Brain?

ON DROPPING OUT, GETTING BACK IN, AND FINISHING AN EDUCATION—IN SPITE OF THE STATISTICS

I see my former history teacher, whose class I had to flee from each morning at 8:20 when I raced to the bathroom to heave and sob in my favorite toilet stall. He realized why I left each day and warned me of my future: "You know what this means, don't you? Not that you would have had much of a chance to begin with, but now you are just finished. I still expect you to show up every day, but I don't know what good it will do you. Girls like you don't graduate anyway."

I wish now that I had been able to look at him and say, "Girls like me don't listen to people like you. Girls like me have raised presidents. We've raised messiahs, and musicians, and writers, and settlers. Girls like me won't compromise, and we won't fail."

—Allison Crews,

21, mother, student, worker, Austin, Texas

While working on this anthology I have received enthusiastic letters and E-mails from teachers of teen parents across North America. One high school teacher, herself a former teen mother, wrote, "I am now fortunate enough to be a teacher working with teen moms like I once was. They have taught me so much, even though they may not realize it. They have taught me that even teens can be the best of moms. They love unconditionally and find the strength within themselves to give more, even after the sleepless nights. They remember how to have fun with their babies, because it was not that long ago that fun was all that was important in being a kid. They know all too well that they are responsible for another life and must provide the best. I know in my heart that they will. They've taught me to look back at the young mom that I was and realize that I too was great at it."

Not only the moms who stay in school deserve our best wishes and praise. One high school teacher and former teen mom—a school dropout who went on to earn a GED and eventually bachelor's and master's degrees in education—wrote, "Few of my peers are aware I didn't graduate from high school. All they know is that I don't like it when they complain about a student who is dropping out, saying they will never amount to anything. I pop off, 'One never knows.'"

In visiting a number of schools and programs for teen parents, I heard arguments for student mothers to stay in mainstream classes and I heard counterarguments for them to be sidelined into special teen parenting programs. The young mothers who spoke favorably about separate programs appreciated the camaraderie of other pregnant and parenting students. One woman wrote that she was able to "gain lasting friendships with other women in a similar situation." Some students in special programs especially liked being physically apart from judgmental or unsympathetic teachers and peers. They liked having a curriculum designed for them, with topics such as prenatal nutrition, the effects of smoking on fetal development, and craft activities for toddlers. Others simply appreciated being in a group where becoming a mom was the norm.

I also heard complaints from separated students. "They don't expect anything of us," one mom in a teen parenting program told me. "We don't learn anything here." Shunted off to a program housed in an alternative high school, she had no access to rigorous academic courses such as chemistry, physics, or advanced-placement history or math. She feared that she was getting inadequate preparation for college. (For more on this topic, see Katherine Arnoldi's essay in Part 8 on the education rights of parenting students.)

The one thing everyone seemed to agree on was that becoming a parent brought innumerable lessons in and of itself, and many said they were learning—whether formally or informally—in a whole new way. Motherhood prompted some to consider going to college when they hadn't given it a thought before. Others found that it sparked a change in their course of study or career plans. One woman described how having less time for schoolwork motivated her to have a sharper focus on it. Several described initially aiming for "sensible" careers in teaching or business, only to find that the soul-baring experiences of parenting compelled them to recognize—and to pursue—their genuine passion in another field.

In the following essays, Jackie Lanni describes her transformation from a "selfish and volatile girl who walked out of her mother's house forever rather than clean up the bathroom" into disciplined graduate student. Judy Moses details the benefits of dropping out in order to see and learn from the world. Katie Huber weaves through sex, drugs, and punk to face off with intrusive students and a short-sighted principal, as she endeavors to collect her high school diploma. And Clea Roddick discovers that being a mother has its advantages when you are trying to stay focused on your life's dream.

Jackie Lanni

How to Get to Law School

Being a teenage mother is something I haven't considered until I learn I am to join the proverbial ranks. I am sixteen, living with my boyfriend, and not going to school. I live in a trashy studio apartment in dilapidated downtown Mesa, Arizona, and have no ambition. How do I get from here to law school? Easy. I have a baby.

Perhaps saying "easy" is misleading. Okay, it's lying. I do not know what being a teenage mother means on that February afternoon when my Fact Plus test shows me a big pink plus sign. I know that I am pregnant and that I will have a baby. I assume that one day I will be a single mother, and I am okay with that. Rather, I am numb to that. A feminist even at sixteen, I know that abortion is my right. I do not consider it. Instead, I try to imagine what being a mother will be like.

I am too naive to know how hard it will be. I, like first-time mothers of all ages, have mental images of sitting in a rocking chair in a sunny room, gazing adoringly into the eyes of my newborn. I want to be different from my own mother. I want to have time for my baby, and I want to protect my child from the abuses my mother wasn't able to protect me from. I want to be the best mother in the world, and I am confident I can do this.

What I know about teenage mothers I have read in magazines and seen on newsmagazine shows. I know we are a population "spiraling out of control." I hear that we are sucking the life out of the welfare system, leeching off honest taxpayers. I hear that we are incompetent and selfish mothers at best, abusive and neglectful at worst. It is said that we commonly drop out of high school, have more illegitimate babies while still young, and ultimately spend our lives in poverty. Although I have no reason to disbelieve this information, I scorn it and vow that I will never be this model of teenage motherhood.

What people think of me and of my future never bothers me until now, when I am pregnant. I know right away that I must graduate high school to avoid becoming a negative stereotype. So, visibly pregnant, I enroll in summer school to try to make up for the semester I have just blown. I stand in line for registration among the tan and well-dressed teenagers, and all conversation around me ceases. I meet their stares, expressionless but quaking inside, and realize that they, like me, have never seen a pregnant teenager before. I can't blame them for staring; I obviously do not belong here among these good students who enroll in summer school to get ahead, not to catch up.

For the first time in high school, I make A's. People in class even begin to talk to me on occasion. Still, I feel isolated as I sit under a shade tree eating my mushy sandwich and reading my pregnancy book while the others drive away in bright cars packed with friends for a fast-food lunch. I belong to my own little world that no longer includes friends and carefree living. I tell myself that my isolation doesn't bother me. I convince myself I like being alone. I am different from these teenagers. They do not pay rent or utilities or take prenatal vitamins. I no longer have rights to their world.

In the fall I enroll in a teen parent program at the district's vocational school. We teen moms must be tucked away from the nice boys and girls; our alleged promiscuity is contagious. As the weeks until I am due melt away and I read book after book about pregnancy, I am more dedicated than ever to completing high school. Not only must I finish, but I must also be able to tell my son that I graduated with A's. It is no longer enough to simply graduate. Some latent perfectionism has taken over my life, perhaps shocked out of dormancy by pregnancy hormones. Nothing is too good for my unborn son, and I will not give him the mother that everyone expects I will give him.

I am hypersensitive to the stares of disapproval I now receive frequently. I see it in the eyes of my obstetrician, an older man who scowls at me, and I quickly change to a different OB/GYN. I see it in the eyes of strangers as they pass me in the street and stare at my belly as if I was not a real person conscious of their staring. I even see it in the expressions of my family, who don't know quite what to think. I know my family does not want me to fail, but they only know the selfish and volatile girl who walked out of her mother's house forever rather than clean up the bathroom. I will make them sorry they doubted me—or proud. Whichever. Their doubt motivates me more.

I give birth. I am shocked at the immense protectiveness and love that wells up in me when I hold my son for the first time. I feel as though I recognize him, as if I would have known him anywhere. Now I know that I must be a good mother to him for reasons other than merely proving everyone wrong. Soon after he is born, they take him to warm him under the lamps, as his temperature is a little low. I call the nursery after fifteen minutes and continue to call them every five minutes until they return my baby to me. I want my baby, and I lie with him all night, refusing to return him to the nursery. He sleeps away while I catnap and awaken every few minutes to look at him. Overnight I go from self-absorbed teenager to typically protective mother, ready to trade my life for my son's without a moment's thought.

I am blessed with an "easy" baby. He sleeps, he eats, he smiles. I am exhausted with high school, nursing, and my two part-time jobs. During the day I attend high school classes. The nursery staff is supposed to call me on the intercom when he needs to nurse, but I don't need them to alert me. Aching and leaking milk, my breasts instinctively tell me when my son is hungry, and I am halfway to the nursery when I hear my name over the intercom. After school I work either at the movie theater across the street or at the gift shop next to it. My son's father brings Alyx to me to nurse when he is hungry. I am too young and tired to know that this pace and this schedule are insane.

Sometimes I eat, sometimes I sleep, but neither often enough. If I wanted to, I could receive welfare benefits and food stamps and drop one of those part-time jobs, but if I do I will be a teenage welfare mother. I feel obligated to do it the hard way, so no one can point a finger at me.

My boyfriend and I move to Denver, and I enroll in a teen parent program for my final semester of high school. I am eighteen and don't know how to drive. I have always been too scared to learn. Now, however, I must learn, as Eric's work schedule will not allow him to chauffeur me to and from school. I learn to drive in two weeks, although not very well. I can only parallel-park because I can't drive in reverse. My sister and some of my friends encourage me to drop out and get my GED. Tempting though it is, I don't consider this an option. I will drive to school, petrified though I may be, and I will graduate.

I go to school and earn A's, this time in the company of "normal" students. They swarm around with their concerns about school dances and part-time jobs, while I worry about how quickly the day care will be able to find me in case of emergency. One day, my son is on the front page of the school newspaper. I glow with pride as, in every class, students ooh and aah over his picture. I take home twenty copies of the paper. In my journalism class I find out that my project partner also has a baby. She, however, refuses to be part of the teen parent program, instead opting for a "normal" teenage life. Her friends do not know about her son, and her parents care for him. I encourage her to visit our classroom and meet the other mothers, to receive the support she does not know she is missing. She will not come; she is afraid someone might see her going into the room. She is smart enough to be ashamed of her motherhood, while I am not. I like to flaunt it. Some masochistic desire in me seeks the looks of shock and disapproval. I feed off of it; it propels me.

The counselor tells me I have enough credits to graduate. I leave after that semester with no ceremony. I simply leave for the winter holiday break and never return. Soon after, I learn that my boyfriend has been sexually involved with other women, some of whom are my friends. With much grief, I leave him and move back to Arizona and my family. Suddenly I have regressed; I am no longer independent, but once again living with my mother, her husband, my brother and sister, and Alyx. Alyx and I share the small, crowded office, and he sleeps in a crib while I take the floor. I wake up every morning with my eyes glued together from crying in my sleep. After a couple of months, my mother finds a diplomatic way of getting me out of her house and back on my feet. She pays the utility deposits and the security deposit for a small, one-bedroom apartment. I am glad to have my own space but unsure of how to be a parent on my own.

I get a data entry job that pays little more than minimum wage, and I cry as I write checks out for my bills each month. Many of these checks are returned to my bank. This situation would not be so bad if my son's father paid child support, but soon after his girl-friend becomes pregnant he calls with important announcements: They are getting married, and he will not be paying child support to me. I have no money for gas, much less a lawyer. My days are filled frantically calling Bank of America's automated customer service line to see which check has cleared and which hasn't.

I work, typing data day after day in a purchasing department for a large corporation. I get a small raise. Finally, I get promoted after one of the women in my department quits. I love the work I am now doing, as I get to make decisions and judgment calls, but the people I work with drive me insane. The office politics literally makes my stomach hurt. Still, I progressively work my way up the pay scale until I can at last just barely pay my bills. I am the only nineteen-year-old in a department full of women in their thirties and forties. I feel as though I am their age.

I get custody papers one day at work. I hire a sympathetic and smart lawyer whom I pay for with my tax return. At the same time my custody and child support case is settled, I meet a man at work. Dave and I fall in love quickly and move in together soon after. My son loves him and I am glad to finally have someone to help me. I am tired of struggling. I am glad to have some attention.

I work, I get a raise, I work, I get a raise. These raises are always small, but I am proud at age twenty to be making $10.79 an hour. I still hate the office politics, but I am paying my bills. As I look around my office one day, I have an epiphany: Everyone in my department is easily twice my age; although my wage is respectable, even enviable for someone my age, it is not for these women in their forties. I realize that if I do not do something, one day I will be forty and working for this same wage. Although I grew up in a house where college was never mentioned, I think that college is the only way out. I have friends in college, and I envy their carefree lives. College looks like a great alternative to working with crazy people whose lives revolve around potluck lunches and coworker dramas.

I enroll in community college and work part-time. I find that college is my "thing"; it seems effortless and exciting. As a single parent I qualify for grants and subsidized loans, which, combined with part-time data entry work, is enough to get by. Dave works full-time, and my days of skipping lunch seem far behind. We buy a small house and start our middle-class life. I feel in control. My life is progressing nicely.

After a year I transfer to the state university, where I continue to excel in my studies. With a good GPA, I am able to qualify for more grants and scholarships. I am a lazy student, but it seems to work for me. My success is easy, and I never feel like I have truly earned it. I work toward my bachelor's in English and along the way pick up enough history credits to earn a bachelor's in that field as well. Women's studies becomes another strong interest, and I pursue a certificate of concentration in that area. Before I know it, I have been in college for five years.

My son loves that I am in college. He loves to brag about my status as a college student to anyone who will listen, and he can recite my majors when asked. Because my schedule is more flexible now, I am able to spend a lot of time volunteering for his school. He is thrilled to have me in his classroom, and when I am there his face fills with pride. "That's *my mom,*" he says to his disbelieving friends. Their moms look like *my* mother. One day another mother, no longer able to contain herself, turns to me and asks me if I am a student or a mother. The other moms view me cynically, although they try to keep their smiles bright so as not to appear shocked at my age. I force my way into the inner workings of the school, smiling all the way. I join the Parent-Teacher-Student Organization, I chair their committees, I am treasurer of their clubs. With time, some of the mothers warm to me, while others seem offended that I don't have the decency to hide that I am a very, very young mother. I am the source of the PTSO's biggest mystery: How *old* is she, anyway?

In my last semester of college, my son tells everyone with pride that I am graduating. I know that going to college has provided something valuable to both of us. More time together sometimes, less time together sometimes. A real view of college life. A real view of a student staying up all night typing a paper. The pride of an A. We share these things, and he knows how hard it is. We also know that it is so important, for both of us.

I decide before I start college that I want to go to law school. In my final semester, I apply to several. My son, meanwhile, is telling everyone, "My mom is going to be a *lawyer.*" I grin a silly grin when he says this. On the top of my mortarboard I carefully paint my thanks to my son and my boyfriend. I lean into the television camera at graduation so my son can see his name on the jumbo screen. My son graduates third grade right after I graduate college. I take a short trip after graduation and return to a letter offering a Merit Scholarship to law school. It means a move, but I can't refuse it. However, I lose my boyfriend of seven years, and I must start my life over again. All of the changes of my life seem to coincide. I am ready, though.

I move to another city an hour and a half away. I rent a small house and decorate it how I like. I make a conscious decision to make friends, to not segregate myself from everyone else. I no longer need the fighting stance I adopted when I became pregnant. I am ready to start a new life, once again as a single mother. This time I don't walk into it scared or unknowing, but welcoming the challenge with new wisdom.

I am now at the end of my first semester of law school. Balancing being a single parent with the demands of graduate school has been the greatest challenge of my life. I have wanted to quit, but I can't. It's not just that I owe it to myself, even though I do—I also owe it to Alyx. Without him, I would not have graduated high school. I would not have gone to college. I would not have aspired to law school. I would not have done half the things I have done, and I wouldn't have taken a fraction of the risks. At first, I had something to prove to everyone else— to the religious right, to the conventional families of the world, to the naysayers and prophets of social doom. Gradually I found that I wanted *him* to see something in me, something that *he* had caused. The gifts he had given me.

I doubt he will ever understand how his life has affected me. Likely he thinks that Mommy went to college because she wanted to get a great job and make a boatload of money. It *is* something we discuss. But I know that I did it because I wanted him to be proud of me, to be proud of *us* and what we did together. I never wanted to use my being such a young mother as an excuse for what I couldn't do for him or myself. I could not face my son feeling that my life had been ruined—or that both of our lives had been ruined—by my early foray into motherhood. I chose to do the opposite; I used my young motherhood as a reason to hold myself to a higher standard than I'd previously ever thought possible.

Being a young mother has given me a confidence I never had, and I am proud to have been a teenage mother. I must admit—I still love to flaunt my teenage motherhood in the faces of the smug, the critical, and the closed-minded. Maybe my accomplishments will never be enough for them and my child rearing never conventional enough, but I can look with pride at my son, now ten, and think, *I have done* something *right*. I don't need anyone to validate me anymore. Don't tell me my life ended when I had a baby at seventeen. I didn't believe you then, and I certainly don't now. My life story *starts* at age seventeen.

Jackie Lanni *is the twenty-seven-year-old mother of Alyx Shea, age ten. While raising her witty little genius, she found time to attend Arizona State University and graduate with honors. She holds BA degrees in English and history as well as a certificate of concentration in women's studies. She is currently attending law school at the University of Arizona and ultimately plans to found a nonprofit legal service/lobbying group to aid women, children, and of course, teen mamas.*

Judy Moses

My Independent Study Abroad

When I broke the news of my pregnancy to my friends and family, they warned that having a baby was going to ruin my life. With a discouraging look and apologetic shake of her head, my best friend cautioned me that dating, having fun, sleeping eight hours a night, and being thin—things every eighteen-year-old ought to value—were as good as out the window with a kid in the picture. The night I told my father I was pregnant, he paced around the living room, shocked and furious. Disappointed that I would have to put college on hold, he tried desperately to assure me that having an abortion was my best option. I sat and cried, fighting back nausea, knowing abortion was not an option at all.

Though everyone seemed to consider it the end of the world, I was extremely relieved to be leaving school, which hadn't gone well even before I'd gotten pregnant. I was a freshman at Virginia Commonwealth University in Richmond, the same city where I had gone to high school. The new friends I'd made in my first semester at college all seemed so sure about what they wanted out of life, confident about the goals they'd set for themselves, and pleased to be in the higher educational system. I was uncertain about what I wanted to study, let alone whether I wanted to study anything at all. I couldn't make myself concentrate on or care about reading assignments or writing essays. I could not find motivation to attend my classes. My heart wasn't in it; I simply wasn't ready. Now, with no feeling of purpose at college and a baby on the way, I had no intention of sticking around.

Peter, my baby's father, was an English guy who'd been living in France for most of his life and had only been visiting the U.S. when I got pregnant. By the time I was cleaning out my college apartment and planning to move in with friends, he'd long since returned to Europe. I had thought I'd never see him again, and any lingering hope I had vanished when I discovered I was pregnant. When he called me from France and said he wanted us to stay together and be a family, I was shocked.

My father stood firm in his belief that an abortion was the only solution which would allow me to lead a full and productive life. Whenever he spoke to me he stressed what a mistake it was for me to have a child. He said he was willing to pay the considerable cost for me to go to another state and have a second-trimester termination. Feeling frustrated and defeated by his lack of support, I decided not to have contact with him anymore.

While living with friends and trying to enjoy my pregnancy instead of treating it like a cataclysmic emergency the way my family did, I was offered a job as a nanny by a divorced father whose three school-aged children would be staying with him during the summer. He wanted me to shuttle them to and from summertime activities at the library, swimming pool, and playground while he was at work. The job was not difficult; I loved spending my pregnant days seeing movies, reading books, swimming, and eating ice cream with three friendly little girls— and I was being paid to do it.

For months I alternated between feelings of excitement and apprehension about whether to move to France. It was scary to think about moving to another country where I didn't speak the language and knew only my boyfriend. Staying in the U.S.—my home—was also frightening. My friends were very supportive of my decision to keep my child and not at all opposed to a pregnant girl living with them—but a girl with a baby?

I worried about how my relationships would change and how I would manage to care and provide for a child on my own. Most of all, I wanted my boyfriend to be with me—to feel the thumping kicks from the baby inside me, to hold my hand during labor, to help me with middle-of-the-night feedings. To just be with me. Realizing how much I missed him and that his offer to live in France was the only way that we would be together, I made up my mind. I wanted to stay at home with my baby and raise my child with her father around every day, things that would not be possible if I was a single mom in America. Moving thousands of miles from familiarity seemed a small price to pay for giving my baby two loving parents.

At seven months pregnant, with my family still insisting that pregnancy was the worst thing that could have happened to me, I cleaned out my room at my friends' home, packed up my belongings, and spent nearly all the money I'd earned working as a nanny to fly to Paris. With my enormous belly propped uncomfortably on my lap in the tiny airplane seat for eight hours, I was still uncertain about whether I had made the right decision. Visions of an exciting adventure *and* of a disastrous mistake both came freely.

The apartment Peter found for us in Paris was a tiny studio flat with tile floors and peach-colored wallpaper. The entire living space was about the same size as my bedroom in my parents' home, but it was cozy and located in an exciting and exotic new place, and for those reasons I loved it. I spent my days there alone while my boyfriend went to work—dealing with a subway system whose workers were often on strike, and often being away from our home for twelve hours at a time. During those long, lonely, late summer afternoons, I read books about childbirth and newborn care. Folding and refolding tiny baby clothes, I memorized phrases in French. Using flashcards I taught myself how to say "I'm bleeding," "I'm having contractions every five minutes," "My water has broken," and "Epidural, *s'il vous plait*." Amused, I reflected that if I'd arrived in Europe under different circumstances, I'd be looking up how to ask for directions to the Eiffel Tower or how to order drinks in a nightclub.

For my prenatal checkups, my boyfriend and I walked three miles every week to and from the hospital where our baby would be born. As hot as it was in late summer and as cumbersome as my body had become, I loved those walks. It amazed me how old France was compared with the U.S. Thousand-year-old churches stood next to buildings built by slaves centuries ago, both still in everyday use. Citing pregnancy cravings for gateaux, I would stop at one of the many bakeries on the way home to fill up on heavenly French pastries. In autumn, as my due date neared and then passed, Peter took his paternity leave and we trekked every other day to my examinations.

My daughter's entrance into this world was more amazing than I'd ever imagined. She needed coaxing to come out—I ended up having labor induced at forty-two weeks—but even so she was persuaded from my body without complications. She emerged looking sleepy and solemn, with huge, dark blue eyes like the ocean the night I flew overseas. When she looked at me, I felt faint with happiness. Her face was heavy and calm, and as soon as she was placed in my arms, her perfectly round pink head rested on my chest and we watched each other, unblinking. Love at first sight, something I'd never believed in, sparked white-hot and all-consuming. The earth spun, and my tiny newborn baby girl and I were the very core of it. A centrifugal force pulled away everything else—contractions that still rippled through me, pushing out my placenta; doctors murmuring in French; the stinging in my shredded perineum; my discouraging, warning family, far away in another country; my uncertainty and fears.

Smelling her baby head of wispy fine red hair scented with

me, I learned how true love felt. I was a mother, right then, and I knew it. No searching, no fumbling around for it to feel real and right, no doubting that she was really meant for me, no question in my mind that I was meant to be her mama. Her father and I cried, thrilled that our little treasure was finally here. I was certain that we would be okay, and I would fight as hard as I could to make sure of it. It was as if the world had been devoid of color and feeling before that very moment, and taking my daughter into my arms showed me the whole world and all of its possibilities.

My daughter Eskarina is now one year old. Being a mother has been overwhelming, draining, even terrifying, but always underneath the difficulty and struggle it has been mind-blowing and beautiful, well worth every frustrating obstacle ten times over. It's true I am not in school and that I don't have as much money or get as much sleep as I might were I childless. My friends were right when they warned me that I wouldn't be able to pick up at a moment's notice to go out and party. But they didn't know about all the crazy mama fun I'd be having without them. Eskarina makes me laugh until I'm near tears with her random babbling at strangers on the Metro. She flirts with the family who runs our neighborhood patisserie, knowing they will give her a cookie. She wakes me up with kisses sweeter than any boyfriend can offer. Having my legs unexpectedly wrapped in a knee-high hug makes skipped nap times a nonissue. With each new skill developed, every inch grown, every smile given to me, she fills me with happiness and gratitude.

What I have learned about myself since getting pregnant and dropping out of college is far more valuable than anything I learned in school. Young motherhood has taught me to become assertive. I question my daughter's pediatrician about the tests and vaccinations he wants to administer, defend my right to breastfeed my child on a park bench when I'm asked not to, educate myself about child development, and strive to feel confident and capable with everything I do.

Though it may not be hot stuff by anyone else's standards, and though pre-baby I would have been appalled by the jiggling of my belly and breasts, now that I'm a mom I feel confident and secure in my body. This body, stretch marks and sagging and all, successfully carried, birthed, and nursed an incredibly healthy child. It may not be much to look at beside that of a childless twenty-year-old, but the night my daughter was born, power unbeknownst to me coursed through me, every agonizingly wonderful moan and scream and contraction bringing me closer to meeting my daughter. Not even caring that I was naked in a room with some half-dozen strangers, I gave birth, my physical being host to some kind of religious, supernatural miracle. Mine is a body that gives life. Wearing extra width on my hips is well worth it.

Becoming a mom has opened doors to things I never would have otherwise experienced. If I didn't have my daughter, if she hadn't been conceived before I was married, before my family deemed it A Good Time, I would never have come to France. Certainly not to live in Paris, and definitely not to live the most exciting, soul-shaping year of my life. Without my daughter I would never have visited London, Frankfurt, Paris, or Nice, finding out which cafés are breastfeeding-friendly and which bistros tolerate diaper changes on their tables when there are no designated areas for such things. In my first six months abroad, I learned more French than I had learned Spanish studying it for five years in school. Now that I must describe my life and all the little things in it using a language that is not my own, my view of the world has changed hugely.

Being a mama has been fiercely empowering. Every decision I make is a challenge and affects her health: Should I let her cry when she is unhappy or pick her up? Should I put her in cloth or disposable diapers? Buy commercially farmed or organic produce? I know that her well-being shapes her world. My role as a mother drives me to fight hard for a safe place for my child, and I'm filled with intense rage when I hear of any harm coming to any child. I want to castrate child molesters, cleanse oceans, and orchestrate world peace. But I also just want to sit and soak in every beautiful moment with my baby, thankful that she is in my life. I feel more hope now that I'm a mother, and I feel more despair. I feel healed, and I feel more hurt.

If this is the ruined life of a college dropout, so be it.

Judy Moses *is an adventurous twenty-one-year-old living in beautiful Central New York with her daughter Eskarina, the two-year-old ball of fury. Judy enjoys music, all-you-can-eat Chinese buffets, 300-plus-point Scrabble games, and world travel with toddlers.*

Katie Huber

What Matters

've always loved school. Not the people at school, but learning. I'd devour everything the teachers threw at me. In first grade I read at a third- or fourth-grade level. I love reading, and I love books.

I think my love for school started because it got me out of my house. I hated it there. My father was abusive, frequently beating my younger brother, myself, and sometimes my mom. As I walked home from school, I'd wonder what the reason would be that day: a toy left on the floor, the cereal put back in the wrong place? Any little thing could set him off. School was a release from the pain.

By the time I was in fourth grade, my father demanded good grades. If I got a B he'd start yelling, then smack me around and kick me before he really laid into me, throwing me against walls, choking me, punching me. "You can do better than B's," he'd say.

So I tried harder. My grades were great, but my interactions with my classmates were horrible. They didn't like me. I was a poor kid. My clothes were from Kmart, not the Gap or whatever was popular at the moment; my hair was never in the latest style; my toys were cheap or secondhand. Nothing about me was good enough for them. So I stopped trying to please the kids at school and developed my own sense of self: dirty flannel shirts, rock music, black fingernails. The kids in forty-dollar T-shirts and designer jeans called me "dirty," a "Satanist," and anything else that they thought didn't pertain to them. I put up with their bullshit until about seventh grade. Then I started punching the people who made any cruel remarks to me. After that, people only talked behind my back.

Seventh grade was also when I lost my virginity, to a seventeen-year-old who was notorious for "popping cherries." I didn't really want to have sex with him. I knew I wasn't ready for it. But after so many years of enduring my father's abuse, I just wanted a guy to touch me and not hurt me. I wanted the gentle caress of his tan, rough skin on my silky, white skin. I wanted to smell his musk cologne mingling with my feminine perfume. I wanted to feel wanted, needed, beautiful. And for a short time, I did. I gave the only thing that was truly mine to a guy who didn't give a shit about me, just to feel like I was special.

The day after that boy took my virginity, my father caught us kissing and beat me so badly that I couldn't go to school—my haven—for three or four days. I became terrified of my father finding out that I was having sex, so I stopped.

Around this time, I started mutilating my body. It was another release. Watching the blood flow from my self-inflicted wounds was like watching my pain seeping out. I used razor blades, box cutters, anything that would make a perfect, beautiful cut. And it was mine! I controlled it! I couldn't control anything else in my life but this.

And then I found something else I could control: my weight. As puberty progressed, I started gaining weight. I wasn't fat, but as I had always been a thin child, this softer body was new to me. It didn't really bother me until my father noticed. As we ate dinner, he'd start oinking and laughing at me. No matter what I wore, he said I looked fat in it. He'd tell me that no guy would ever want me and that I was a disgusting pig.

I became more and more self-conscious. Believing that I was

fat and disgusting, I hid my body in clothes two sizes too big. I skipped breakfast and lunch, and at dinner I just pushed the food around on my plate.

I didn't realize at first that I was hiding my body and not eating enough. After a while, when my father stopped saying things about my weight, I realized that I wasn't as big as I had been. I still believed I was fat, but this, like the self-mutilation, was something I could control. So I kept at it. Soon, his comments were about how skinny I was. He said I was disgusting now because all my bones stuck out. I was five-seven and had gone from a healthy 150 pounds to a sickly 92. One night at dinner, as I pushed my food around, he told me, "If you're gonna starve yourself to death, you can do it in your bedroom. I'm not wasting money to put you in the hospital."

At age fifteen I took a trip to Ohio to see my grandmother. As I was hugging her and saying good-bye, she started to cry. I asked her what was wrong, and she said, "Honey, I can feel all your bones." At that moment what I had been doing to myself became clear. Slowly I started eating again.

My parents had been divorced for several years, and my father had managed to get custody of me. My mother was finally able to get custody of me when I was in high school, and when I moved to her house, things did get somewhat better. I was no longer afraid to bring my report card home, and I knew that I was loved. But my self-destructive behavior was so firmly in place that I couldn't stop it. Vodka, straight up, no chasers, was my drink of choice. I went through about a half gallon to a gallon a day. Since I was living with my mom, I had stopped talking to my father and was no longer afraid of him as I had been. I started getting into sex again. I went to parties where I'd end up sleeping with at least one guy, and sometimes two or three. By the time I was sixteen, I had had over twenty different sexual partners.

During my freshman year of high school I strayed from alcohol and got into drugs. I went from marijuana into cocaine, LSD, morphine, and anything else that would numb me for a while. Some of my grades started to slip. I got really weird, was into controversial rock singer Marilyn Manson, mutilated myself more often, and lashed out at anyone at school who so much as looked at me funny. I slept with any guy who glanced at me, and I had pretty much determined that my only purpose was to get fucked-up and to please the guys who wanted to get me into bed—though I also enjoyed having sex. I went through a lot of stormy relationships with guys who pronounced their undying love for me and then slept with my "best" friends. The few guys who did treat me with respect and love scared me, and I would quickly break things off with them.

My mother tried her best to help me. She tried counselors, medication, talking to me—anything she could think of—but mostly she never failed to let me know that she loved me and wanted to help. The counselors I went to were more interested in how I was performing at school than in how I was feeling. My junior high career was filled with certificates, medals, and plaques commending my academic excellence. Even throughout my drug and alcohol abuse, self-mutilation, and eating disorder in high school, I managed to do well in school. Whether it was because of personal ambition or an innate desire to please my parents, school remained vitally important to me. The counselors seemed to think that if my grades were good then I was dealing with the things I had been through.

Three or four months before my seventeenth birthday, I went to the mall with friends, and this dirty punk-rock guy named Tyson with neon-red hair just like mine caught my eye. We talked for a few minutes, then parted. I had a huge crush on him. Over the course of the next few months, we kept running into each other, like it was fated. One night we ended up going to the house where he had been staying with friends. We stayed up all night talking. I think that's the night I fell in love with him.

I stopped doing drugs because Tyson, who was a recovered drug abuser, was strictly against drug use. But we drank. A lot. And I wanted to drop out of school. I was stressed. I was sick of the yells of "Freak!" down the hallway, sick of the ridicule because I was a punk, sick of it all. Tyson didn't want me to leave school. While I was glad that he cared about my education, I was also upset with him: How did he, a dropout himself, have any right to tell me not to quit?

I found out I was pregnant on a Friday, before a weekend when I'd planned to drink. My period was a month late, so I did a pregnancy test. If I was pregnant, I didn't want to drink and hurt my baby. While I hoped against hope that I wasn't pregnant, I tried to face the possibility responsibly.

When two purple lines appeared, my mind raced. I stood there in the bathroom for a moment, struggling to comprehend what this little plastic stick was telling me. In shock, I showed Tyson the positive test. I watched as his face went white and his hands madly searched for the bathroom counter.

"Are you okay?" I asked worriedly. "Are you going to faint?"

"Ugh," he replied. "Are *you* okay? Do you need to sit down? Need some water? Are you feeling okay?"

I laughed and told him that I was pregnant, not dying. He begged me not to call my mother, claiming that she would kill him, but I insisted. After all the pain and worry I had put her through, I had come to realize that she was my best friend, always there for me, doing her best to steer me onto the right path, and catching me when I strayed—which was often. I had to tell her.

"Mom," I said over the phone, "I have some news that's kinda good and kinda bad."

"What?"

"I'm pregnant." I held my breath.

"Well, honey, how is that bad?"

Release breath. Unclench fists. Thank God.

"I was afraid you'd be pissed at me. I mean, I just started my senior year."

"Well, I do wish you could've waited at least a couple more years, but you should graduate before the baby comes. And besides, how could I not be happy? I'm going to be a grandma!" I could hear the tears in her voice.

So *I* started to tear up. I was so relieved that she wasn't angry. As I stood in the living room, the phone still in my hand, I realized that my life was no longer just about me. Everything I did from now on would directly affect this tiny little person whom I could feel growing inside me.

Although I didn't look down on pregnant girls who dropped out of school, I didn't want to be one. I didn't want my child to grow up feeling that it was his or her fault that I didn't graduate. I wanted the best for my child. And, for me, I knew that graduating was one of the best things I could do. I knew it would be difficult. I would be eight months pregnant when I graduated, but I knew I could do it. I wanted to prove it to myself, mostly, but also to people like my father who thought I couldn't do it. Throughout my life he had said that I could never accomplish anything. He was wrong. "They" were wrong. I could do it. I was strong.

So I did it. Even though people expected me to drop out. Even though, as soon as I had a tiny little baby belly, strangers were asking me if I was still in school. It pissed me off! These people assumed that, because I was pregnant, my brain had suddenly disappeared.

My school was on block scheduling, which meant that we had four classes per day, each an hour and a half long. I had only told my closest friends that I was pregnant, but by the time I was six months along it was obvious. To my surprise, I really didn't get much of a backlash from people at school. I got along well with most of my teachers, and they were happy and excited for me. When I told them I was pregnant, they congratulated me and made me promise to bring the baby to school so they could meet her. My English teacher even told me that I didn't need to ask her to use the bathroom, I could just go when I needed to.

The bigger I grew, the harder it became physically. My locker was downstairs, and all my classes were upstairs. So, between each class, I had to go up and down a flight of stairs. By my seventh month I was so big that I couldn't fit behind the desks anymore—I had to sit sideways. People I didn't know just looked at me and didn't say anything, but I didn't care. Realizing I was going to be a mother made what they thought of me seem so inconsequential. After all, they were just faces in a sea of people who didn't even know my name.

My new way of thinking made dealing with high school easier. Though I had always enjoyed learning, I used to face each morning before school with trepidation. Now that I realized I didn't need other kids' approval and that what they said or thought meant nothing, I began to thoroughly enjoy school.

I had one problem with my principal. Toward the end of the school year, all soon-to-be-graduates were required to attend an awards ceremony that lasted about three hours and had no bathroom breaks. I went to the principal and explained to him that because I was almost eight months pregnant and had to go to the bathroom at least twice an hour, I couldn't attend. He got very upset and short with me, saying that unless I had a doctor's excuse, I had to go and deal with it, that it was my problem I was pregnant, not the school's. I replied angrily that when he had a six-pound baby sitting on his bladder, he could tell me to "deal with it."

Thankfully my doctor was an awesome guy, and he readily gave me a written excuse. And so, at exactly eight months pregnant, I waddled across a makeshift stage and accepted my high school diploma with immense pride.

Being a teen mother isn't easy. I'm one of the "lucky" ones, according to society. Tyson has stood by me throughout everything. We had been engaged for almost a year when we found out I was pregnant, and we were married April 6, 2001, when I was six months along. My mom, brother, grandparents, aunts and uncles, and Tyson's sister and her husband were all thrilled and totally supportive.

I have a new life now. Through my family's love and support,

I have stopped the drinking, drug abuse, and self-mutilation. I have realized what is important to me. It's not money. It's not being popular. It's being surrounded by friends and family who love and accept me. It's the way my daughter smells after a bath, her crooked smile, her tiny hands and feet. Most important, as a mother, it is my child.

Katie Huber, *almost twenty-one years old now, delights in being mama to her wild and crazy daughter, who is almost two years old. She and Tyson do go head-to-head sometimes, but they still love each other like crazy after four years. On June 4, 2003, Katie lost her kitty, one of her oldest, dearest friends. She dedicates this essay in memory of Gee-Whiz, thanking her for all the love she shared over their fourteen years together.*

Clea Roddick

Stages

The lonely and empty place that I inhabited during my pregnancy still pokes little holes into me. The sharp jabs of others' unspoken expectations and unconscious stereotypes pierce into brain and heart until we do it to ourselves. I do it. I doubt myself. My four-year-old daughter is much more confident. Her bubbly investigation of the world has caused her to realize that some people have no house or food. She says we are lucky. I wish I could go back to my pregnant teenage self and give myself what no one else did. I would respect and rejoice. I would prove that a great purpose was really there all along: to teach my bright child the importance of her dreams. But first I had to learn that myself.

A blackness used to cover me, a drowning feeling that I would never follow my chosen path. I remembered singing to the cows and horses of my childhood ranch, dancing in the field where no one could see me. All I wanted was to get up on stage, and it had finally begun to happen—a family band, the chances at folk festivals, the rush of lights and people, making music that was danced to, and my romance with the piano.

Pregnancy was not in this picture, Charlie told me. "Mommy" and "success" didn't share many sentences. Apparently I was throwing something away, and I was too young and too stubborn to realize it. There was only one person who was okay with me remaining a musician. She used to fall asleep in her swing as I droned out accordion ballads.

When I began to take back my life, the first swamp from which I had to remove myself was Charlie, Chale's father but still a tortured little boy and not ready to have an adult relationship of any kind. On most days I would do absolutely everything to keep the air peaceful; on others I didn't have the strength. I just wanted to lie still, cocooned inside the last bit of spirit that remained my own, in that one place where he couldn't see me or reach me.

It has taken me years to admit that I was abused. Now I know that abuse includes more than just hitting. I was bound by a web of manipulation that I couldn't even see until I finally crawled away. When I moved back home my mother was studying to become a social worker, and she had a "Circle of Abuse" diagram among the papers on the kitchen table. Later, I sneaked into her desk to read it again and again. Every word described what had been my life.

Sometimes, when I think about what I've done since I decided to raise my child alone, it seems almost like someone else's life. I want to tell you that I had the strength to take my freedom and go where I thought a door had been slammed on my fingers. Somehow I dug a tunnel through the remains of high school, working on outreach courses while Chale was sleeping, resisting the sleazy advances of a lonely teacher. Approaching graduation, I applied to more than five different programs and finally decided on "Integrated Environmental Planning," a good, sensible occupation. But when I read about the college's music program, my heart strained so much that in an irrational burst I decided to audition. Being accepted flipped a switch inside of me, and I knew that I had to change programs and follow my true passion.

I packed up the multiplying family of stuffies and moved again, this time over a thousand kilometers from my family. On the second day I called home sobbing because I didn't know anyone and it was terrifying to be so completely alone. I felt intensely paranoid that I might be making the wrong decision for Chale's future. My mom said I could come home. My father said, "How will Chale feel if she finds out you had this opportunity and didn't take it because of her?" Later, Chale and I discovered Lakeside Park and scratched pictures of unicorns on the wet beach.

Going to college to study Contemporary Music and Technology gave me back my life. I had never felt so vibrant and fulfilled. Stressed-out students accused me of being too happy, as I beamed and sang in the hallways. I wrote songs about the past: *"I know why / You keep me here / It's to fix as you break it my dear / And to mend / The threads that you bear / Seeds you spill I still grow with care . . . And it feels like it isn't enough. . . ."*

I went to Chale's day care every single day to arrange her soft blankets for nap and to pat her sweet little back, determined to keep a strong bond between us. Sometimes her chubby two-year-old face would turn over and order, "Mommy, just go. Just go back to music school." Chale began to emerge as a radiant and articulate little person, shining in the company of other children, and I soon became friends with her excellent caregivers. When they confided in me that I packed healthier and better lunches than other parents and that Chale had passed a kindergarten entry test at the early age of three, I realized that being a young musician on a student loan didn't make me any less of a mother.

Being a mother made me a better student. I always had an excuse to stay home and study ear training and harmony while my school friends were out pursuing expensive hangovers. I was the only single mother in my whole program—and the only mother at all—who took on a full course load and persevered. Sometimes the rehearsals and projects and classes whipped me into a dizzying, frantic spin where the pressure was so intense that I felt like I just couldn't keep a grip. A chance to stride onto the stage would come just in time, and I could belt out *"Hold on, I'm coming . . . ,"* pretending to be Etta James and turning the audience into my clapping puppets.

Just before I graduated, the two teachers whom I admired most spoke to me privately, making me cry in tired relief. I got such a feeling of self-worth to realize that the faculty truly admired me for struggling to excel while raising a child alone.

If you can bring your jaded heart around to hope for a fully packaged happy ending, I can tell you about the talented and beautiful prince I met. His fresh beeswax lip balm banished the sweaty stink of unshowered bodies from the cramped little practice rooms. It was months before I believed in his respect for my careful parenting and reclaimed virginity; before I believed that one man could be everything another was not. I now believe. I spent this morning in his recording studio, finishing my demo CD.

Chale became a purple winter faerie on Halloween. We sewed a felt star onto a wooden spoon and decorated it with beads and sparkly ribbons to make her magic wand. She has no memory of me in sad desperation, wishing to be something else. I can't deny that I'm still butting my head against the traditional obstacles that worm their way into my mind, and there are times when I cry out in frustration, but I am learning how to trust myself. Being my daughter's primary role model has driven me to become capable and proud, and I hope that she will learn to live true to her own soul.

Clea Roddick *is a young musician with a reputation for intimate and energetic performances. She grew up on a ranch in northern Alberta, Canada, where her musical career began with performing in a family band. She graduated as a keyboard performance major from Selkirk College in British Columbia in 2000 and is now self-employed as a music instructor. She also teaches creativity and songwriting workshops for teenagers. Currently, Clea lives in Calgary, Alberta, with her daughter and her partner. She is recording an album in their home studio.*

Speak Out!

If you ran a middle school, high school, college, or university attended by pregnant and parenting teenagers, what free services would you offer?

Yummy food for moms and their kids. Let pregnant and nursing moms eat in class! Parenting, breastfeeding, and childbirth classes.

Prenatal care by midwives.

Birth and postpartum doulas.

Lactation consultants.

Nutrition counseling.

Free or reduced cost birth control and other health services.

Computers.

Transportation.

Tutoring.

Study spaces.

Parents' clubs.

Job placement.

Job skills.

Career planning.

Resume preparation.

Financial management and planning and guidance.

A course on how to deal with government aid and social workers.

Sex education, including how to avoid unwanted pregnancies and STDs .

Counseling.

Relationship support groups.

Body image workshops.

Child care co-ops and play groups.

Field trips for both parents and kids.

Clothing exchange.

Volunteer opportunities.

Massage therapy.

Legal assistance for dealing with the court system, getting child support, etc.

Housing referrals / resources etc.

On-campus housing for teens and their children.

College information and counseling.

SAT preparation courses.

Mediators for working out parenting plans between moms and dads.

A mommy-needs-help hot line.

Child care, child care, child care—during classes and after school.

I wouldn't hand anyone anything. I'd make it a cooperatively run school.

PART 5

Encounters That Empower

ON BEING CHALLENGED AND STANDING FIRM

"Are you his baby-sitter?" a girl of about eleven years asked.

Suddenly, I was no longer enjoying a carefree afternoon at the pool with my seven-year-old. I am fifteen again, with a burgeoning belly, trying hopelessly to ignore disapproving glares from people I pass on the street. I am sixteen and trying to readjust to classroom schooling while my swollen breasts leak through my blouses, much to the hilarity of my male classmates. I am back in my high school psychology class, listening to the teacher berate teen mothers' intelligence. I am in a graduate professor's office, after she has learned that I am a twenty-one-year-old single mother with a son in kindergarten, listening to her extol the virtues of her decision to wait until after college and graduate school before marrying and becoming a mother.

I swallowed and looked hard at my curious young acquaintance. I am the one who fretted through pregnancy and struggled through twenty-four hours of labor, unaided by drugs, to birth him as a nearly ten-pound baby. I am the one who hunted for the perfect preschool; who held back tears beside him through hospital visits for whooping cough, a hernia surgery, and a broken forearm; who spent hours helping him with his homework. I am the one he tells, "I love you, Mommy."

"No, I'm not his baby-sitter. I'm his mother."

The little girl seemed surprised. "You don't look old enough to be his mother."

I simply smiled at her and said, "Well, I am."

—Dana L. Philipps,
25, mother, Ph.D. candidate,
molecular biology, Bristol, Connecticut

In the summer of 2002 I sent five essays from this anthology to an acquaintance who works in publishing in New York City to get her feedback. After reading the stories she replied, "Now when I walk by the many young mothers and their babies hanging out on their front stoops in my neighborhood, I see the young women differently, and I no longer look away." It was a satisfying response. The young mothers hadn't changed, but as a result of encountering a handful of young moms' personal essays, my acquaintance had.

The stories in this section illustrate encounters that expose each writer's self-doubts or challenge her self-image or sense of self-worth. Each of these women seizes the opportunity to act with compassion, share knowledge, or simply reflect on and reassess the intrinsic value of her own unique and complex life. Elizabeth Strater bypasses both her own chagrin and an older couple's startled looks to offer them assistance with their fussy newborn. Lennon Sundance shows what it takes to be a perfect school volunteer. Caitlin Crane's striking poem celebrates her son's imminent birth in an unusual setting. And Julie Cushing opts to spend a day talking to students in the very high school from which she fled just one year before.

Elizabeth Strater

Waiting Room Lesson

was sitting in the pediatrician's waiting room with my three-month-old daughter. She sat quietly on my lap, looking through the book of photographs as I turned the pages. My nose was pressed against the top of her head, smelling her warm, powdery smell. She made soft noises as I tapped the pages and repeated the names that matched the smiling faces of her extended family. I bent over her, trying to ignore the cool disapproval on the faces of the other parents in the waiting room.

I looked younger than my nineteen years. Since my pregnancy began to show, strangers had looked sadly at me, smiling sympathetically or shaking their heads. One unforgettable encounter on the subway in late pregnancy still sounded in my ears.

"Oh, is the baby kicking you?" a woman asked with saccharine sweetness as I rested my hand on my taut belly. I nodded politely and looked away. "You aren't old enough to be married. . . . Was this a planned pregnancy?" she continued, nastily pleasant as I turned my face toward the window. I smoothed my shaking hands over the elbow, heel, or shoulder that rippled unseen beneath the surface of my skin. "Are you still in touch with the father?" Her voice had taken on the slightest antagonizing pitch. Choking with rage, I said nothing, and she got off at the next stop while my face burned. I looked down at my overlooked wedding band. I was glad she hadn't seen it. I didn't need a wedding ring to tell me this baby, while not planned, was fiercely loved and wanted. From the day I knew I was carrying her, I was determined that this flutter of a child would never think she had not been wanted. I didn't need to justify my pregnancy to anyone.

I paused between photos of Great-Grandmother and Auntie Kate, and my daughter's hand patted my arm softly and her wide baby eyes looked up at me. Next to me in the waiting room sat a well-dressed woman, her body still swollen from pregnancy. Her hair was a salon-expensive shade of blond, smoothly pinned up. The setting in her engagement ring would have paid my rent for years. Her face, beneath the makeup, was showing the laugh lines of a woman in her late thirties aging gracefully. I thought idly that she was old enough to be my mother.

In a car seat at her feet slept an impossibly small newborn. I had seen that beribboned cashmere outfit in the window of a high-end baby boutique on St. Claire Avenue. As I looked at the little red face, my daughter suddenly felt large, substantial in my arms. The baby began to stir, tiny mouth opening and closing like a fish. Soon a nasal squall began to rise.

The woman carefully unbuckled the straps of the car seat. Her husband began poking around in the designer diaper bag, while she sniffed at the baby's fist-sized bottom and decided it must be hunger that had roused her. She looked around the small, cramped waiting room. I could see a wet stain spreading across her breast, leaking through her ironed blouse. She looked briefly at her husband and began to unbutton her shirt, starting at the collar. By the time she had unfastened enough to unhook her nursing bra, most of both breasts were exposed.

Blushing furiously, her husband draped her with a blanket, then his jacket. The baby arched her back and screamed. Her tiny tongue protruded from her lips, and I could hear the desperation in the woman's whispers.

"John, she won't latch on! I can't see what I'm doing with that blanket in the way!"

The husband protested over his wife's absence of modesty, but even when he removed the jacket, the hungry baby cried on. I could see tears well in the mother's eyes.

I cleared my throat. "Would you like some help?"

Startled, she looked at me, and her husband's expression mirrored hers. My face burned, and for an endless moment I knew what they were thinking: Who was I to offer her help? My hair slid into my eyes, reminding me I had not had time to ·vash it that day. My daughter was picking at the fringed hole in the knee of my jeans. My face, bare of makeup and pinched from sleepless nights and early morning feedings, made it clear that I was barely out of childhood myself. Who was I to help anyone?

In that silent pause in the waiting room, the mother's eyes slid down to my daughter, plump and pinkly perfect. I silently lifted my shirt and slowly brought my daughter to my breast. When my nipple brushed her cheek, she instinctively turned and opened her mouth. Her lips flared in a textbook-perfect latch. I unlatched her gently and offered her the breast again. She opened wide and we repeated our wordless lesson. The woman next to me took a breath, looked down at her still-screaming daughter, and followed my movements, bringing the already open mouth to her breast. Like magic, the tiny jaw began to work, and tension ebbed from mother and daughter as milk began to flow.

I was aware of my surroundings again. I showed her how to unbutton her shirt from the bottom, to be more discreet. When she began to stroke her nursing baby's hair, I turned away. Her name was called, then mine. As my daughter finished her meal in the privacy of the exam room, I was struck by the power of my own body. My daughter's sturdy arms and rounded cheeks have sprung from nothing but my body. Since conception her growth has been sustained by my blood, my milk, my life.

The doctor entered and ended my reflection. He carried out her well-baby evaluation, hailing my daughter as a model of perfect infant health and development. Descending the stairs to the street, I saw the couple from the waiting room buckling their daughter's car seat into the leather interior of their late-model Audi. Over the roof, the new mother's eyes met mine, and she smiled warmly. For one moment in that waiting room, we had been brought together. We were both women, and that was no small thing. I smiled back and crossed the street to head home.

Elizabeth Strater *is a twenty-two-year-old student, gardener, and weekend gourmet in Toronto, Ontario. Her two-year-old daughter is thriving and teaches her more than any class. She is a gutsy survivor of a massive migrating millipede population, and sends many thanks to the night shift workers at the garden center of Home Depot.*

Lennon Sundance

Mom in Boots

spent the morning feverishly tearing through my closet; my different identities lie lifeless on the bed, the chair, the floor. Striped socks and a polka-dot dress? Nah, too Ringling Brothers clownlike. Velvety black dress? No, too Morticia. Knee-high boots and a skirt? Did I want them to think I was working the streets after midnight? I wanted to find an outfit that was cool, yet not too embarrassing. I settled on a cherry ballerina skirt, the color of my hair, and a lace top. It was as if I was preparing for an important date. And in a way, I was—a date with a classroom full of eight-year-olds.

I was trying to be the "good" mom volunteer. Astera's eyes had lit up like carnival lights when I'd signed on to help with her class's art activity. I hopped in the battered station wagon and chain-smoked the entire way to school, checking my reflection in the rearview mirror at stoplights. Smoke curled throughout the car. Not wanting to smell like a smoky barfly—I needed to be a proper role model—I stopped to buy mints. I pulled up in front of the three-story brick castle of knowledge and checked my hair, my makeup, my composure. *Please,* I begged God, *don't make them think I'm too slutty or weird. Just this once.* . . .

My paranoia wasn't completely out of line. I was often perceived as an older cousin or sister of Astera. When I told people

I was her mother, I felt their acceptance begin to dissipate like a steamy haze rising from a crystal-clear lake. Some would shake their head in disbelief; others sized me up with their eyes. A mother? Dressing in fishnets and knee-high leather boots? Piercings? Tattoos? It's true, I was nineteen when she was born. On my first outing with her—she was scarcely pushing three days—an elderly man in elastic-waist khakis shook his head. "Too young, too young," he muttered. At early childhood classes, I was usually the youngest by eight years. Unlike the rest of the moms, I didn't knit or do needlepoint. I wasn't married to a lawyer, doctor, or CEO. I was on welfare, and job opportunities weren't jumping out to greet me. My greatest fear was that I would spend the rest of my life being stereotyped as the under-educated, poor, young parent who plastered glossy magazine covers as the newest epidemic and curse of modern times.

As I entered Astera's school, the smell of youth and authority mixed in the air: metal, rubber-soled shoes, pencil shavings, and the bleach used to try and cover it up. Schools always bring back that familiar, pit-of-the-stomach nauseating feeling that would wash over in me in waves during my younger days in those halls of hell. Yet there was a sliver in time when school seemed filled with primary-colored carpets and rainbow-embellished walls. There was also a time when my mother seemed cool. I remember vividly the day she crossed over from being a fun mom volunteer to an embarrassing relative I didn't want to claim. In kindergarten, she used to cut out oversized Charlie Browns and Lucys and laminate them for our wall.

"Hey," I'd whisper to the kid next to me at mat time, "my mommy did that."

But in second grade she did something that horrified me. She became . . . "The Lunch Lady." She was a line Nazi, making sure that we kept our mouths shut and our feet moving forward as we received lumps of mushy food on plastic trays. She was a recess wrangler, pulling kids out of playtime to stand against the wall as they glared in my direction. But the worst embarrassment lay in my mother's inability to stop being a mother to me when she set foot on my turf. She'd pull me out of line and smack me on the head if she thought I was being too lippy. I'd hear her scream my name out on the playground, her chubby hands defiantly wagging in the air. Then came the never-ending taunts from Tony and Dean and Will: "Mrs. Bush grabbed my tush!"

The movie reel of my mother continued to play as I made my way down the cement hallway to room 135. The class was full of giggling girls and boys whose arms flailed like those of mechanical windup toys. In the corner I spied two other volunteer moms, smartly dressed in khakis, with neatly coiffed hair. *Shit,* I thought, *competition.* Now I'd have to be *really* good.

The kids were making bas-relief self-portraits in honor of Renaissance Week. Why couldn't they have worn floppy hats and jousted instead? I had never taken an art class in my life, so the idea of keeping kids from poking each other's eyes out seemed like a more manageable task for me to undertake. The masks were contorted images with Picassoesque eyes, clumps of clay for noses, and absent mouths. The parents were supposed to help the kids fashion clay mouths, but the teachers didn't know that my kids drew better than I did.

"How do you make lips?"

"How do you carve hair?"

The kids all raised their hands in unison. Anxiously, I tried to help out, though I clung to Astera's side of the room. I needed her support to get me through this hour, instead of the other way around.

Down the row of desks a student named Mai Vang (not her real name) looked desperate. She stared at her blob of clay face and sighed. Bravely, I made my way to her. I held two lumps of semidry clay in my palm like a peace offering. She wanted to know how to make lips.

I kneeled, making eye contact with her. "Here, you make two worms outta clay. Look in the mirror at your lips. See? You have nice *big* lips."

She looked at me in confusion, her head cocked to the side, her eyes slightly watery in the light.

"I mean, I mean . . . What's the politically correct term . . . ? FULL! Yes, full, that's what I mean."

Astera's teacher looked at me as if I had slapped the poor girl across the face. Muttering underneath his breath, he shook his head disapprovingly. I only made out the words "politically correct," but his exhausted and snide tone was enough to confirm my fears. He thought my big-lips remark was racist! I wondered if he was going to send me out in the hall for a spell, a place I was too familiar with as a kid.

I had failed as a good mom volunteer. He'd never ask me back. Astera would be so ashamed! The end of class hurried by as my mind twirled like jump ropes spinning double Dutch. I felt my mistake burned to my forehead, a fat, juicy F for failure. Failure to speak inoffensive kid language. Failure to rise above the doom-carrying gene passed down to me from "The Lunch Lady."

It was the clothes I wore, right? Blame it on my appearance. But the truth is that I am not a politically correct mommy. I have never read Doctor Spock or watched parenting shows on *Oprah*. As Astera and I sit glued to the television screen, I refer to the girls on the gross-out show *Fear Factor* as the "ones with the big boobs." I say "hell," "damn," and "bullshit" more often than a surly teen but not quite as often as a 1920s sailor. We have frank discussions about sex and birth control because of all the PG-13 coming-of-age teen flicks we watch together. We giggle like gossipy preteens and speak Valley Girl slang—"Oh, ma God! Can yu believe she wore that to the Pretty Princess Prom? For *real!*" We role-play with dolls who have collagen-injected lips, miniature waists, and curvy hips. Laughing our heads off, we change their platform diva shoes and pick out slinky club clothes for them to wear.

Maybe I am not what society deems an appropriate role model, yet I wouldn't have my relationship with Astera any other way. For this sliver in time, my daughter thinks I am cool. She genuinely likes me, and she talks to me about real stuff: boys, politics, fashion, and sometimes even feelings. I know that someday it won't matter if I am cool or not. I will fall prey to the inevitable label of "Embarrassing Mom." I will either be tragically unhip or try to be too hip.

So, dammit, let's watch *American Idol* and gossip about who got cut and who made it. Let's talk about glittering spandex tops and red vinyl boots. Let's be as close as we can be while it is still possible to hold hands or be seen in public together, without seeming "lame" in the eyes of moody preteens. And someday, after she's done thinking that I suck, we will come full circle.

Lennon Sundance *is a frantic mother of two wonderfully raucous children, Astera and Ezra. She currently is playing the role of urban pioneer, referee, poor homemaker, kid taxi, and college student pursuing a degree in writing and literature. She lives in a creepy old house near downtown Minneapolis that is a constant work in progress, like herself.*

Caitlin Crane

#9 Bus

He unfolds like a Japanese fan
and I can feel his slippery feet
kicking my ribs like fence posts,
his head growing between my bones,
jumping with hiccups.
I can feel where his heart is beating
and where his fists, juicy plums,
beat out moon-music.
I want to move my swollen feet,
dance,
brave and hysterical,
down the narrow aisle.
I want to say to
this woman sitting next to me,
watching rain from the open window drip onto her sweater,
"My son is singing, can you hear him?"
To the bus driver, who has never heard of reggae,
who spent the seventies in a cathedral with Elvis,
I want to say,
"Listen, he is singing God songs."
To the pretty girl with red hair and two babies,
who drinks orange juice out of a water bottle

and coughs into her fist
I want to say,
"Why are your eyes apologetic?"

But when I turn to speak,
my mouth open and half a word hanging out,
I can see it in their skin.
Their faces thin over hard lines,
over, "Get her out of the welfare office, get her out of my wallet."
Over, "Another one."
And, "Poor baby, poor girl. She doesn't even have a chance."

My son is coming,
And I don't have the time to wait for you.
My son is coming
and he will dance to your echoes of injustice,
his face to the sun.

Caitlin Crane *is an eighteen-year-old single mother extraordinaire. She is a full-time college student in Portland, Oregon, pursuing a degree in creative writing and planning on teaching high school. Her only son, Malakai, is a four-month-old genius who plans on ending world hunger.*

Alumni Day

"You're not on the list."

"What?" I asked, too busy straightening my chubby-cheeked baby's hat to pay attention to the sour-looking woman watching the door at my old high school. I stared up at her blankly, just in time to catch her eyes as they made a slow, disapproving line from my drooling son to me.

"The list here, of people who registered. You aren't on it," she huffed impatiently.

"Oh . . . ," I replied uncertainly, wishing for once that I had actually stopped and read the rules before I took the plunge. I was here for Alumni Day, a thinly veiled attempt to pressure students into going to college by telling them how cool and fun it is, and I was starting to think that maybe I shouldn't have come at all. Less than a year ago, I had run through those doors and not turned around once, been miles away even before they fully shut. Why in the world had I wanted to come back now?

I've heard that the only people who return to high school are the ones who live in the past or have something to prove. I could be the poster girl for the "I'll show them!" category. I didn't do well in high school, and toward the end I wasn't having any fun anymore, either. The joy of carefully choosing the perfect outfit to shock the other students and dreaming up new ways to achieve notoriety had faded and given way to classes taught in the backseat of a Volvo and forged sick notes that allowed me to spend school days smoking pot instead. I wasn't stupid, but failing and skipping class tended to lead people to that assumption. Getting pregnant during senior year only solidified their belief. Considering my history in this building, it was ironic that today education was my main goal. I could find no logical reason why I wanted to prove to the other alumni—whom I'd never cared about before—that I was intelligent, responsible, and, most important, that I was still managing to be cooler than all of them and a kick-ass mama to boot. Most of my infinite motherly wisdom would probably be lost amid the Ivy Leaguers and sorority girls, but having just settled into the mama groove and feeling pretty good, I wasn't going to waste an opportunity to flaunt it.

Along with my peers, my teachers and other grown-ups had expected me to fail. I knew from the moment that my belly was visible underneath my T-shirt that it would define me, that as soon as my son was born people would realize how our birthdays matched up and furrow their brows, giving me sidelong glances. Had I been a more obedient teenager, perhaps their judgments would have hindered my success. But obedient I was not. Rebellion was my forte, and knowing that the only thing I was thought capable of doing was failing gave me a sense of freedom I had never experienced. I had no expectations to live up to but my own. If I didn't make it, no one would be shocked, they'd just shake their heads smugly and say, "I told you so." Any success would be multiplied tenfold because it was thought impossible of a girl in "my condition." My effectiveness at screwing with others' limited definitions of "mother" only bolstered my ego, and with support from the only person that mattered—myself—I began to learn. I was able to do things my way, and so I did.

After a few long, staring minutes, the woman at the table sighed and handed me a form. She didn't approve of my being there, but it was obvious space wasn't full. With a hint of unsettled nerves and a feeling akin to morning sickness, I wrote my information down on the alumni sheet. Name, graduation year, school, major. I felt a tinge of embarrassment as I wrote down my college. It was only a community college—the "thirteenth grade." So many of the other kids there were at "real" schools with names that prompted impressed little "Aahs," and they probably managed to do almost as well as my five A's with half the effort. I imagine college life is much easier when you are not dealing with crying babies or leaking milk.

In an attempt to still my shaking self-image, I took stock of my accomplishments: among them, acing finals with a newborn, raising a healthy nursling, acting to bring about social change. My son, cocooned against me in his sling, had marched with me on our state's capital numerous times, where I carried banners and chanted protest songs similar to the ones of activists gone before. We were participating in bigger things than just student groups and fraternities, I told myself. We were part of generations united by the eternal struggle for improvement. I answered to the noble title of "mother." I was aligned with an age-old group of women who had birthed new life, healthy and strong, from within. My nausea subsided, but only a little. I am powerful and I am phenomenal, but nothing can shake me like facing the people who watched me grow up.

I had had a purpose in coming here today, a mission to grab the last few brains not yet warped by traditional high school ideals, but I was starting to lose confidence in both the message and my ability to present it. In my conservative school system, how would they cotton to my statements that high school is only a small sliver of life and that getting pregnant doesn't wreak the rumored havoc unless you want it to? Perhaps what I was most afraid of was that no one would understand. That they would look at me and only see a chubby, stretch-marked stereotype, a statistic, a joke. So many of the girls that get pregnant seem to just fade away, almost as if that's what they are supposed to do. I didn't want to be that girl. I wanted to show everyone that we don't just dissolve into the background and lead our mundane lives. We march to our different drumbeats from our ragtag toddler band, and we take the paths that pass by toy stores and the park; we stop to wipe off sticky hands, to nurse and change diapers—but we eventually cross that same damn finish line, sleeping child in our arms. Would my journey be seen as less valid, simply because it was different?

The eager principal herded the parade of graduates into the cafeteria, bringing forth memories of a similar orientation when we were nervous, skittish freshmen, worried about finding our lockers and the right bus home. The cafeteria hadn't changed much, either. It still smelled of soggy French fries and students sweaty with the rigors of high school, still had chairs that didn't announce their brokenness until they were sat upon, still sported sticky patches on tables that predated me. Teachers lined the front of the room like middle-aged cheerleaders, trying to look thrilled at seeing students whose faces they only vaguely remembered. More faculty members positioned themselves strategically around the room in order to prevent things from becoming too fun.

The organizer then launched into a perky soliloquy of the day's plan. We would talk to students in various classes about college life and answer any questions they had. She encouraged us to talk about "special circumstances" we encountered, but she was careful not to look at me.

Following the announcements, we were allowed to socialize. I wasn't any better at this than I had been in high school, but at least now I had my son as a distraction. We set up our own little camp, complete with colorful toys and scattered Cheerios, at the same corner table where I used to eat, and I tried to adopt the "go away" body language that had worked so well when I was a student. Unfortunately, giggling and flapping about, my son turned into a magnet for all the people I was trying to avoid. The teachers were patronizing and self-righteous, managing in one glance to display that, yes, I was bad, but they were pious

enough to accept it. They kept their distance, but they stole sur-
reptitious glances and chatted overanimatedly, hoping to make
up in enthusiasm what the event now lacked in class. The girls
who approached me were pejorative, even thankful, glad that it
was me that was chosen to be the someone "it" had to happen
to. Their ignorant queries conjured up high school as they questioned me snottily about my son: his father, his race, his parents'
marital status. Deciding that this would be a learning experience
for my small child, I answered politely and even allowed them
to stroke his soft head, secretly hoping some of his charm would
rub off on them. Despite all the conversation, no one asked the
questions I wanted. No one brought up the merits of
breastfeeding. No one mentioned styles of discipline or parenting. Things that had become so important in my world played
absolutely no part in theirs.

After what seemed like hours of discussing my son's name,
age, and father, we were hustled out of the cafeteria. Despite
attending that school for four years, I still didn't know where
the room I was assigned to was located. I walked down the hall,
breathing in the shared memories that emanated from its walls.
Remembering the still-fresh pains of being an awkward freshman on up to a slutty senior took my mind off the reason I was
there. The dark, angst-ridden high school student in me wanted
so desperately to come out, to hike up her skirt and give everyone
the finger, but found she clashed too sharply with the responsible-
mother image I was hoping to present. Reading the room number posted on the wall put the past back in its place. Using my
Lamaze breathing, I stopped and meditated in front of the door
for a moment, telling myself that I could be more than simply a
nineteen-year-old lecturer who doesn't know when to quit. I had
never felt that I belonged, so why should this have been any different? Perhaps because the divide between us was so gaping
and definite, so fundamental and basic . . . perhaps because no
matter how hard I tried, it wasn't just about weird clothes and
cut classes anymore.

The room was bland, as high school classrooms tend to be, with curling inspirational posters attempting to distract the eye from the water stains and spitballs lodged in the ceiling. The desks were arranged in typical high school fashion, and as I walked in I silently thanked the teacher for having faced them away from the door, so I wasn't immediately on stage as soon as I entered. Before I was even at the front of the class, I was easily the main attraction. The students peered cautiously at the dozing boy in my arms. I could see them quizzically trying to estimate my age, my youthful face and the fruit of my womb giving contradictory messages.

When it was my turn to speak, I wasted no time. I told them about getting pregnant senior year and my eleventh-hour decision to continue my education. My voice got louder and stronger with every sentence. Pencils ceased tapping idly and notes stopped mid-pass as two dozen pairs of eyes fixed hungrily on me, giving my squirming son and me their full attention. After all, I was the stuff of trashy talk shows and charged political debates, and I was right here talking to them. And they listened.

Perhaps they sensed the difference in me from the other speakers, heard the truths I wanted to tell them. Perhaps they only watched me like an after-school special, but they did listen. I felt like a cross between an *en vogue* celebrity and a deer in headlights as I began sharing with them the story of my life. I talked about attending the alternative school, graduating pregnant, and being so proud. They laughed at my tale of being too big to fit in the desks and managed to look concerned in all the right places when I told of Dylan's stay in the Newborn Intensive Care Unit. I told them about the fear of what was to come and how those fears dissolved the moment my son was in my arms. Even the teacher had to smile, offering her grudging approval when I mentioned my 4.0 GPA and finely honed ability to nurse a baby while typing a research paper.

No one asked the questions I wanted, but now I offered all the answers anyway. I forgot about my rigid plan for dramatically altering everyone's worldviews by forming them into small versions of myself, little moons to orbit my planet. Instead I worked on kicking up some dust and putting a few dents in the stereotypes, asking them to question the prejudices they held and to wonder why everyone vilified pregnant teens—who were doing the same thing most everyone else was, just with different results. I knew that very few people could relate directly to what I was saying, but I hoped that they would gather up some of my information, file it away, and years later look back at it and say, "Hey, that weird chick with the kid was right."

Listening to the sound of my strong voice outlining my own metamorphosis, I couldn't help but feel pretty good. I knew that the strength showing was just the tip of the iceberg. People often ask how young mothers do it, and my first thoughts are always *How do you* not *do it? How do you not go to school when you have a child? How do you not work insanely hard for the very best when you have someone who will depend on you for the rest of your life? We do it like everyone else does: We do what we have to do.* Other times, I sit back and ask, "How do *any* of us do it?" Motherhood is rewarding but exhausting, and there isn't an abundance of support or understanding for all that we do. Mothers are amazing, and young mothers are especially so because of all the additional roadblocks we face. When I'm immersed in the mundane activities that come with mothering, sometimes I lose sight of how incredible parents are. Outlining my progress in front of a rapt audience reminded me to never forget my own power.

Feeling a rush of bravery, I launched into a description of the confidence my mothering had given me, and how I would someday be running the world—not in spite of my son, but because of him. "This is the only way I know it—and the only way I'd have it, if you want to know the truth," I said.

I paused to adjust my babe in his sling and wondered how to tread lightly around sensitive issues. Remembering the teenage ability to be extremely candid—and then remembering that I was, in fact, one of them—I thought, *To hell with sugarcoating,* and chose honesty. I told them they could be me, but they didn't have to be. They should be armed with enough knowledge, anecdotes, and condoms to make teen parenthood about choice, not chance. My life doesn't suck, and no amount of guilt or "concern for the public good" will make me say it does. I don't have a typical teenage life, but why is that a bad thing? I'm young enough to recall that high school is *not* the best time of anyone's life. My life is different now, it's true. I don't live fast anymore. I drive in the slow lane, and I spend afternoons in hammocks finding patterns in wind chimes and raindrops. I flow along lazily, pointing out every piece of scenery, and I can make a walk down the street last an hour. I blow bubbles in the bathtub and happily ponder my child's eyes for an entire afternoon. I know the magic of a soft voice in a quiet room and the heaven of a baby asleep at the breast. My son has given me balance, harmony, a perfect complement. I know what is real, what's important, what matters, and what doesn't.

"This is not misery," I said. "And don't let anyone tell you it is."

In truth, there may have been only one mind changed that day. Other people might not want my life, but my purpose wasn't to make it look glamorous. I was honest and I was true to myself, my son, and my beliefs, and that's really all I could ask for. The Sorority of Teenage Mothers is an elite crew of wonder women, but few people know that until they're inducted. Looking back at my son, sitting snugly in his car seat pondering his feet, I knew that the only approval I needed was granted with his raspberries and messy smiles. There are bumps in the road, and I certainly fall down at times, but I can look around and think, *I love this, skinned knees and all.* Feeling contented, I let it all sink in, a mantra of "Life is good" running like a marquee through my mind. With the happy call of "Mamamamama" from the backseat, I knew that there were two people on this planet who wouldn't change any of it for the world.

Julie Cushing *is a mama, writer, student, mentor, and activist. She is a social work major at the University of Texas and plans to someday save the world. She's a managing coeditor at www.girlmom.com. Her passions include breastfeeding, the pursuit of social justice, and attaining reproductive rights for all women. She lives in Austin with her girlfriend Allison, stepson Cade, and Dylan, whom she gave birth to on September 29, 2000. Mothering is easily her greatest joy, and she's still as amazed with her son and herself as she was on the day he was born.*

Speak Out!

If your life were a TV sitcom,
what would the show be called?

"Saving Grace"

"Mi Vida Loca"

"Crash Landing"

"Debbie's Dilemmas"

"Through the Eyes of a Teen Mother"

"Motherhood Improv"

"A Miracle"

"You Can Breathe Now, Kat!"

"My So-Called Life"

"Where the Hell Are My Keys?"

"And a Mommy, Too!"

"The Hidden Life"

"Scraping By"

"She Can Do Anything!"

"Real Life!"

"Wishing I Could Have a Quarter-Life Crisis, But I Can't Because I'm Too Busy"

"Sexy Young Mama"

"Dancing Like No One Is Watching"

PART 6

Toilet Paper or Milk?

ON WORK, MONEY, AND
FINDING A CAREER

Most challenging to me as a young mother was balancing school and work and parenting—while not being able to complain about it. I always felt like I had to make it look easy, to prove to the world that the assumptions about me were wrong. When I got older and my friends started having children, it was strange to hear thirty-year-old moms with houses and husbands and cars complaining about how hard it can be to raise a child. I never felt like I was allowed to admit that.

—Lydia Prentiss,
28, mother, student, Takoma Park, Maryland

Millions of women work while pregnant or raising children. But how many successfully work, raise a child, and go to school? Over and over, I heard from young moms who were struggling to do all three. A former student from my teen moms' writing class attempted to take college classes while holding down a part-time job. She wound up dropping the classes. "It was too insane," she said. She and her child didn't see each other enough, and she wasn't able to focus on her schoolwork. "It wasn't worth it," she added. "I can't do it all right now."

Making tough choices between work, education, and family was a common theme in the writings I received. Young mothers found that their willingness to work often bumped up against constraints: time required for school, lack of affordable, high-quality child care, or difficulty finding a wage that would cover their living expenses. One writer mentioned welfare policies as a frustrating limitation: "One day I was pulled aside by my case-worker to be told that the government was changing its rules and that I couldn't go to school *and* be on welfare. I could quit school and stay on welfare, or I could lie about being in school to stay on welfare, but if the government knew I was in school, my benefits would be cut. *What?* Can you imagine anything more stupid than saying, 'Stay home and do nothing and that's okay. But try to further your education and you'll be cut off'? . . . I promptly got off welfare and went to work part-time while staying in school . . . putting my kids in less-than-optimal child care situations."

Some women didn't think much about money issues when they first became pregnant: "Expenses such as medical bills had never occurred to me, much less the expense of raising a child. I figured my dad would support my baby, but I was in for a big surprise. I had to drop out of school in order to work full-time to pay my living expenses." Others expressed tremendous grati-tude for their families' ability and willingness to support them until they could get on their own financial feet.

I heard many examples of frugal living and resourcefulness: "I didn't expect to spend much on our new baby, since I was planning to breastfeed and launder my own cloth diapers. When the washer broke, I washed the diapers by hand. When the dryer broke, I hung them on the clothesline. It required extra planning, since in the dead of winter the diapers took two days to dry, but it worked. When the washer broke again or the car broke, I figured it would be cheaper to learn how to fix them than to replace them, so I bought a book and some tools and learned how to fix stuff."

The essays here reflect difficult decisions, the juggling of priorities and values, and the writers' willingness to set aside one or more priorities temporarily in order to devote time and energy to others. Jennifer Lind thinks she's found a way to escape the predicted poverty and prejudices suffered by young mothers, only to discover that in her chosen field of work she's losing her family and herself. Shannon Minydzak fulfills her valued commitment to her country but learns that taking care of her son isn't always compatible with all that entails. Katherine Robins's assisting another teen mom to give birth on a starry Texas night provides her with an opportunity to reflect on the importance of her choice of work. And Jenne Herbst throws all caution to the wind to follow her heart's desire—and flee from life on a Midwestern farm—by adventuring with her young daughter into Hollywood's persnickety film industry.

Jennifer Lind

The Letter

I stood in the unemployment line with tears streaming down my already puffy face. In my hand I clenched the list of places I had applied to and the check I had been sent for last week. Thirty-five dollars. My feet ached.

"Date of birth?"

Two weeks shy of my nineteenth birthday.

Clickclickclick, never looking up. "Reason for meeting?"

I thrust the check and the list, crumpled and slightly sweaty, in front of her. "It wasn't enough," I said. "It barely covered the gas I used in driving to all these places."

The woman at the counter looked over her glasses at me and gave a cursory glance at the list. She sighed.

"This check is based on last year's income," she said, looking back down at her keyboard. *Clickclickclick.*

Tears ran into my mouth and down my chin as I explained to her, again, that I had been a junior in high school last year and that this check was based on my summer job, which was not even a fraction of what I had been making this year.

She took off her glasses. "I guess you'll just have to get another job quickly then. Would you like to see one of our career counselors?" She handed me back my papers.

I shook my head and turned toward the door. I recognized in

line behind me the father of a boy I had once dated; he wouldn't make eye contact with me. In my car, windows cracked to air the fumes pouring in from the floorboards, I glanced at the list. Ten companies, ten interviews, ten different attempts to hide my huge belly. Ten times listing my boyfriend as emergency contact. No one would hire a girl seven months pregnant. I pulled a pen out of the glove compartment and signed the check. I had a WIC appointment and I needed to see about heat assistance—it was getting colder outside. Maybe, just maybe, thirty-five dollars would hold off the phone company another month . . . so that I could call my mom . . . try to work things out. My tears tasted like aluminum.

More than a year later, I took a job selling computers for the Christmas season to prove a point to Tim. We battled in whispers, because the neighbor upstairs screamed at us every morning through the floor about the noise of our alarm clocks and the neighbor below blessed us when we sneezed. I hated the new apartment. In fact, I loathed just about everything at that point, including myself. I no longer found time to write, and my book of essays and journal were stored in boxes in the basement. My friends had stopped calling as soon as I came home from the hospital with my newborn son Jon, too busy with starting college and spreading their wings. My school counselor had told me just to forget about college because I wouldn't get admitted. I envied them all. I was caged in my ratty little apartment, and they had cut me off. I was more alone than I ever cared to be, my only company my year-old son and the music lessons being played on the piano in the first-floor apartment. Do re mi fa so la ti do do ti la so fa mi re do, again and again, until I could actually feel the entire building moving in rhythm to the scales.

I spent a lot of time in the basement doing laundry. I was turning my back on the world, and I was beginning to turn my back on Tim. I took the sales job to prove that I *could* get work

other than as a gas station attendant—my postpartum job—and
that I *could* take care of this family and get health insurance.
That was the reason we were married now, right? For the non-
existent insurance and the right to set foot in my parents' house
without my father threatening him bodily harm? I was an angry
soul, and selling computers seemed an easy buck. Tim was a
computer repair guy; I could learn from him. I found a day care
and started the job, determined to hate everyone I worked with.

My performance on the job was shaky, my customer relations
were average, and I was shy and wore the same two outfits all
week long. Yet after a few months, they told me that Jess, the
golden star of sales, needed an assistant and she needed one fast.
Had I thought about transferring into the Corporate Department, and did I know Jess? Did I know anything of her reputation? *No?*

I was promoted immediately.

Within one week of starting work for Jess I became known as
the candy coating over a bitter pill, walking behind Jess and fixing the hurts she created. I discovered her last assistant had left
after two days; she couldn't take the pressure, and she couldn't
handle Jess's reputation. I didn't care about either one. I was bitter and angry, and I needed more money to get my family into a
new apartment. I developed a dental assistant's smile and voice,
a *this isn't going to hurt a bit we're only strapping your hands
down for your own protection that's a good girl open wide for
the needle* sort of manner. Jess was ruthless and rock-hard with
the other sales reps, and I was willingly blind and sympathetic.
The two of us won deals whoring my naivete and innocent eyes
to the customers. I won awards for being "The Longest-Lived
Assistant to Jess," nobody realizing that I was having the time
of my life.

No one crossed me with my big bad boss looming over my
shoulder. People forgot how young I was and respected what I
said. No one asked about Jon and then did the math in their
head. No one questioned when I ordered wine at luncheons, even

183

though I wasn't yet old enough to drink. Jess threw phones at me over lost deals, but she seduced long-distance customers in a voice that dripped corn syrup and musk. She made them love her. She would call them every day and make them squirm in their leather office seats, if only they would buy. And they did love her. They bought and bought and bought while we ravaged the company for perks and special parking. Because they loved her, we got what we wanted, and because of that, I loved her. She made the company millions, herself a six-figure income . . . and they scraped my pittance commission off the top of her sales.

The pay was never enough, but we moved out of our four-hundred-square-foot apartment and into a two-story town house. My coworkers hated Jess, but they pitied me. They'd pull me away for smoke breaks to ask how I was doing. "It sucks," I said, "but it pays." I would smoke my ciggy in less than a minute and dash back up the stairs, forgetting to eat lunch. They ran to the printer for me so I needn't leave the phone, brought me coffee to my desk. You couldn't be hungry when the phones were ringing; you couldn't think about the kink in your neck. A year passed so quickly that I missed the one-year anniversary of my being with Jess; I was startled when they brought me another piece of paper to hang on my wall and took me out to lunch. I missed my first "review" meeting because I was so busy that day.

My son learned to talk at day care and called me "Hat" rather than "Mommy" for two months. I lost fifteen pounds from not eating, and then I gained sixty pounds in under four months from a combination of starving and evening bingeing. I didn't understand my crinkled-up shoulders and chest pains. I never ate, so how could I be getting fat? I subsisted on the four-gallon drums of animal crackers that we kept in our cubicle. I adjusted the waist on my work pants with elastic bands like I had when I was pregnant, and I ate even less. My hair started to fall out and the pager, my God, the pager never stopped. It buzzed during morning coffee, during sex, and at 3 A.M. Always

Jess. Always needing me. Her life had started to fall apart, and I was so busy trying to keep hers together that my own was disintegrating fast. Tim and I saw each other so infrequently that our relationship was little more than sharing a bed. I didn't even notice. Because the pager never stopped buzzing and Jon never stopped crying and the money was never enough. But, goddammit! I was next in line to be promoted to having my own client base. I couldn't slow down now. I couldn't. I wouldn't.

The day came when the pager was the only part of my wardrobe that still fit. I wore jeans because I could pull them up and zip them even though they weren't dress-code acceptable. So that no one would notice what I was wearing, I remained in the cubicle until well after everyone had left. That day, Jess walked into the office around 3 P.M. and left at 6. The phone stopped ringing blessedly long enough for me to realize that this was the second week that I had been running her business alone. That in the last week she hadn't even shown up long enough to turn on her computer and yet she was making $375,000 a year, while I was making less than $35,000.

Around that time, Tim got a new job an hour away and could no longer pick Jon up from day care, so I had to leave work at a normal hour in order to get our son. Jess stormed the head office and they hired another assistant for us. Suddenly, for the first time in two years, I had evenings free if I wanted them. Tim was still a ghost who stole the covers at night, but at least I saw Jon. He hardly knew who I was anymore, but at least he was no longer calling me "Hat." When Tim quit the new job within a few weeks for a job closer to home, I never told the office. I now had an excuse to leave when I wanted to, even if it was a lie. Lies had become commonplace there.

In a few months I joined a writers' workshop for thirty-eight dollars—more than that stupid first unemployment check. I paid the money painlessly, and I remember thinking about how far I had come, how once that money had been a week's worth of pay. I thought of how much I had lost in the process of then till now. Tim and I were talking about divorce.

The first night of the writers' workshop I stepped outside the glass doors of my office and felt the cool dusk air on my cheeks. I sat for a minute on the hood of my car and smoked, tucking my skirt up unladylike around my legs and lying back. I was out early, but it was Friday and everyone had gone so there was no one around to see me. The day had been hell, but tonight! Tonight was writers' group, and I had a few minutes to spare before the hour drive to the class. I looked at the stars coming out and wondered when the last time was that I had seen daylight during a weekday. Usually I was up before dawn, at the office by daybreak, out again after dusk. Home again in the dead of night.

The wind stirred my hair, falling from its scrunchie, and I took a deep breath of the spring humidity. For the first time in years I felt like acting my age. Right in the parking lot, I pulled on a pair of jeans under my skirt and maneuvered out of my dress and into a sweatshirt. Then I let down my hair. Tonight I was missing my family, but I had something I had to do. Tonight the results of the real-estate license exam I had taken were sitting on the kitchen counter, and I had passed. Barely, as I'd had no time to study for the exam before I took it. Tonight I was forming an escape plan. Tonight I was going to write again after so many years away. I hadn't put pen to paper in two years. Tonight people were going to see me. Writing. Not in a suit. Not with makeup. Just me. And they weren't going to care how much money I made or how old I was. Afterward I would politely decline going for beers and make my way home to my waiting family—at least, I hoped they would invite me for beers. I had hopes about a lot of things for tonight. I pulled off my gold earrings and felt their weight in my hands. I smoked another cigarette, tossed my earrings into the bushes as an offering, and turned off the pager.

I sat down at writers' group and started before the assignment was given. It was a letter that had begun in my head on the drive here, a drive filled with cigarettes and Dunkin' Donuts coffee. It was a letter to Jess at first, but then it became a letter to me. I wrote about who I was and who she wasn't. I wrote about my sticky child and dirty house and how I could no longer play the game, pretending at the office that I was something I was not. Clean. Polished. Structured. Conformed. I wrote those things out of my soul. I wrote away the mannerisms and figures of speech I had picked up, my burnished and well-polished reflection of her. I wrote away all the times that I had bitten my tongue on her behalf. I wrote away the clothes and the sacrifice and the loss. I wrote away *her*—Jess—and that part of myself that was becoming her. I wrote to the woman on the other end of the letter to stick her cell phone up her ass.

I got up, poured myself a cup of tea from the waiting lukewarm pot, and sat down again to pen out my resignation letter. Suddenly, I had an urge to bake cookies and paint a mural. I wanted a walk in the woods. *Welcome back*, I thought, and I smiled.

Jennifer Lind *is a twenty-six-year-old divorced mother living in the woods of New Hampshire with her son Jonathan and daughter Allison. Since leaving the corporate world she has worked repossessing cars and as a real-estate agent, project designer, stay-at-home mother, landscape gardener, Avon lady, waitress, baby-sitter, art model, photographer, data analyst, clinical affairs assistant, secretarial temp, and doula. Currently she works in a medical device testing lab and volunteers as a doula with a group of women who volunteer free labor support services for every mother, regardless of age or income, at a local hospital. She is also working toward her bachelor's degree in health science. You can contact Jennifer at stonesinthegarden@yahoo.com.*

Shannon Minydzak

Navy Mama

graduated high school near San Diego with a 3.5 grade point average and honors. After working for two weeks at Wienerschnitzel, a fast-food joint, I decided that I had to do something more worthwhile to ensure a good future for my two-and-a-half-year-old son Adam and myself. I joined the United States Navy as a hospital corpsman. In September of 1999 I shipped out to boot camp, crying as I left my son behind with his grandmother.

While in boot camp, I received two letters from my family telling me how Adam was doing, and those were the only two times I cried. Other people cried because of the stress, because of being exercised until our muscles gave out. I cried because I missed my son. I regretted leaving him and often felt like I had abandoned him. But I needed to build a life for us. One letter from my mother said when she picked Adam up for a visit, he ran out of the house and nearly bowled her over because he was so excited. He kept asking for me, and all she could think to say was, "Mommy went to the navy. She'll be back soon." I cried because of that. I also received a card from his paternal grandmother when I was about to graduate boot camp. They had Adam try to sign his name, and he got an A and the M right. I cried because of that.

I graduated and went to Corps School, calling home as often as I could. Every month I had a two-hundred-dollar phone bill from calling Adam so much. He wasn't talking very well, but he could say "Hi, Mommy" and "I love you, Mama," and he could tell me the shows he was watching on TV and stuff like that. I loved hearing his voice. I lived for those phone calls. I missed him terribly and longed to get back home. At the end of March I received my first set of orders. I was being sent to Naval Medical Center, San Diego! I was ecstatic! In April of 2000 I graduated as an E-1 hospital corpsman and boarded a plane bound for San Diego. I had friends waiting for me at the airport to take me home.

I spent two weeks at home visiting Adam, family, and friends. Then I had to report to the hospital, without Adam. I was planning on looking for a house right away to move out of the barracks and move Adam in with me. They had me start work in the Pediatric Intensive Care Unit. Unfortunately, they had a stipulation for all new corpsmen out of Corps School working in the Pediatric Department: No move-out chits would be approved until you had been there for six months. I had to wait at least six months before I could even be put on the waiting list for navy housing, and the waiting lists are at least two years long. After six months, I got put on a list, and I waited. And waited. After a few months, I checked on my status. I had moved two spots. I was number 23. A little over a year later, I got my house.

I am now twenty-one years old and have been in the navy for just over three years. I am stationed in San Diego, about two hours away from home. I have my own house, which I share with Adam, almost six years old now, and my wonderful husband, whom I met on base while living in the barracks. We got married September 8, 2001. We are expecting a child by the end of November 2002. We have orders to leave San Diego (with Adam!) and transfer for at least three years to North Carolina. I have a job that I can't get fired from and a steady paycheck. I pay taxes, I support my son and myself, and I defend your right to free speech and freedom. I am a productive member of society. I am not the exception, either.

Shannon Minydzak *is twenty-one and still in the navy, but she plans to get out next year to be able to spend more time with her children. She works in a navy pediatric clinic in Jacksonville, North Carolina. Shannon lives with her husband, Dennis, and her children, Adam and Jacob. She is currently pursuing a bachelor's degree in nursing and hopes to ultimately become a pediatric respiratory therapist.*

Katherine Robins

Birth of a Midwife

"Buuuzzzzz . . ." The clinic doorbell woke me.

It was only midnight, but I was exhausted. Only six hours to go until my shift ended.

"Buzzzzz."

Warm, sultry air kissed me as I opened the door of the birth center for a laboring woman and her parents.

"Oh, she's probably not really in labor . . . ," her mother was saying as I led the young woman and her mother to the exam room, while her father mindlessly took a seat in the waiting room. The young woman was wearing a delicate light blue blouse and flared black pants, her hair cascading over her shoulders and down her back, thick and dark like the Texas night sky outside.

I looked over her chart:

Isabelle Herandez, age 16. Height: 62 inches. Weight: 145 lbs. Gestation: 39.2 weeks. Estimated due date: July 23, 2001. Father of Baby: not involved.

"You can check her if you want. She says she hurts . . . but I think she is really okay, you know. . . ."

Isabelle stared straight up, her dark eyes fixed on one of the tiny ceiling holes above the exam table. Under her warm skin I felt the gentle waves and rolling of the baby moving beneath my hands. I measured her swollen belly and listened to the swift gal-loping of the baby's heart. *Ba-dum, ba-dum, ba-dum.* Her eyes closed and her brow furrowed slightly. The top of her belly became rounded as the skin grew taut. *Ba-dum, ba-dum, ba-dum.* I watched her chest rise and fall as she breathed in deeply. Her brow creased deeper and she shut her eyes more tightly.

"Breeaathhhe," I whispered. A shallow, labored breath escaped from her dry, pursed lips. Her fists were clenched at her sides, and her forehead glistened with sweat under the bright fluorescent light overhead.

"So we'll probably be going home tonight. . . . See, she isn't really doing anything. . . ."

As I led them down the hall to a birth room to get settled, her father commented to me, "You look so young." I smiled, remembering the many times I had heard that since beginning my apprenticeship at the birth center.

When I returned a few minutes later, her mother, who was sit-ting in a chair in a corner, sighed and said, "Well, it'll probably be a long time. . . ."

From the other chair in another corner, her father, a man with shiny dark hair and a long mustache, tight blue jeans, a large belt buckle, and pointy cowboy boots, nodded in agreement. Lying on her side facing away from her parents, Isabelle quietly moaned with a contraction. As I looked into her pleading eyes, I was brought back to my own son's birth six years ago.

"What did you expect? Of course it hurts! Maybe you should have thought of that before you went out and got yourself pregnant—this is what you get for having babies when you're still one yourself!" Her icy glare and harsh voice linger well beyond the moment when she turns and leaves, closing the door all but a crack. Alone, I sit in the bathtub and stare ahead into the darkness, taking little comfort in the warm water that used to be my refuge. Oh no! Oh God! Here it comes again. Starting low, inside my back, it takes hold of me, creeping slowly but surely around to the front, powerfully clutching everything it

grazes in its path; it has me by my belly with such a painful grip that I am paralyzed, unable to say anything or call for help. Maybe I am going to die here, alone, in this bathtub, in this hospital, and it will be because of that damn nurse who won't help me. I can't just get out of this tub myself—I dislocated my knee a week before and am on crutches. She had told my family about an hour before, "Oh, she's fine. She'll be fine. You can just go home, get some sleep, and I'll call you when she needs you," and so they had left.

"Well . . . you're fine. . . . Yes, of course it hurts . . . ," her mother said with a slight chuckle laced with irritation. She turned to me. "So, we'll probably be here a while, huh? She doesn't look like she is progressing much. . . ."

My first inclination was to tell her to shut up, that Isabelle was working very hard, and how dare she constantly undermine her. I placed my hand softly on Isabelle's lower back and started massaging, back and forth, slowly and firmly, trying to rub out the pain. I turned to her mother and replied softly, "She is working very hard and she is making a lot of progress. She is so strong. See how well she is handling these contractions? She is doing it perfectly." A sense of calm seemed to wash over Isabelle, and her shoulders loosened and relaxed. She closed her eyes as she rested, waiting for the next contraction.

I am jolted awake by the horrible gripping pain again. Oh, I can't do this. . . . I can't stand it anymore! I need something . . . someone. . . . Why am I here alone? I search for something to bring me back to reality. . . . Through the crack in the door I can make out part of the clock, the small black hand taunting me that I have been in this bath for almost five hours now. I look again at the closed door and pray for it to open, but it never does. Defeated, I succumb to the pain as my tears hit the frigid bathwater with tiny splashes. Finally, my tight belly begins to loosen as the contraction recedes. . . . My eyelids are very heavy and, too exhausted to think, I fall into the harbor of a listless sleep, forgetting that in a very short time I will be forced awake again.

I watched Isabelle's face as she grimaced with her contractions. Inhaling deeply, I matched my respirations to hers, silently letting her know that I was still with her. When the intensity of each tightening subsided, the deep wrinkles in her forehead smoothed and her tightly shut lips relaxed and became full again, and she'd rest in a place of internal serenity, comforted by the moments of reprieve from the waves of labor.

I see a beautiful countryside with rolling green hills and farmhouses. There is a river running happily through it. Oh, wait—that river is inside of me, making its way through me, flowing out gently from between my legs. I am the land, my fair-skinned rounded belly and pendulous breasts are the lovely rolling hills, and the warm river is flowing out of me, so peacefully. The river spreads its warmth around my thighs like a ray of sunshine on a crisp winter day. . . . Startled awake by the pain, I feel great pressure in my bottom, like a heavy bowling ball, trying to push its way through me. Pressure, pressure, pressure, unrelenting. . . . Maybe I have to go to the bathroom. . . . Something is happening. . . . Where is the call button?

As Isabelle's moans became louder and she grew more restless with her contractions, I knew that she was in the transition phase of labor, which is the most difficult time for many women. Her mother, who had been asleep for the past several hours, startled awake.

Isabelle looked up at me and tightly grabbed my hand. "I can't do it anymore!" she said in desperation, her upper lip beaded with sweat.

"Oh, Isabelle, stop it. Of course you can." Isabelle turned toward her mother, shooting her an angry glance. "Isabelle," her mother said in an authoritative yet embarrassed tone. Ignoring her challenge, I positioned myself directly in front of Isabelle, shielding her from further confrontation by her mother.

I hear the door open and the brisk heavy footsteps of the nurse approaching. "Well?" she asks snidely. Suddenly consumed with anger at being dependent on this wretched woman, I try to lift myself out of the bathtub. My knee doesn't cooperate, sending sharp shooting pains all along my leg as I try to bear weight on it, warning me not to push it any farther. Time is of the essence because if I am immobilized by another contraction, the nurse may leave again. "I'm getting out!" I tell her defiantly. "I don't care what you say. I am ready to have this baby." She looks at me for a moment, obviously irritated that I have challenged her authority. "Well, it's been a while. I suppose we can check you now."

"You are doing it. You are doing so well. It won't be long, and I will be here with you. You will see your baby soon," I reassured Isabelle loud enough for her mother to hear, wanting her to appreciate what her daughter was experiencing. Now focused, Isabelle raised her head with a look of determination, and our eyes met, mutually acknowledging that she had the power within herself to give birth.

"Yep, it's almost time. Who should we call?" "What do you mean it's almost time? What about my epidural? I am supposed to have an epidural." With superficial sweetness she replies, "Sorry, honey, too late. Now, who should I call? You're having this kid within the next few minutes." Out of desperation and sheer terror over the imminent pain that will accompany the unmedicated birth, I break into tears. This is not how it's supposed to be. . . .

Isabelle grabbed both of her legs behind her knees and brought her chin to her chest. Her face reddening with effort, she pushed through several contractions. "That's the way! You're doing great! Stronger! A little stronger! Push right here! That's it—perfect! Okay, now rest . . . just rest until you feel like pushing again. . . . You're doing such a good job." Flushed and sweating, Isabelle closed her eyes as I placed a cool washcloth on her forehead.

Isabelle asked quietly, "When will she come out?"

"Soon. It won't be too long now. You're going to feel a lot of pressure and probably some burning as her head is moving down right before she is born."

"I am ripping in half! I am splitting apart!" I cry to the nurse and the midwife. The nurse flatly says, "You're fine." Goddammit, I am not fine! I am splitting in half the way my brother and I used to split the wishbone after Thanksgiving dinner. I am not fine! "It won't be long," the midwife, whom I've only met once, tells me as she peers up over my belly from her seat between my legs. I hear myself making deep, guttural noises as I struggle to push. My mother and Matt, my boyfriend, are now on either side of me. Matt is rubbing my arm incessantly, rapidly repeating, "You're okay, you're okay, you're okay," as he seems to be hyperventilating. My mother, very concerned, puts her arm around me and is saying, "It's just you and me, sister. We can do this." What do you mean it's just you and me? It's just me. "You're okay...." "It's just you and me." "You're okay...." My mother, irritated at Matt, reaches across me and swats his hand off my arm. "Leave her alone! Stop it!" she says protectively. Matt protests, "I can be here! She's having my baby!" The nurse keeps counting. "... one, two, three ..." "You're okay! You're okay!" "... six, seven, eight ..." Oh my God, get me out of here! This is too much! My vagina is on fire! I can feel it being stretched too thin, too wide.... It's going to rip.... I can't do this anymore. "You're okay!" "... two, three, four ..."

With each tightening, I could see a little more of the baby's head coming into view, wrinkled and glistening with shiny black hair. "She has lots of hair. Do you want to feel her head?"

Isabelle's eyes sparkled, and when she reached down and touched the baby's head she broke into a smile. Taking in a deep breath and scrunching her face up tightly, she pushed with newfound determination as she anticipated meeting her baby. She let out a scream when she delivered the baby's head. "It's okay— your baby's head is out now...." As I gently supported the baby's pink little head between my hands, her eyes just barely started to blink open. I was reminded of how privileged I was to be here, to be able to witness this truly amazing event. "She is beautiful. Just one more push with the next contraction."

The midwife places this warm, slippery, pink little body on my bare belly that is now flaccid like bread dough. I am no longer aware of the chaos around me but am completely awestruck by this beautiful, perfect baby. Between my breasts he strains his neck to lift his little head. Raising his eyebrows, he looks curiously into my face with big, blue eyes framed with long black eyelashes. I feel overwhelming warmth and love for this amazing little creature—the sensation is almost indescribable, and he somehow just came out of me. . . .

As I placed the baby up on Isabelle's chest, her eyes grew wide with amazement. Her face lit with joy as she realized that she had just given birth—this was her baby. Isabelle was mesmerized, gazing into her daughter's eyes, large and dark like her own. She seemed unaware of her mother talking in the background to my midwifery instructor about her healthy baby, how she didn't even think that Isabelle was really that close to delivering when she came in, and how it was too bad that the baby's father wasn't here. I suggested that Isabelle and the baby rest and encouraged her parents to go out and eat breakfast for a couple of hours.

As I watched Isabelle and the baby sleep peacefully, I realized that Isabelle had given me a gift. Until this birth, I had not fully understood why I had been called to midwifery as my profession, other than an intense fascination with pregnancy and childbirth. While the labor and actual birth of my son was a traumatic and terrifying event for me, I felt a tremendous sense of accomplishment and empowerment that I was able to endure it and successfully deliver my beautiful son. Assisting Isabelle led me to understand my desire to work with young women so that they feel supported, accepted, and strengthened through their own birth experiences.

Isabelle's baby slept in her tiny pink and white striped hat, one pink booty poking out from under the baby blankets, her sweet little lips moving in and out as if she were dreaming about nursing. Isabelle, lying on her side, stirred from sleep as she instinctively placed her hand gently on the little bundle beside her.

Take this birth with you, Isabelle, and remember what a powerful woman you are. Remember it when people try to bring you down or criticize you. Please, don't listen to them. Know that you have your own inner strength that will carry you and your baby; let it be your shield. Look at what a wonderful mother you are already.

I walked quietly to the door, turning back toward Isabelle one last time, silently thanking her for this experience and for helping me renew my dedication to be of service to young women through midwifery.

Katherine Robins *lives with her two wonderful children, Samson and Lily; her good friend, Angela, and Angela's son, Riley; and their beloved cat, Daphne Rose, in a small town in Oregon. She became interested in midwifery when she was sixteen years old and pregnant with her son Samson. With tremendous love and support from her family and friends, she completed her bachelor of science in nursing degree at the University of Washington and is currently a student in the nurse-midwifery program at Oregon Health & Sciences University. She feels passionately about providing midwifery and health care services that are empowering to young women and their families. After graduation, she plans on eventually opening a freestanding birth center and health clinic as a certified nurse-midwife and family nurse practitioner.*

Jenne Herbst

Cows, Colleges, and Casting

Growing up on a farm wasn't absolutely horrible, but I knew that it wasn't the life for me. I watched my father wake up every morning at 5 A.M. to milk the cows. We could never venture too far from home, because my father had to be back in the evening to milk the cows again. The daily milking schedule, as well as the weather and how it affected the crops, determined our whole existence.

There were good things about farm life, of course. My father was usually home when my brother, Joe, and I got off the school bus. I enjoyed the numerous animals around us. There was no discrimination between "girls' jobs" and "boys' jobs." Everyone helped out to make sure the work got done. My mother and father expected both Joe and me to bale hay, shell corn, and feed the cows.

However, the tedious tasks of farm life just weren't for me. I wanted to experience things that I read about in books. I wanted to be able to write about those experiences. I wanted my daughter Caitlin to see that there was an amazing world outside of Minnesota. I knew that a college degree would afford me the opportunity to give Caitlin and myself those experiences. St. Olaf

College accepted me, and even though it was fifty miles away and didn't offer family housing and I couldn't afford to live off-campus, I trusted that it would all be worth it.

I was going to do the responsible thing—major in English and become a high school teacher. I would be the first one in my family to leave farm life and graduate from a four-year college, and teaching looked like a sensible choice.

College was amazing to me, but I felt like I was leading a double life. At school I was discussing my thoughts and ideas with the professors and the other students. I was responsible for getting my work done and turning it in on time. In my "mom life," I was responsible for making sure Caitlin had enough to eat, getting her to bed, and discussing the finer points of Barney and Baby Bop.

As a parent, being an English major was a wonderful choice. I could do my homework and read Caitlin a bedtime story at the same time. Her grandma Vicki read her *The Very Hungry Caterpillar, Green Eggs and Ham,* and *Is Your Mama a Lama?* I read her Shakespeare, John Donne, and Aphra Behn.

I tried hard to make my mom life and my college life come together. I could bring my college work home, but it was much more difficult to bring my home life to college. The professors and students did not know what to think of me. Most students were spending their free time trying to figure out how to get alcohol into their dorm rooms on a dry campus. The professors were used to students who lived in the dorms and could partici-pate in a lot of activities on campus outside of class. Since St. Olaf doesn't have family housing, the faculty was not used to some-one who was already a mother and needed to plan her activities around parenting responsibilities. I used the long drive between home and school mentally preparing for whomever I needed to be—the college student comparing and contrasting socialism with democracy or the mother reading *Go, Dog. Go!* ten times in a row without stopping.

A sign right by St. Olaf College inspired me. It reads, "Welcome to Northfield—Home of Cows, Colleges, and Contentment." Every time I saw that sign I would think, *I'm going to college to get away from the cows and find my contentment.*

It took a while to find my contentment. Although I loved English, my heart wasn't in becoming a high school teacher, and I believe the only people who should be teaching are the ones who love it. I also loved drama, and one of my English professors encouraged me to take a class in the theater department. When I took "Introduction to Theater," I knew right away that I had found my home. Bedtime stories for Caitlin became much livelier. She now had the German film director and playwright Fassbinder and the playwright Christopher Durang to put her to sleep, and a mother who would perform all the roles.

Even though a major in theater felt right, I still didn't know what I was going to do with it. I didn't want to be an actor—I knew my performance skills were something only my daughter would appreciate, not the world at large. I could barely draw stick figures, so designing sets was out of the question. I could sew, which made costuming a possibility, but I am a perfectionist, and the sewing done on theater costumes is not perfect; it's done very quickly, just enough to hold the costumes together through a few performances and look good on stage from the audience.

Most parents are not pleased when their children come home and say, "It's the theater life for me." My practical farmer parents thought that I had lost my mind. Adding to their concerns was my status as a single parent. They were convinced that Caitlin and I would be destitute.

I needed to figure out what I wanted to do in the theater, and I needed to prove to everyone that I could do it. I took a job as a stage manager. The pay was higher than that of any other work-study job, and it would allow me to learn about all the different theater positions. The first show I worked on was *Pericles*. The director, one of the professors in the department and my advisor, allowed me to help with auditions. I had the chance to watch the actors prepare, and sometimes I sneaked up into the booth and watched the auditions. When callbacks were held a few days later, the director had me sit in on them.

Professor Pinnow posted the cast list and asked me what I thought of his choices. There is nothing I love better than giving an opinion, and I let him know that I didn't agree with some of his decisions. I listed the reasons why one actress would be better than the actress whom he had cast. I told him that I would have switched the roles of two actors and gave him my reasons for the switch. As I spoke I noticed that he was smiling, and I wondered what was going on in his head.

"You know, Jenne," he told me, "there is a job where you can get paid to put actors into roles. It's called casting, and I think you would be great at it."

"Casting?" The practical side of me kicked in. "Do you make a lot of money?"

"I think the money is good, but most of the jobs are in Los Angeles or New York."

I knew that I had found my calling. Casting would get us off the farm, I could support Caitlin, and, the best part, I would be paid to give my opinion.

That night I told Caitlin, "Mommy is going to be a casting director." She looked up and smiled. Of course, being only three years old, she had absolute confidence in everything I said or did. Yet, it was through her that I regained so much of my old self-confidence. Her trust sustained me through all of my theater classes and the icy Minnesota winter drives to college.

Casting is a far-fetched career choice, but then again I hadn't expected to find out that I was pregnant the night before I was supposed to begin my senior year in high school. Life is funny that way. When I thought I was going to Columbia College in Iowa to major in international business, I found out that I was pregnant and wound up going to St. Olaf College to major in English. And then I ended up in theater, someplace much better than I had ever imagined.

I began doing research into the casting profession. I read anything that mentioned casting. When I watched films, I noticed the casting director's credits. I indulged in watching *Entertainment Tonight* and reading *People* and *Entertainment Weekly*, all under the guise of doing research.

I found very little information on becoming a casting director, but I did learn that the best way to enter the profession was through an internship. The best one was the Academy of Television Arts and Sciences Internship Program. It was highly competitive, not just because of who was sponsoring it but because it was paid, whereas most internships were not. As a single mother on Aid to Families with Dependent Children, I figured this was the only way I was going to make my dreams happen. I sent in my application and kept my fingers crossed.

When I learned that I didn't get the internship, I got a really sick feeling in my stomach. I wanted to throw myself onto the bed and yell, but Caitlin was napping right beside me, so I put my face in the pillow and sobbed. Everything that I had endured for four years poured out in those tears. Staying up late to study and when I was finished, Caitlin waking up, wanting to play. Driving a hundred miles round-trip from my parents' home to college. Feeling driven to find a way off the farm and offer my daughter and myself more opportunities.

Not getting the internship was a blow, but a couple of days after I found out, I decided that we would move to L.A. anyway. I was determined to become a casting director. I knew that I had the talent to put the right actor in the appropriate role. I also knew that if I didn't take a chance I would regret it. Putting myself through college as a single mother had given me tremendous self-assurance, so in September of 1996 I took out a loan from my grandparents, packed up the car, and moved my daughter and myself to Los Angeles.

So, how did it go? Well, being a mother prepared me well for my time in Hollywood. I was able to handle anything thrown my way with panache. I had gained the patience and compassion needed to work with actors when they go to their "deep, dark, actor place." I used my "mom voice" when I needed to close a deal with an agent and he was acting particularly cocky. As for those "tyrannical" directors, let me just say that they have nothing on a three-year-old.

The rest is history.

Jenne Herbst

CASTING EXPERIENCE

Casting Director:	**Vagina Monologues** (2001 and 2002)
	NC State University
	Undone*—35 mm Short Film (2000)
	*Winner Best Short and Best Actress at
	NoDance 2001
Casting Associate:	**2gether**—MTV's First MOW (1999)
	Road Trip—Feature Film (1999)
	Lord of the Rings—Feature Film Trilogy (1999)
	Cast Away—Feature Film (1999)
	Fantasy Island—Series for ABC (1998)
Casting Assistant:	**Nash Bridges**—Rysher Series for
	CBS (1997–1998)
	Before Women Had Wings—MOW (1997)
	Quicksilver Highway—MOW (1997)
	The Inheritance—MOW (1997)
Casting Intern:	**Touched by an Angel**—Series for CBS (1996)

EDUCATION

St. Olaf College—Northfield, Minnesota (1992–1996), Bachelor of Arts Major: Speech Communications/Theater; Minor: Women's Studies

Jenne Herbst *lives in Raleigh, North Carolina, where there aren't many cows. She recently married a wonderful man named Stuart, and Caitlin is now in middle school. Since moving to North Carolina, Jenne has cast and directed* The Vagina Monologues *at North Carolina State; she will also cast and direct this play in the spring of 2004. She currently works as a temp and in her spare time is reading; writing plays, short stories, and a young adult book titled* The Bright Blue Line; *seeing too many films (is this possible?); and clapping and cheering whenever she sees casting directors' screen credits.*

Speak Out!

What's the single biggest issue, obstacle, or challenge teen parents face today?

Lack of support, whether it's from the government, parents, teachers, friends, or babydaddies. Every parent needs help with stuff, whether you are a teen or not. And it's so hard to get.

> Overcoming society's belief that all teen mothers are going to become failures.

Feeling like we should measure up to middle-aged, suburbanite parents, and not thinking for ourselves about parenting issues.

> Preconceived assumptions about how I became pregnant and how I will be as a mother.

Finding a way to support our families without being slaves to state assistance programs.

> Discrimination.

Lack of resources—child care, parenting classes, help with getting a car seat, etc.

> Fathers don't want to take any responsibility, and mothers end up holding the bag—mentally, monetarily, socially.

Republicans.

Not receiving the help and respect that any parent or human being deserves.

Lack of role models—women just like us who made it!

The economy.

Suddenly having a family to care for before I knew how to care for myself completely.

Maintaining a balance between being a mom and being a teenager.

Disrespect for our authority as parents. How are we supposed to learn and trust our parenting instincts if we are told constantly that we are wrong?

Lack of information, on everything from housing to schools to how to take care of ourselves.

Education, hands down! There are very few resources for us mothers.

Exhaustion. We're fighting so hard not to be seen as failures that we can barely let go, even for a moment.

PART 7

Emerging From Darkness

ON HEALING FROM ABUSE AND ADDICTION, AND LEARNING TO LOVE AGAIN

William didn't come back to the hospital until I was being discharged with my new son a week later. Within the first six weeks of being home, William had bro-ken my hand with a screwdriver and threatened to take the baby. I had William thrown in jail for domestic violence. After being afraid for so long, I had become the lioness, protecting my cub.

Tristan was my divine intervention. Without him I would have never found the strength to stand up and get out of a deadly situation. Without my son I have no doubt I wouldn't be here today.

—Anna Phillips,
34, mother, health care assistant,
Seattle, Washington

Some of the women who sent me their stories conceived their babies in love, some in carelessness, some in violence. A number planned the pregnancy, either with a partner's consent or without. Others conceived the first time they had sex, thinking it wouldn't happen to them. More than one writer wanted to have a baby to create the loving family that she lacked. Some women forgot to take their birth control pills—just one pill, or just a few—or they used the notoriously unreliable withdrawal method. Various writers talked of consenting to having sex halfheartedly, giving in to a partner's badgering or threats of abandonment. Still others agreed to have sex hoping it would strengthen a shaky relationship or prove that they were lovable.

One sixteen-year-old former gang member wrote that she became pregnant as the result of a rape at age fourteen. An older family member had helped to set the situation up and stood by in a nearby room while the girl was being violated. Today she has no involvement with the man who abused her, the man who fathered her child. She has ended her gang involvement and her use of drugs. She goes to school, and she gleans lessons on child rearing both from the day care her child attends and from parenting classes.

She wasn't ready to have a baby, she wrote. But the relative who betrayed her is also a young mother—neglectful and abusive, the young woman said—and when she witnesses that relative's bad choices as a mother, it helps her to make good choices for her own child.

Such determination—to turn a bleak situation into something bright and positive and joyful—echoed through so many of the essays I received. In this chapter, motherhood works like a salve to soothe Stephanie Sylverne's wounds from a difficult childhood. Latisha Boyd faces a tragic loss that challenges her to discover her inner strengths. Sarah Tavis confronts a debilitating relationship and asks herself, *Who do I want to be?* Kelly Busch descends into a frightening addiction and searches for the way out. And Rita Naranjo survives a lonely foster care upbringing to embark on a career in social change.

Stephanie Sylverne

Turning On the Lights

My daughter was conceived in my shame: shame in my body, shame in the act that made her, shame in my need to feel loved. Don't look at my thighs, don't look at my breasts, don't expose me—for fear that you won't love me anymore. But please, please, give me a baby to prove your love for me. I finally got that baby, yes, but in the journey I unexpectedly got something more.

In the eyes of the world around me, a seventeen-year-old pierced and pregnant high school dropout was not exactly on her way to enlightenment. The general consensus from friends and family was that becoming a mother would further damage my already complicated life. Admittedly, my outward actions pointed only to impending disaster in raising a child. My parents were devastated, embarrassed, angry, and horrified, to say the least. Despite the criticism from my family, I felt in my heart that my growing belly was more than just a financial burden, more than a social liability, more than yet another project I would grow tired of and throw by the wayside.

I cannot remember exactly when or how my self-hatred began. In kindergarten, I wore a pillow inside my Halloween bumblebee costume. I sat at the short, round table in my class thinking that everyone in the room was staring at my fat belly.

Even after stashing the pillow underneath the table, I sat in rigid terror that someone would know it was mine and everyone would laugh at me. When the teacher found the pillow, I sat silent as she asked repeatedly to whom it belonged.

I recall that moment as the beginning of many years of torment at the hands of my classmates. I was the outcast, the chubby girl sitting at the edge of the playground, partly hoping someone would play with me and partly hoping they would all, just this one day, leave me alone. The only weapon I had was my brain, and even that was attacked. Taunts of "teacher's pet" and "smarty-pants" were soon added to the "fatso" and "tub-o-lard" variations that filled my school days. Being found out as the only Jewish girl added even more colorful vocabulary to their arsenal. Throughout grade school, classmates broke my glasses, spit on me, pushed, chased, pointed at, and whispered about me. They said I had cooties and lice and that I smelled. When I sat in a chair, boys would make wood-splitting noises as if the chair was breaking. When a teacher had us roll paper across the floor to draw outlines of our bodies, one girl told another, "She better use two pieces."

The height of the shame came when I was sexually attacked at ten years old. This cemented what I thought was my total lack of worth. I spent the next six years despising everyone, especially men, and either wanting to die or wishing I had the guts to open fire on everyone in my path. I became cynical and angry and self-destructive. I had one-night stands with any guy who would show me a few minutes of attention and afterward try to scrub away the feeling of his skin. Sex made me feel dirty and used. Obviously I was too fat, I would think, and that was why he didn't like me anymore.

By this time though, I wasn't really fat. Sure, I had a size-10 body more suited to a twenty-five-year-old than a fifteen-year-old, but I was neither too big nor too small, so I didn't attract much concern about my mental health. Nobody thought I was overweight enough to be overeating, and I wasn't small enough to be marked as bulimic or anorexic.

I did go to some counseling, mostly for anger and stress management, but I never talked about my inner self-hatred and I certainly didn't say anything about being abused. I hardly even consciously acknowledged it. The counseling I got barely touched on surface issues that were just symptoms of a deeper problem.

When I was fifteen I met my first real boyfriend. The first time we slept together I had an anxiety attack and sobbed right in front of him. Surprisingly, that didn't scare him away. He told me repeatedly that I was beautiful, and even though I finally felt somewhat safe, I never let him take away the blanket or turn on the light. He was different from the other guys I had been with. He liked me in all the ways that I wanted to be liked—he recognized my intellect, brought me to dinner with his family, and took me to his senior prom. Thanks to his continuous attention and soothing words over the months we were together, I gained some assurance in being loved and in the possibility that I was attractive. His unconditional affection healed a vital piece of my self-worth.

Toward the end of that relationship, I met a man who would in two more years become the father of my first child. I knew the moment I looked at him that my daughter would have his eyes. I was instantly attracted to him; it was what most people would call love at first sight. Early on he said, "Can I ask you a personal question?" I said I didn't mind, and he said, "Were you ever molested?"

I was shocked. "How did you know?"

"I can just tell," he answered. A few months later, he convinced me to tell my parents and emotionally supported me to go into therapy to deal with the abuse. During the group therapy I learned two important things: that many, many women are sexually abused in their lifetime, and that many of them are abused in far worse ways than I was. It did not have to be the defining disaster of my entire life. I could be a survivor, not a victim.

But my boyfriend and I had a volatile relationship. We were madly, passionately, and deliriously in love with each other. Unfortunately, we fought with the same intensity. I wasn't trusting, and he was untrustworthy most of the time. Often, I didn't know where he had been, whom he had been with, and what he was doing. I needed constant reassurance and attention from someone who didn't have a clue how to handle me. We would have debilitating breakups almost every few weeks, even though we always ended up back together.

Part of what kept me glued to him was that he understood my boundaries and hang-ups. He was in no way sexually threatening to me, so my confidence could thrive little by little. On some inner level I knew that the relationship wasn't healthy, but I chose to ignore the red flags. All I wanted was someone who would love me, no matter what, whether I gained fifteen pounds or cut off all my hair or cried in my sleep. Still, the emptiness inside gnawed at me, until I came to the conclusion that having a baby would probably fill that void.

My diary from that time is filled with baby names and musings about what our baby would look like. I had dreams of being pregnant, of a dark-haired baby with my boyfriend's blue-green eyes. In a small way, I thought that getting pregnant would heal a missing piece in our relationship, but really it was more about what I wanted. I didn't have as much concern about our instability as I should have. I justified conceiving by imagining that if I were pregnant, I wouldn't feel fat anymore. A pregnancy would hide my big thighs! For nine months I would not have to worry about eating; everyone expects pregnant women to be big. I have yet to come across any other women who got pregnant in order *not* to feel fat.

When I found out I was pregnant, I wasn't afraid or upset in the least. I was jubilant. I couldn't help but smile. The one other person I thought would be happy turned on me in a heartbeat.

He told me in no uncertain terms that he wanted nothing to do with me ever again, whether I had the baby or not. My family, to say it lightly, was devastated. It was pure hell in my house for months: "You will have to do this alone—he won't be there." "What the hell were you thinking?" "You are not ready to have a baby!" "There is no way you are having this baby."

But I was obsessed with my pregnancy. For the first time in my life, I didn't pay attention to the numbers on the scale, fret over what size I was wearing, or dive into guilt about what I was eating. For the first time I thought my body was working exactly the way it should. Even though my condition had sparked a war at home, I spent a lot of time feasting on every available book about pregnancy and trying to find joy in my little kicking stranger. It seemed to me like everyone wanted to knock me down when my self-esteem was finally, for once, rising.

Still, by the last trimester everyone was more or less accepting and excited about the new baby. I had packed on about fifty pounds and I didn't care. I no longer cried in front of the mirror when trying on clothes. I was consumed with love for the little person kicking me in my giant stomach. Every day was exciting, some new milestone being reached. I was back together with the baby's father, but he began distancing himself again as my due date approached. One day at his apartment, we got into a major fight, and in front of his friends he said, "Shut up, you fat ugly bitch." My bubble burst. My face flamed with anger and embarrassment. I ended up running out into the hallway, where I sat moaning and sobbing on the stairs. He came out and offered a half-assed apology, and although I went back into the apartment, that day changed my feelings for him forever. I weakly vowed to stop subjecting myself to his cruelty. I was sick of letting everyone use me as a punching bag. I still went back and forth with him for a couple years, mostly out of habit and comfort, but something in the back of my mind had snapped. I never forgave him for that day.

Samantha was born on July 16, 1997, at nine pounds, eight

ounces and twenty-two inches. My body finally did something right. At eighteen years old, an age when most girls are just starting to have feelings about growing up, I became a woman. It didn't matter to me anymore what my peers thought of me, because I was now somehow above them. Their parties and boyfriends were so trivial. Yes, I was a size 12 three months postpartum, but I had a baby, so my body didn't apply to the same childish beauty standards anymore. I couldn't fathom why any young mother would feel shame for having a baby when it initiated her into a more fulfilling life where more important things mattered than who would be your dorm mate.

In the years after Samantha's birth, I struggled off and on with my self-esteem. I didn't scheme for painless ways to kill myself or fill my diary with vicious words and violent scribbling the way I used to. My empathy for others blossomed dramatically, since any child could now be my child. I still had trouble in a mirror, but my standard was no longer nearly as rigid. I had many more good days than bad. I had taken my GED while I was pregnant, so I went to college, where my intellect could express itself without being attacked. I no longer thought I was lucky to have the attention of a man and became far more powerful in my relationships with them. My on-again, off-again relationship with my daughter's father finally ended when I had the strength to realize I didn't need someone to love me if it wasn't in the way I deserved.

My life came full circle at my four-year-old daughter's preschool Halloween parade. I stood outside like all the other moms—armed with a camera, waiting for our quickly grown babies to turn the corner. When I saw Samantha coming, my eyes filled with tears. She looked so innocent and shy, peeking up and waving. In an instant, instead of noticing Samantha, all I saw was five-year-old me, embarrassed in a bumblebee costume, wanting to hide. Here I was, twenty-two years old, standing away from everyone else, not feeling accepted into the "older" mothers' club grouped together and pointing to their preschoolers.

Once again I was alone on the playground. Suddenly I felt that even as far as I had come, that little girl was haunting me, crying for someone to listen to her. I remember thinking, *Is it ever going to end?*

I fled the first moment I could and drove down the street, sobbing. I wasn't sure why I was crying; I just knew that for my daughter to experience even a fraction of the pain that I had would be unbearable for me to handle. Like many times before, something snapped. I knew I couldn't live like this anymore.

I always tell my daughter that she is beautiful, but I also make a point to tell her she's smart. I've seen others limit their child's food intake for fat content and I check myself every day to make sure I don't do something like that. I tell her to think for herself; I tell her that what others say about her doesn't matter. I want to encourage her in art, in reading, and in empowering competitions like team sports, something I never had the self-esteem to participate in. I never listen to people who say I should put her in modeling, pageants, cheerleading, or anything else that might contribute to her making a connection between her appearance and her worthiness. The older she gets, the more my eating habits and complaints about my body become apparent to me. Now that she is five, such a critical age in my own life, I am starting to realize that my body image disorder no longer affects only me. I have to change not only for my sake, but also for hers.

My daughter's presence in my life is a daily reminder of how valuable I actually am. She gave me the key to unlock my inner power to be a woman and to be unleashed from the body of the lonely little girl I once was. When I look at her, I am reminded who I was, but I am also reminded that she is a whole new person whose worldview I shape in all kinds of ways, both large and small. I can't allow myself to scream and cry about my body anymore. I can't allow myself to be in doomed and violent relationships. I can't decide to throw away my education or to lie in bed all day, stuck in deep depression. I can't allow my version of womanhood to be wrapped up in the thickness of my thighs. It is a daily struggle to remember how much she learns from me, even when I think she's not looking. It is in my hands now to quiet the rage and finish resolving my past.

Stephanie Sylverne *is a twenty-four-year-old single mom to a worldly and inquisitive six-year-old named Samantha. They reside in the Chicago area with no pets and a lot of junk food. Stephanie spends her free time plotting, reading, writing, avoiding telemarketers, watching the Discovery Channel, contemplating the meaning of life, and taking Samantha to soccer practice. She swears that one of these days she will finally finish her BA and move on to graduate school. Her dream is to become a professor, author, and world traveler, and to raise a free thinker like herself in the process. Friends describe Stephanie as an overopinionated pessimist who takes tarot cards far too seriously and spends a ridiculous amount of time arguing religious philosophies.*

Latisha Boyd

Growing Up Too Fast

I was raised in New York on Eastern Parkway, between the Jewish community and the Hispanic and Haitian community. The middle was the African-American/Caribbean community—the "block"—where the noisy people came to hang out, that place where everybody knows everybody and everybody's business, from when the last government check came to who's sleeping with whose baby's daddy.

When I was fifteen, I moved with my favorite aunt to Kingsboro, a small project in Brooklyn and one of the worst in the area, though back then I didn't know that. The projects were a different life for me: The same gossip existed there, but it came from a community of guns, sex, and drugs, where black people paid fifty dollars for rent while driving a Lexus or BMW, where guys wore expensive jewelry to prove how much drugs they sold, and where girls wore Gucci clothes and carried Fendi handbags just to walk through the projects to the A train.

In Kingsboro I met my first love, M.T. At fifteen, he was already a father, but it didn't matter to me because it was the norm back then, in 1988, to have a baby or be pregnant. That was part of the gossip—who would be pregnant before high school? I was one of the "lucky" ones because I was sixteen when I met my boyfriend and started having sex, not twelve.

Unfortunately, I wasn't lucky enough not to get pregnant. My mother was furious over that pregnancy, so she decided we had to terminate it. I couldn't understand why she was so angry. Up until then, she hadn't paid too much attention to my needs or to what I was doing. I wasn't even living in her house. But she had a reputation of being pretty, sexy, and respectable, and she had a dream that I'd finish high school. Her reputation had so much weight that it was difficult for my sisters and I to do anything that wasn't acceptable. She wanted me to be the good gossip on the block, since I was the baby of her three girls and my sisters already had children of their own. She reminded other people's kids to say, "Yes, please" and "Thank you." Even when she was drinking, kids knew not to be rude around my mother because she would put them in their place and then send them home to their own mothers. People loved that about her.

I wanted to have a baby. I first got the urge to become a mother when I watched M.T. with his daughter. I was spending a lot of time with them and often felt jealous that he had somebody loving him. She would cling to him, always following him and needing him to pick her up and hold her. I wanted someone to love me, to cling to me and need me like that.

I hadn't had that kind of love myself. My sisters were eight years older than me and my mother hadn't made the time to bond with me or introduce me to my father or any paternal relatives. I didn't know any of my grandparents, cousins, aunts, or uncles on my father's side. I had difficulty believing that I was wanted, and I called myself a bastard child. I'm not sure if I believed it or if I just wanted to hurt my mother's feelings.

My sisters and I have different fathers, but they have love from their paternal relatives. I have one memory of my father taking me to Burger King when I was about five years old. Talking about my conception with my mother was too painful, so I accepted the bits and pieces she gave me without any question. I knew my father was real, and I knew how he died. I guess my mother thought that was enough.

M.T. and his family shared a bond. It was dysfunctional, but still, it existed. I knew that having my own baby, I could create my own bond and prove to my mother that I could be a better parent than she'd been. I wanted to provide a child with the comfortable home that I never had.

I left my dysfunctional home, where my mom and sisters were addicted to drugs, to move in with M.T. who sold drugs, and his family, whose friends drank alcohol. In the beginning, I fit right in. His mother knew I was having a difficult time with my mother, and she admired the fact that I wanted to finish high school. Her offer to live with them as long as I attended school was like a blessing to me. I thought that living with my "man" made me a grown-up. I challenged any adult who told me I was still a kid.

After a couple of years and my second pregnancy, which I miscarried, M.T. became abusive and controlling. He had another girlfriend who lived three buildings away and two other girls who claimed him as their babies' father. I took beatings and humiliation from him, yet because he said he loved me, I stayed with him. My mother used to abuse me and then tell me she loved me too, but I didn't believe her. It was easier to believe M.T., because I had never heard those words from a man and because when my mother said them she would be drinking. M.T. was my sole provider of food, clothes, and shelter. He was my father figure, male role model, and sex partner, all in one. He was the only man I had ever had in my life, so I stayed.

After my miscarriage, my urge for motherhood became stronger. I had graduated from high school and had nothing to do. M.T. was still hanging out with other girlfriends and staying out late, regardless of the fact that I was still sleeping in his bed every night, even when he wasn't there. The next year, at nineteen, I gave birth to my son. I'd prayed for a boy, not only for someone to love me but so that M.T. would love me again as well. He already had a daughter, and his other kids were "daddy's maybe"; how could he resist the woman that would have his son under his own roof?

Yet, as I lay in the hospital, I didn't want to go back to M.T.'s house, and I didn't want to go back to my mothers'. I knew by now that M.T. was selling drugs. With dysfunction on both ends of the scale, I had to decide which household I'd be able to handle with a baby. My mother never knew how to be there for me when I was growing up; at least M.T.'s mother could help me with the baby in the middle of the night. I went back to M.T.'s. I thought having M.T.'s son would stop the abuse. It didn't work that way. The more trapped M.T. felt, the more he abused me, and he began putting me out on the streets.

Those first six months of my son's life I spent homeless, living with one relative after another. I was always packing clothes and cans of milk and pushing them around in the bottom of the stroller, not knowing where we would sleep. Instinctually I had certain things organized: I knew what days my son needed to go to the clinic and when to pick up his milk. When I visited them, my mother and my friends didn't have a clue what I was going through, and most days I ended up at M.T.'s relatives' homes. I spent most days in the welfare office trying to get an income so I could then get an apartment. I had to gain some independence for my son and me: I didn't want him to grow up seeing his father abuse me. Finally, M.T.'s aunt helped me get my first apartment. This was my first step toward empowerment, toward creating a new me—a woman who took care of her son's needs. I took care of him emotionally by kissing him and hugging him and telling him how much I loved him. I took care of him physically by making sure he had clean clothes and medical care. I took him to birthday parties with other children and made sure he always had food and a clean, comfortable bed to sleep in at night, not like the one I had as a child that broke just from sitting on it. Those were the things I'd always wanted my mother to provide for me.

When my son turned one I wanted more for us, so I enrolled in a nurse's aide program. I took care of my baby in the day and went to school at night. Although his father and I were not together, I was still having sex with him. I didn't know whom else to turn to when I was lonely. M.T. had been my main companion for five years, and I had promised him that I would never have sex with anyone else. He in turn promised he would always love me. Not understanding the cycle of power, sex, and control, I let him abuse me.

The more I began to do things for myself, the stronger I became. I started going to church to ask God to help me provide for my son. I became involved with the community through church activities. I began to read the newspaper and watch educational programs on television. I took my son to the library, and I would take out self-help books.

M.T. saw the changes in me and wanted to be around me more. I didn't want to be involved with him, but I wanted my son to have his father around, so I gave us another chance to be a family. It lasted less than three months. I expected him to be a husband to me and a father to our son. We were no longer teenagers, but he still had not gotten a job or finished high school. His thing was selling drugs, and I didn't need that money anymore. I had a job in a nursing home and my son was enrolled in day care.

I had help from family, too. My sister Natalie was seeking help with her own personal problems, and we were helping each other. M.T.'s mother was a good grandmother, and she was in my corner one hundred percent; without her I don't know how I would have managed. My relationship with my mother was still strained, but I did visit her. After going through so much drama with M.T., I had begun to see her differently. I think it was easier for me having a baby in 1991 than it had been for her in 1971. When I had my son there was less racism, better access to resources and services, and more openness about sexuality. I didn't have to fight racism on the front line but from the middle. I had learned how to build my faith by attending church. My life experiences also helped me to understand her drug addiction and her lack of affection.

I'd always feared two things. The first was to be rejected by society—labeled a victim of poverty and not recognized for taking care of my son as well as I did. The second was his father not being around to see our son grow. The first I had the control to change through life experience. The second one did come true. On July 10, 1993, my first love was killed in the very project in which he was born, raised, and made most of his living. This tragedy changed me. At times I'd depended on the money he gave us; now that he was gone and had never had a job, even Social Security couldn't help us financially. But even more, it was his presence that had mattered. Like me, now my son would experience that ache in his heart of not having a father.

I would sit in a corner, crying and screaming for hours, asking God, "Why did this happen to me?" I'd think, *The man who was everything to my son and me is dead.* For months I lived in the dark, not seeing the people around me. I was unable to care for my son, who spent most of his time with M.T.'s mother.

I knew I couldn't continue to live that way. I had to do something so my son wouldn't go down that same path.

I got into counseling to get help with my grieving. I read self-help books. I gradually went back to church and joined a bereavement group. One day on the subway I looked up and saw an advertisement that read, "THINK EMPOWERMENT." It was for Audrey Cohen College, today known as New York Metropolitan College. In September of 1993 I enrolled, majoring in human service. I took a lot of women's studies courses, which helped me learn to love myself.

With faith and support from my sister and M.T.'s mother, my healing process began. Within a year, I was able to fully care for my son without relying on his grandmother. With my faith and support groups in church and encouragement from my sister, my son and I got much healing support. The next year I marched down the aisle at my graduation, overwhelmed with joy to hear my name called to receive my first college degree, for professional studies in human service. In the audience were my son, now five, my fiancé, my mother, my best friend of twenty years, my favorite aunt who had always taken me in, my cousin, my future father-in-law, and my supportive sister Natalie, who was always there for me, even during her own struggle. My son's other grandmother was cheering for me from home.

This was the very first time I had experienced joy, the first time I had lived in a moment of happiness, the first time my face felt pain from smiling so much. It was the first time in a long time that my mother had hugged me and kissed me without her being intoxicated. This day was phenomenal. Who would have thought the birth of one life could change the outcome of another? My son had inspired me to reach for the stars.

Latisha Boyd is a mother of two beautiful boys. She currently resides in Maryland, where she is a social worker in the community, having obtained her MSW from Adelphi University. In her spare time she enjoys designing and facilitating empowerment workshops for women and young girls. Latisha spends most of her time with her children, and she enjoys listening to Gospel and jazz. She believes the key to happiness is to believe in a higher power, to love yourself first, and to not be afraid to ask for help.

Sarah Tavis

Grace and Mama in the World

At nineteen, I didn't date men for their potential as a father. In fact, I didn't date men much at all. I was fresh out of my first year of college, and I was living in my first apartment with a few friends I'd met in the dorm. School and partying were much more important to me than men. I was still a virgin, and, unlike most of my friends, I was waiting for that special guy who would fulfill all the culturally induced fantasies I had about love. I wanted to be a part of the cult of goo-goo-eyed, giggling lovers who take long walks on crisp fall days, share intimate secrets while snuggling in bed, and never fight. I was Sleeping Beauty, waiting for Prince Charming to knock me down with his puckered lips.

When I met him, he didn't knock me down. He knocked me up.

Sal was gorgeous. Tall, dark, and punk rock. We met at a friend's. He was there with some chick, but that didn't stop him from drawing a picture of a fetus on my thigh. My first journal entry about Sal read, "This guy makes my uterus itch." Three months later, I was pregnant and had a raging case of chlamydia.

It took me years to appreciate the irony of that first night, that first journal entry.

Shortly after Sal and I started dating, I moved into his sister's one-bedroom apartment. Angela had the bedroom, and I managed to fit my single futon into a crevice in the kitchen. The manager of our apartments called it a breakfast nook. Angela and I did almost everything together, including enough mescaline and acid to give my grandchildren hallucinations.

About three months after Sal and I started dating, I suspected I might be pregnant. One night at a party, as I confessed to my best friend about my possible pregnancy, Sal found his way into the bedroom of some girl who lived at the house where the party was. The next day, when I found out about Sal's sexual adventures, I was determined to be done with him. A week later, I found out I really was pregnant. Suddenly, everything changed. So, Sal was an unfaithful creep. He was also the father of my child. What the hell was I supposed to do now? In just three months, I'd gone from naive virgin to pregnant teenager. All of the crap I'd been fed about teen moms reverberated in my panic-ridden head: *welfare, food stamps, shame.* Forget about school, girl. Might as well get a job at the nearest fast-food joint, frying various animal parts for minimum wage.

It was the day after I'd gotten back from Mardi Gras in New Orleans that I found out I was pregnant. That night, I wanted to say a prayer for my baby. But I didn't know who to pray to. So, instead, I asked the universe to protect my baby from all the psychedelics I had unknowingly flooded her with during my Fat Tuesday celebrations. Then, I promised I wouldn't do any more drugs while I was pregnant. At that point, I was unwilling to make any promises beyond gestation.

I remember calling Sal, who, a few weeks earlier, had moved in with the girl he'd screwed at the party. I huddled on the bathroom floor, paralyzed with fear and nausea, in the space between the toilet and the kitty litter. Although I'd rehearsed the phone call all day—I'd tell him I was pregnant, and he'd tell me he loved me and would be right over so we could work things out—when he finally got on the phone I froze. I felt like a snake, cornered and poised for attack. "I'm pregnant and I'm getting an abortion. You need to send me three hundred dollars by next week." I hung up, so afraid of Sal's response that I couldn't continue the conversation. Then, too exhausted to even take off my clothes or run the water, I climbed into the tub, collapsed in a heap, and sobbed until Angela came home and comforted me with clichés: "This will pass," "Give it time; time heals all wounds," and "Sleep, then you'll feel better."

I never wanted an abortion. I was scared to death of the whole abortion process. I had nightmarish visions of a vacuum tube being inserted into my body to suck out the fetus I was afraid to carry. I also feared I might regret not having this child. The fear of the actual abortion and of the sorrow that would remain after my womb was vacuumed was more pervasive than my fear of having a baby.

Despite my abrupt proclamation to Sal, I knew right from the start that I wouldn't have an abortion. But I was still scared about becoming a mother. I didn't know how I was going to cope alone with a baby. I didn't want to work at a fast-food joint or get on welfare. I didn't want people to feel sorry for me because I got pregnant. I wanted to finish school, travel, be young, and have fun. It didn't help that the after-school specials on television and the sex-education classes in high school made the life of a teen mom out to be hellish: the crappy job, the crying baby, the stigma. I was well aware of these negative stereotypes, but I was also looking forward to the positive prospects of parenting: breastfeeding a new babe; the intimacy of sleeping with a small, snuggly body; the first smile. As the oldest of six children, I'd witnessed these things firsthand through my mother. I wanted to experience all that motherhood has to offer, but I wanted to experience it in my mid-twenties, not in my late teens.

I suppose that for a few days I thought my life was over, especially during that phone conversation with Sal. But I also realized that I would still be able to do all the things I wanted to do—and be a mama, too. It was just gonna be a hell of a lot harder. In his novel *Memoirs of a Geisha,* Arthur Golden writes, "We lead our lives like water flowing down a hill, going more or less in one direction until we splash into something that forces us to find a new course." I think this is an apt description of my feelings during this time. This baby was my splash.

By the time I was five months pregnant, Sal was living with his sister and me in a larger, but still cramped, apartment. We were not a couple, but I was working on it. There was something about carrying this man's child that allowed me to forgive the cheating and forget the hurt and humiliation I felt from Sal's unfaithfulness—all in order to give my baby a family. That we would be a fucked-up family hadn't occurred to me. I just wanted a family. I wanted our baby to have Saturday morning snuggles in bed with Mom and Dad. I wanted to have family meals, family vacations, and family birthday parties. I wanted to give our baby the childhood I'd had—Christmas Day spent with both Mom and Dad. Not Christmas morning with Mom and, later, Christmas dinner with Dad.

When Sal went to jail for an old probation problem, we spent the last four months of my pregnancy writing daily love letters, letters of preparation. We made plans for our future. We wrote about Sunday evening dinners, soccer games, family picnics, birthday parties. We had everything figured out. I felt safe in the sweet reassurance from Sal that I would not have to raise our baby alone.

When our daughter, Grace, was born, Sal was still in jail, but they let him out for the birth. Afterward, he went back to jail, and our daughter went into ICU for "possible pneumonia." My mom and grandmother came down for a few days, but I mostly spent those five days in the ICU alone, breastfeeding my healthy girl, while the two-pound baby whose incubator was next to Grace's crib regularly went into cardiac arrest. Lonely nights in the ICU taught me my first lesson in single motherhood: I was it—the only person who was going to be a constant in Grace's life. It was Grace and I against the world.

When Grace was a month old, Sal got out of jail, and the first few weeks were glorious. Sal was the dad he'd talked about in his letters. He changed diapers and, late at night, rocked a crying Grace back to bed. He washed dishes and folded clothes.

Soon, however, I was home all day with Grace while Sal worked, then home all night with Grace while Sal played—often until the early morning. The night before I started work again, and Grace started her first day of child care, Sal was out until five in the morning. He came home without the car, but full of excuses and apologies. I was livid. I was scared about working again and anxious about Grace feeling safe at her new child care center. I needed support, and Sal was raising the level of stress in my already maxed-out life.

One unusually chilly November night, when Grace was about one month old, we were waiting at a bus stop next to the highway. I had just gotten my first Depo-Provera shot (I wasn't taking any chances with future "accidents"), and Grace had just had a blowout in her diaper. She and I were both covered in spit-up, and my soggy, puke-stained bus schedule told me that we would have to inhale car exhaust for another thirty minutes. About ten minutes into our wait, a blond woman in a gold Jaguar pulled over to see if I needed a ride. I was mortified and quickly turned her down while wearing my best *I like waiting for the bus on cold nights with my shitty newborn* smile.

After she drove away, I also felt deeply offended. I imagined that the woman in the Jaguar viewed Grace and me as a good deed, a sympathy story to tell her friends over coffee the next morning. I also imagined that she was looking at my situation and assuming that I was not a good mother.

That night was pivotal for me. I couldn't stand the thought of being someone's pity case. I didn't want to see myself as a bad mother, and I'd be damned if anyone else did, either. I realized I could be proud of my parenting. I knew I was a damn good mom, even if I had to wait at a bus stop on a cold winter's night with my baby covered in vomit and poop or pay for my groceries with food stamps.

Sal and I split up when Grace was three months old. He was "ready to move on" and wanted to date a woman he knew at work. We stayed in the same house for almost another month, with him waffling between this woman and me. I couldn't stand it anymore. My naive dream of a family was dissolving and once again I was faced with the prospect of creating a family alone with my girl. One evening during that time, while Sal was holding Grace, he told me he was planning on going out that night, and I slapped him. After he left, I wrote in my journal, "I've lost it. I've gone too far, and I'm afraid that if I don't let go of Sal, let go of this anger, I will be unable to be the kind of mom that Grace needs: calm and centered—not full of anger and hurt. I can't believe I hit him while he was holding our baby! That is NOT ME! It is not who I want to be! I have to LET GO!"

Soon after I wrote this, I made a connection between the incident with the lady in the Jaguar and the night I slapped Sal. Encountering the woman in the Jaguar, I was ashamed of who I thought she perceived me to be: an unfortunate young mother in a sad situation. On the night I slapped Sal, I was ashamed of who I feared I was becoming: a raging and abusive self-appointed martyr. I did not see myself as either of these women, and I knew I had to remove myself from Sal, both physically and emotionally, in order to be the woman I wanted to be—and the mother I wanted to be.

When Grace was four months old, Sal moved out, and Angela and I moved into a roomy house with a great yard. Single motherhood was not what I had hoped for when I signed up to be a parent. Fortunately, I had Angela on hand to lend moral support and serve as a built-in baby-sitter. Yet, as I adjusted to life without Sal, I realized there were several perks to single parenting. The biggest one was that I did not have to spend every waking hour with Grace. When she had daddy time, I had me time: time to be twenty years old; time to go to school, be young, and have fun.

Of course, there was also the downside to single parenting. This one was big. It was the *My tax money is paying for you to feed that screaming toddler* look I got almost every time I went grocery shopping and paid with food stamps. Or the "How old *are* you?" asked by the perfect stranger on the bus. I worked hard to combat the food stamp shame, the ugly stares on rainy days at the bus stop from people driving by in heated cars. I got the looks, and at first they hurt. For a while I pretended to be married. Talked about the fictional husband and our "family" whenever someone said, "You look too young to be her mom."

When Grace was born, my mom told me that I would grow up with my baby. At the time, I didn't pay much attention to this statement, nor did I ponder what my mother might have meant. As Grace got older, however, I realized the importance of her remark. I think what she really meant was that in order to be a good mother, *I* had to grow up. I had to stop living like a self-indulgent teenager. I had to stop looking for the next party and start looking for the right college.

Not receiving a college degree was never an option for me. Both of my parents are teachers, and education is valued highly in my family. Often, I felt like my life was dichotomous: single college student in the morning, food stamp–paying single mama at night. And, yet, I think it was the chance to be a single college student that allowed me to deal with long lines and disrespectful caseworkers at the welfare office. I was not going to be buried in the pit of poverty. I had found the door leading out of the welfare office, and education was my key.

I also knew I could no longer date men who were anything less than respectful and mature, kid-loving and patient. In fact, I realized that if I were to date at all, I needed to do it while Grace was with her dad. I was not willing to introduce her to a man unless I was serious about having a relationship with him. I did not want different men floating in and out of her life. Ultimately, this meant that I did not date much.

Most important, I realized that I had to make responsible choices that were beneficial for both Grace and me. After two and a half years of working full-time, schooling part-time, and meeting very few parents my age, I knew it was time to find the right community in which to raise my daughter. I also needed to get myself into school full-time. By now, Sal was seeing Grace very irregularly, and Austin, Texas, was getting so big that I had a hard time finding anything that came close to resembling "community," especially for a young, single, left-of-middle mom like myself. My best friend had graduated from Evergreen State College in Olympia, Washington, and she'd been trying to convince me to move to Olympia for years. Drawn by the promise of a kid-centered community and the chance to finish college, and with the cash from my income tax return in my pocket, Grace and I moved to Washington State when she was two and a half.

The decision to move was difficult. It meant leaving family and a great job and moving Grace twenty-four hundred miles from her father. Yet for me, the decision to move to Olympia was probably as important as the decision to have Grace. The transition from Texas to Washington was unbelievably smooth. I was still on food stamps, but most of the cashiers at the food co-op were too. I received a smile instead of a sneer each time I paid for groceries. Rent was cheaper in Olympia, so I could afford a better house. I received enough financial aid to work only a few hours each week at a cushy work-study job: the campus child care center, with Grace one of the kids I supervised! Also, working at the center gave me ample opportunity to meet young, like-minded parents. The community I'd longed for was finally materializing.

My first class at Evergreen was a poetry class. Not only was it exactly the kind of learning situation I had been dreaming of for years—interdisciplinary and mostly student-led—but it was also the class where I met my husband, Jay.

When we met, Jay was in the middle of ending a relationship with the mother of his three-month-old son. Sound familiar? It was the same age Grace was when Sal and I split up. Faced with Jay's circumstances, I felt like an old hand. I'd been through the volatile mediation appointments, trying to hammer out parenting plans, visitation schedules, and child support. I was familiar with the anger, fear, and pain that both Jay and his ex were experiencing. As a passive observer of Jay's battle for visitation, I relived my own painful memories: Sal's empty accusations of drug use. His futile attempt to prove me an unfit mother so he could get custody and not have to pay child support. Months of lawyer fees and waking up tearful from nightmares about losing my girl, just for Sal to give up in the end, calling me the night before he was supposed to take a piss test to say he'd do whatever I wanted.

After over a year of court battles and lawyer fees, we were exhausted and fearful about having any future with Jay's son at all. Yet two years later, including several heavy discussions full of apologies and lots of listening, we are figuring out our own definition of family. Family is Grace and Mama. Family is Grace and Mama, Jay, and Grace's new baby brother, Dimitri. Family is also Grace, Mama, Jay, Dimitri, and my stepson and his mother. We spend holidays together, plan birthday parties together, and stay at each other's homes during visits. My stepson's mother even refers to our kids as her stepchildren.

We still have several kinks to work out, but we've definitely created a viable version of family that works for everyone involved. Grace's stepfather is the man who goes to the school conferences, takes the training wheels off the bike, and strings the piñata at her birthday parties. I work for a small nonprofit that provides childbirth education classes and parent support groups for young families. I love that while facilitating parents' groups, I can offer young moms a safe and nonjudgmental space where they are listened to and their choices and experiences are validated. While working, I often think, *Damn! Where was this when I became a mother?* It feels like I've come full circle: I am able to offer young moms a chance to form the community and support I so desperately needed.

Becoming a mother at such a young age has been damn hard work. It was definitely not the easiest path to choose, but I am glad I chose it. I can't imagine any other choice would be as satisfying, as important. Like most parents, I find pleasure in parenting. It is rewarding and exhausting. At times I feel like I have sold out—ditched all my fellow single moms. At the grocery store, I smile at the young mama in line behind me, yearn to commiserate, to connect. "I know you are a great mom," I want to say. "You did not make a mistake!" There are days where I miss my old family—our time as Grace and Mama vs. the World—but mostly I am thankful for our blessings. They are many.

Sarah Tavis *lives in Olympia, Washington, with her daughter, Grace; her husband, Jay; her stepson, Finn; her son, Dimitri; a whiny cat named Rose; and a lanky German shepherd named Gus. She works for a nonprofit, the Mary Sheridan Foundation, which provides childbirth education classes and parent support groups for young families, as well as doula scholarships. She loves her job! She has also come out of the broom closet as a full-fledged witch who is raising her children to love the original mama, the earth. You can contact Sarah at s.tavis@comcast.net.*

Kelly S. Busch

The Fix

When I became a mother at the age of seventeen, I wanted to be able to parent by myself and to learn my own lessons. Nevertheless, I didn't anticipate the intense loneliness I would feel once leaving my parents' warm house for a small basement apartment. I had no money to go out with my friends or even to pay someone to watch my daughter. I found out that the people who had professed endless friendship to me only a year before had vanished, just like Kayla's dad. My fun and entertainment was cable TV, which I couldn't really afford, on a small 13-inch screen.

My mom had become my best friend, the only one to whom I could express my feelings. "Mom, this sucks," I told her during one of our daily phone calls, tears forming in my eyes. "I feel alone when I wake up, and I feel alone when I go to sleep, and I feel alone in between waking and sleeping."

My daughter was often sick with asthma-related problems. Consequently, I spent countless hours dealing with miserable, overworked, underpaid nurses at the hospital, and subjected to their judgmental comments: "Are you married?" they would ask me. "Looks like you've been too busy to go to school." Their words hurt, crushing my spirit.

One night during a fit of coughing, Kayla stopped breathing

for a few moments. It was something that had happened several times before. Just as I was going to call 911, she started breathing again. Knowing she was out of danger, I called my mom to take us to the hospital. Still at the hospital the next morning, I called the receptionist at my school to say I was in the hospital with Kayla and wouldn't be in classes that day. She replied icily, "If you don't want to make an effort to attend, you might as well not come back."

There was no way I was going to leave my daughter in the hospital alone. Kayla only wanted me, and why should I have denied her that?

Kayla was released from the hospital that afternoon, because the doctors could find nothing wrong with her. In the weeks that followed that experience, I started to feel that it was hopeless to try to complete my education and that I had failed my daughter and myself. I began dropping classes, one at a time, until I had only one left.

During the summer holidays, I met a man. Marcus said he wanted to love both Kayla and me, but one morning, a few weeks after we met and he moved in, he brought destruction.

"I need a fix," he told me as we were lying in bed. "It eases all of my pain, all of the sorrow. You should try it," he added.

A few days later he brought home two syringes, and a week after that he stuck my vein with a poison so sweetly tantalizing that I forgot about love, forgot about my daughter, and forgot about myself for a whole year. My intense love affair with morphine and the syringe almost killed me. I was on a path of self-destruction, and I brought my daughter along the dark and winding path of death. She was a year and a half, and so innocent, yet exposed to insanity beyond belief.

I was highly unstable when I was a junkie: One minute I was happy, and the next I would yell and throw things against the walls. Once my daughter watched as I picked up our living room chair and threw it against the cement wall in our apartment, all because I wanted a fix.

It was not unusual for Marcus and me to sleep until late afternoon. By that time, my daughter was starving and had crapped herself, smearing it all over the crib that imprisoned her. I would yell at her when I woke and saw this, even though deep in my heart I knew it was my fault, not hers.

The saying "Never trust a junkie" is absolutely true. I was manipulative and deceptive. I conned money out of my parents and stole money from them anytime I could. I often used my parents to watch my daughter so Marcus and I could score or sell drugs, and I continually lied to them about what I was doing.

The first time I tried to quit morphine was when my apartment was being watched by the police. They wanted Marcus for something he wouldn't tell me about. I decided to stay at my parents' house for a few days with Kayla, and that's where I went through withdrawal. I told my mom I was just sick; I never told my parents I was a junkie. They only found out what was wrong with me six months later, after my cousin had watched me fix.

All of the windows in my apartment except for Kayla's bedroom window had been kicked in, because Marcus and I had a lot of people angry with us. We were scamming money out of people in order to support our morphine habits. I thought that if I moved and didn't tell Marcus where I went, my life would return to normal. I found another apartment with the help of my dad, and one of his stipulations for helping me out with the rent was that I not tell Marcus where I was living. I kept true to my word for a little while, but it wasn't Marcus who was making my life insane, it was my love of morphine, my aching need for it.

The grip of the addiction was strong. I can't count how many times I attempted to quit. Some of my attempts lasted months and others only days. I knew that if I couldn't quit morphine, I was going to have to die trying. One week after my last fix on August 2, 1998, a guy offered to bring some morphine over to share with me. At first I told him to come over, and then a half hour later I changed my mind and told him not to. He called again an hour later, and by that time my skin was crawling and I wanted that morphine so bad I would have killed for it. I told him to call me at 9 P.M., after my daughter was asleep. Up until the very moment that my phone rang, I was determined to do his drugs; free morphine was more than I could pass up. But when the phone started ringing I just sat in my rocking chair, rocking and chain-smoking cigarettes. I sat there for the entire twenty-two times he called, each time letting my phone ring until it would ring no more. I don't know where my strength came from, but I sat there for over an hour while the phone rang, knowing exactly what was on the other end of the line. When I woke up the next morning, devoid of guilt, I knew I was going to make it, because I had *never* turned down free drugs, especially morphine.

With sheer determination to succeed for my daughter and myself and the strength of God beside me, I made it out of my darkening addiction alive. I was broken and withered, and my daughter was terrified of me. Rebuilding torn relationships only happens over time, and it took my daughter and my family a long time to trust me.

Twenty-five days after the last time I stuck a needle in my vein, I returned to a different school with my friend Sheri, whom I've been friends with since we were sixteen. The support I received there—a community high school with additional support services based on assessments of students' needs—is why I am here today. I found addiction support, parenting support, and life support. I was one of many young moms in that school, one of many with problems, and there was support staff to assist in our success. But I soon discovered that the guy who opened the dark path of the needle to me, Marcus, also went to that school.

"I don't think I can go on," I said one lunch hour as I walked into one of the support staff's office at the school. I had just seen Marcus with a guy he'd sold me to for morphine. They were outside smoking, and I had just walked outside when they started throwing pennies at me, saying hurtful things.

"Well, Kelly," she said, taking a seat beside me. "Before you tell me what happened and we get the dropout forms, tell me the reasons why you want to stay. Before today, why did you want to graduate so badly?"

"To show myself I can do it, and because I don't want to provide Kayla with a substandard life," I told her with tears rolling down my cheeks. "I want to achieve in order for her to and because that would make me feel so good. If I can be an example for Kayla, then I can be one for others as well."

My reasons for staying were far greater than those for leaving. I could put up with seeing Marcus and that guy; I had to. I graduated that year, receiving the "Spirit of the Blues" award at my graduation ceremony. It is an award given to the person who has overcome so many obstacles that graduating is an absolutely amazing accomplishment.

I had felt such shame about myself before. But after that moment, realizing all I had come through, I felt a great pride. I was so proud to be a mom. My daughter was my greatest source of strength, my inspiration. I knew my journey was far from over, and I knew education was the only way of me achieving my dreams and goals for both of us.

I took a correspondence course through the University of Saskatchewan and started speaking to youth from all across Canada about my experiences.

"How can you live with yourself, knowing all you have done to both your daughter and yourself?" someone once asked me at a conference where I was speaking.

"I have come to the realization that everything I have gone through has helped me grow to become the person that I am today," I told him, not even feeling an ounce of shame. "There are times that I don't understand why I have to walk the path of life that I am walking, but I know that God will never give me more crap than I can handle. Every experience I go through, good or bad, is for a reason."

I am almost twenty-five now, and my daughter will be seven

shortly. Today we have a typical mother-daughter relationship: I am always getting after her to clean her room, and I have never missed a soccer game that she has played. Today I am composed of strength and integrity, honesty and compassion. I am creative and resourceful and I am determined to always be true to myself, Kayla, and God. I work at a high school with "at risk" youth and I love my job, but I still depend on welfare. I run into obstacles in life, but I have learned that where one door closes, another one opens to greater opportunity, and all of the challenges of life help us realize our potential.

Kelly S. Busch *is a prairie horticulturist. She lives in Saskatoon, in Saskatchewan, Canada, with her daughter. She attends the First Nations University of Canada and is currently working toward earning her Indian social work degree. She has worked with youth on various projects, including serving as youth coordinator for a conference on teen pregnancy prevention. Writing is as much a part of her life as breathing. This is the first time Kelly has been published.*

Rita Naranjo

From Hopelessness to Inspiration

have had many days when I felt so hopeless that it was difficult to lift my head to look up at someone.

I was taken away from my mother when I was only four years old. Over a ten-year period, I lived in a series of foster homes. I grew up with overwhelming sadness, hurt, and mind-boggling confusion. For a long time I didn't understand why I'd been taken away from my mom. I spent many nights crying and crying, hiding my anguish from the people around me. Nobody ever gave me a hug and explained what was going on or that someday things would get better.

At age thirteen, I got arrested for possession of crack cocaine with the attempt to sell. When the cops got me, I had over four hundred dollars on me. I was put on house arrest and I was checked up on a couple of times a day. At this time I was back with my mother, only because I kept running away from my group home placements. I was so tired of being moved around from place to place. All I wanted was to be with my brothers, or at least see them more than twice a month. I hated my mother. I figured that if she loved my brothers and me she would stop using drugs and do what she had to do to get us back. Her attempts always failed; she broke all her promises. My mother could not tell me she loved me without me shouting back at her, *"You are a liar!"*

By the time I turned fourteen I felt as though I had exhausted all sense of hope. I was back with my mother and brothers, but she continued to be heavily addicted to drugs and had no control over me. I was in high school, but I never went. *Why should I?* I thought, *nobody cares whether I go to school or not.* I spent as little time as possible at home, because I could not stand to see my mom in her drugged-out condition. The image of her being high had always haunted my dreams while I was younger, and it was now a frontline reality. I saw my mother smoke crack and drink and then become completely incoherent. It hurt me deeply to see her that way.

That year my mom, my six-month-old twin brothers, my ten-year-old brother, my thirteen-year-old brother, and I were evicted from our apartment. One brother who had gotten in trouble was put back into foster care. The rest of us were on the street with nowhere to go, and we had lost almost everything from the apartment. We were able to pack only one or two small suitcases and whatever could fit in a tiny car along with six people.

I was still on probation. When my probation officer came to check on me and I wasn't home, he put out a warrant for my arrest.

Being homeless did not impede my mother's ability to obtain and use drugs. Nothing else seemed to matter to her. We tried staying with some of my friends, but our stays were brief; people did not want my mom at their house.

Eventually my mom was arrested, and Child Protective Services picked up three of my little brothers. I could not believe that my family was falling apart again! I was scared, but I was mostly in shock. What gave me comfort and confidence was that I knew how to survive on the streets. I had friends that I hung out with—my "crew," my "road-dogs." We could burglarize any house, steal almost any car, sell any drug, and even rob people. I was good at planning, strategizing, and carrying out all these illegal acts. I felt like people owed me. I did not feel bad at the time because I knew the rich people I stole from would be able to buy more things. I was not concerned with material things. I was robbing and stealing to survive. I just wanted the bare necessities, food and shelter.

My mom was in jail for three months, for being under the influence and for child endangerment. All this time I gained and maintained much respect from my friends; they knew my situation and saw me as a survivor. I was the only female around most of the time, but growing up as a major tomboy, I was tough and demanded respect. Though I was not known for being some easy female, some guys are very persistent and will not quit until they get what they want. And that is what happened. One of my so-called friends kept pressuring me to have sex with him. I was hesitant because the year before, when I was thirteen and had run away from a group home along with some other girls, I had gotten drunk and then was raped. I was very unwilling to have sex after that. Nevertheless, I eventually agreed to have sex with him, in part because I thought that maybe he really liked me. Those were truly false hopes. Believe me when I say it was not enjoyable. It was literally a *wham, bam, thank you, little girl* experience. He went to jail two days later for having a sawed-off shotgun, and he remained there for a long period of time due to repeated probation violations.

While my mom was in jail, I was convinced that how I was living was probably how I'd live for the rest of my life. When she got out she came looking for me. She knew where my stomping grounds were, so it wasn't hard to find me. She arrived in a van with the attorney who represented her. I stood there cursing them both out and telling them to get the hell away from me. I did not want to give my mother another chance. I did not want to fall for another false promise. I told them I would rather stay on the street than go home. I was also afraid that her attorney was going to turn me in, since there was still a warrant out for my arrest.

Mom and the attorney eventually drove off without me. As angry and resentful as I was, in the back of my mind I knew I should go back home. I had a strong feeling that I could be pregnant. I was not sick at all and had never really kept track of my monthly cycle, so I am not quite sure how I knew. When my mom came to find me again, I went with her, half-relieved and half-resentful. As usual, she acted like everything was okay, like nothing traumatic had happened to her children.

When I found out I was pregnant, I could have screamed and cried and thrown up all at the same time. I lay in bed that night in the dark, wide awake, and began to cry. I could not believe that I was going to have a child. I felt that I had taken a hopeless turn. How could I be a mother? What did I have to offer?

I turned myself in to the juvenile court system to take care of the warrant that was out for my arrest. I did not want to get arrested while I was big and pregnant or after I had my child, because they might try to take her away from me. I was not going to let that happen. The court set a date for me to "surrender," and the authorities ended up taking me into custody, pregnant and all. They didn't ask how my life was going outside the courtroom, and I was not about to tell them.

In Juvenile Hall I received prenatal care. At my first doctor's appointment they spent a lot of time talking about the option of ending the pregnancy. They gave me booklets and information brochures about abortion—right after they had let me hear the baby's heartbeat. I left there feeling completely lonely and ashamed. They had treated me like a child who had absolutely no potential whatsoever to provide anything positive to another child. They may have had good reason to believe that, but I was determined to prove them and everybody else wrong. No way was I going to kill my baby.

I went right away to enroll back in school. The local public school officials did not think it was a good idea for me to attend their schools while pregnant—another form of rejection. I refused to let them discourage me. They had referred me to Ocean Shores High, a continuation school with a teen parent program and on-site child care. I headed straight there. My first impression was very positive, and I looked forward to going to school—a completely new experience for me.

All my education up to this point had been very unstable and of poor quality. I felt completely ignorant in math and had much difficulty with writing. I must have been at a low grade level, because in the beginning it was hard for me to do the work successfully. Somehow, my self-confidence kept me going, even when things seemed too difficult.

February 17, 1995 was a very painful but joyous day for me: the day that my daughter Sativa was born. I had been having pains since early in the afternoon the day before. Around 10 P.M. I knew it was time for me to head to the hospital. We did not have a car, and the hospital was about a mile away. I did not call the ambulance, because we would not have been able to pay the bill. The only alternative was to walk. My mom walked with me to the hospital late that night. Labor lasted for a really long time, and I thought that I was going to die. I forgot all that when I saw my precious little girl.

Soon after I had Sativa I returned to school. I was a whole new person, more focused and determined. My home life continued to be hectic and unhealthy, but school was my safe haven, a place of serenity that surrounded me with encouragement and support. For the first time in my life, people actually had something positive to say to me. They told me how smart I was. They told me I had the ability to pursue my dreams.

I focused on finishing high school so that I could move on to higher education. I knew that was what I needed to do to make it in life. I did not want to be poor and worry about how to put food on the table, and even though part of me did not believe that I could succeed, I forced myself to keep trying anyway. Nobody else was going to be there to take care of my daughter and me. Sativa's father was out of the picture, and I refused to be dependent on any man.

At times I was at my wits' end and wanted desperately to leave the craziness at home, but I would have violated my probation if I'd left. Searching for a legal way out, I went to my probation officer and asked if I could legally emancipate. She told me I had two choices: to go back to Juvenile Hall or to go back into foster care. Either way, she said, I'd probably lose custody of my daughter. I stayed at home. I was not going to let it drive me insane. I kept my mind and heart focused on school and my daughter.

When I was sixteen I went to my court review hearing. The judge was so impressed with my progress in school and in life, he said, "I don't see any reason for you to continue on probation; therefore, your case is officially being closed." I wanted to jump straight up out of my chair with excitement, but I figured I should maintain my composure just in case the judge decided to change his mind.

As soon as I got home, I acted on impulse: I packed my bags and left. Life at home was unsafe. My mom was recovering and going through withdrawals and because of that was always violent and angry. I was so determined to get out that I did not give a lot of thought to where I would go. My daughter's father was out of jail now, and I ended up with him and his family, but life at their house was not any better. Everyone was doing drugs and getting high, and I could not stand it. I moved from one place to another, but was continuously surrounded by drugs. Eventually my daughter's father and I cleared a bunch of crackheads out of an abandoned house that was undergoing foreclosure and moved in. I got the utilities turned on. During this time I was selling marijuana to make ends meet, but I did not want to engage in any more illegal activity; the thought of losing my daughter terrified me. After much deliberation I applied for public assistance. I hated the thought of having to do this. Not only was I a "teen mother" and a "former foster child," but now I was about to add another negative label—"welfare mother." I humbled myself and did what was necessary.

I thought my life would never see stability; nevertheless, I kept on going to school. I spent hours on the bus with Sativa or pushing her stroller to and from school. Many days I wanted to cry from exhaustion and discouragement, and some days I had to talk myself out of giving up, but I was also thankful that I was able to take Sativa with me to school, where I knew she was in a safe and healthy environment.

When I was still sixteen, I started taking classes at the local community college. I had heard from my counselor at school that I could take those classes and get college and high school credit simultaneously. I thought this was a great opportunity for me to get ahead, and it enabled me to graduate early from high school. I graduated when I was seventeen with a GPA of 3.67. People at school asked me to give the commencement speech at graduation. The local newspaper interviewed me, and the article appeared on the front page of the local section on graduation day. My spirits were higher than they had been in my entire life.

Now I wanted to get out of the abandoned house and away from my daughter's dad. I felt he was holding me back and was not willing to change his lifestyle. Plus, I was not emotionally attached to him. We had stayed together up to this point because we had a child together. Just a few days after I had started looking for an apartment, I came home from school to find my windows and door boarded up. I think God decided to bless me once more, because I met an older couple who let me rent their cute one-bedroom rental house only five minutes from the beach. They even gave me the key before I had the entire first month's rent paid.

I was seventeen when I moved in. I finally felt a sense of security. No more drugs and violence. At last, it was just my daughter Sativa and me.

By now I was a full-time student at MiraCosta Community

College. I had child care and a stable home. A few of my brothers and their friends found my living room floor to be a place of comfort. I was fully independent except for the assistance I was receiving from the state, but I used that to my full advantage. I got a campus job doing outreach and recruitment at one of the local high schools and I loved it. I was making a difference. Even though I planned to major in business, I still wanted to help people.

One day, a really nice woman came to my house to bring my brother a basketful of household supplies. She told us about a project that she had started called the Former Foster Speakers Panel. She explained that participants talked to foster parents and social workers about their foster care experience, offering their insight and understanding. My brother Gino and I agreed to get involved.

I was completely overjoyed with the response to my first speaking engagement. People lined up to tell me how inspiring my story was and how much I had impacted them. I liked the feeling it gave me and was interested in making it last. That started my community activism, and the more I spoke, the more it changed my outlook on life. Before, my main interest had been to make money for my future and spend some time helping others. But one day as I sat outside the conference room where I had just spoken on a panel in front of hundreds of people, I decided to get my degree in social work. I wanted to be an activist and change the system.

Because of my speaking engagements, my reputation and network began to grow. People wanted me to speak at fund-raising events, at teen mother graduations, and at many other gatherings. In the meantime, I was moving further along in school and had more to talk about. In the year 2000 I graduated from MiraCosta Community College and I gave birth to my beautiful son, Amir. Before that, of course, I met the perfect man. Right after graduation I transferred to San Diego State University.

Everything that I have gone through—both good and bad—has had an impact on my ability to make a difference. I still have much to learn, but I already have a lot to offer. I want to be the mother that I never had. I want to be a friend to a foster child, the friend I'd always wanted when I was younger. I want to complete and succeed in higher education when nobody else in my family has. I want to make changes where nobody thinks change can happen. I know I want a lot of things, but I believe that they are all realistic and achievable, as long as I work hard with hope, truth, sincerity, and determination on my side.

Rita Naranjo *is a Colombian-Italian-American twenty-three-year-old mother of two children: Sativa, who is eight, and Amir, who is three. She is currently in her final year at San Diego State University as an undergraduate in the School of Social Work with a minor in anthropology. A former foster youth and teen mother, she is dedicated to giving back and determined to make a difference. Rita is very active with groups and organizations focused on making positive changes within the foster care system and hopes to inspire and empower young mothers. You can visit her work Web site: www.rohan.sdsu.edu/~consensu/. She is the one with the bead necklaces and head wrap.*

Speak Out!

What kind of animal best describes you as a mother?

Opossum—very nurturing and gentle, yet if attacked or her off-spring are in danger, she will fight ferociously to protect.

A protective mama cat.

Hippo—slow and gentle-looking, but can be very fierce.

A mama bear—don't mess with my kids or you will have to mess with me!

Probably a bird . . . I was protective when I needed to be . . . allowed them to spread their wings and fly when they were ready.

A tiger.

Maybe a cat . . . keeping my daughter close, dragging her around! But also encouraging her independence while I watch over her.

Bear—because they are really loving and protective, but kind of lazy.

A kangaroo. Like a kangaroo mother holds her little one in her pouch, I like to keep my son's sweet little body close to me while he's little enough to be held and touched.

Dolphin.

Maybe a dog. A peaceful animal that sleeps with its baby and stays by its side until it's time for the mother to move on.

Lioness.

Maybe a monkey.

Killer whale.

PART 8

Mama Power

ON FIGHTING FOR OUR RIGHTS, KNOCKING DOWN STEREOTYPES, AND CHANGING LIVES

I had been summoned by the department for committing the ultimate welfare sin—failing to find child care for one of my workdays, leaving my husband at home every Wednesday with our child instead of going out to make money.

"You need to put your daughter in the first day care you can find with an opening," scolded my caseworker. "This is the Work First program, and that means work comes first."

"Work does not come first for us," I replied. "My family comes first, and I'll wait for a day care that provides no less than the highest quality of care. You can take away our benefits, but I refuse to put my daughter in a substandard child care situation."

They took away my benefits, and I brought it to a fair hearing before a judge, where I won my case.

—Jade Souza,
21, doula, homeless-youth worker,
mother, Olympia, Washington

Sophia, a doula client, had emigrated to the U.S from Central America two years before I met her. She was eighteen years old, had been married for two years, and was expecting her first child. Quiet by nature, she spoke very little English, and I was one of the few Spanish-speaking doulas in our area at the time.

Although she desired a natural birth, Sophia could not choose one of the area hospitals with a lower rate of medical interventions. Her Medicaid program dictated that she give birth in a teaching hospital where a high rate of use of medical technology for birth was the norm. As her labor progressed slowly, the time-conscious doctor on duty recommended various interventions, and both she and a resident gave Sophia intermittent vaginal exams. Each time, the resident checked her first, and the doctor examined Sophia immediately after.

One of my roles as a doula is to help my client have a positive birth experience. I could see that Sophia hated being checked once, never mind twice in a row, and her tense silence through each uncomfortable ordeal was particularly wrenching to me.

After her second double exam, and after the doctor and the resident had left the room, I asked Sophia if she understood why they were both examining her. She said she didn't. I explained, "The woman who checks first is a doctor-in-training. She's getting practice by doing exams on you. The doctor then checks to see if the resident's assessment is correct.

"You have a choice," I went on. "You don't have to allow two exams."

Right away she said, "I only want one exam."

"Then you have to say that the next time they come to examine you."

She spoke up the next time, and that was the end of the double exams.

Birth complications led to Sophia's needing a cesarean section. Her baby's head was tilted sideways, presenting a larger diameter than would fit through Sophia's pelvis. To put it simply, the baby was stuck in a bad position.

The doctor, however, speaking through a translator, explained the problem to Sophia like this: "Either the baby is too big or you are too small."

I was furious. Sophia was from a culture that highly valued a woman's ability to bear children. Hearing that she was "too small" had to be adding unnecessary stress in an already disheartening situation. And it wasn't the truth.

I left the room to speak to the doctor. I couldn't find her, but I did find the head of the hospital's obstetrical department. I asked that someone please explain to Sophia that she needed surgery because of the baby's *position,* not her or the baby's size. He assured me that the correct information would be delivered.

When no one came to offer clarification, I attempted to explain it to Sophia myself. As she was about to be prepped for surgery, her own family practice physician arrived, a compassionate woman with a working knowledge of Sophia's native language whom I'd met on a prenatal visit. I asked her to explain what was really going on. "Of course!" she exclaimed, going immediately to Sophia's bedside.

Sophia surprised me by asking her doctor to do one more vaginal exam to make sure that the surgery was necessary. That exam confirmed the baby's asynclitic position.

Sophia gave birth by cesarean section to a healthy six-pound boy. When I visited her the next day, I asked, "Do you understand why you had the surgery?"

"Yes," she replied. "Because either the baby was too big or because I was too small."

Words can devastate, and words can unlock doors. Sometimes all it takes to give voice to our truth is a nudge, a reminder, or a bit of encouragement. Sometimes we wait until we are unbearably uncomfortable or until we realize that if we don't speak up, we will be! The women in this last chapter didn't always know how to give voice to their truths. They grew into their voices. They negotiated tricky paths to places and situations where they felt compelled to act to make the world a better place. Katherine Arnoldi's journey has led her to advocate for educational rights and financial aid for young and single mothers. Jessica Allan Lavarnway comes to teenage motherhood not via birth but through her heart and her bold steps into our legal system. And Rebecca Trotzky-Sirr demonstrates how even monolithic institutions can be successfully targeted for positive social change.

Katherine Arnoldi

Life, Liberty, and the Pursuit of Education

was a teen mom. The mom part was like any mom: I loved my daughter with every molecule of my body, with every thought, with all my spirit and all my emotions.

I wanted her to have a beautiful life, with complete liberty and freedom from obstacles that would impede her growth or harm her. I wanted to provide her with an environment that would give her a chance to find her own happiness. I wanted her to laugh, to smile, to learn, and to experience joy. I was just like any mom.

The teen part of me was like any teenager. I was a person becoming someone, a person just beginning on my journey to discover who I was, where I should be, and what I should do. Like any teenager, I had no training, little education, and little ability to support myself. Life was still something that adults did, and I was not yet an adult. I was confused about my place in the world. I was still trying to sort out the criticisms from my mother, the competitiveness and derision from my high school environment, and the negativity pervasive in my ailing Rust Belt city.

But suddenly I was ninety-nine percent mom and one percent

teen. I was ferocious. I may have never shown anyone my feroc-
ity, but I was. I knew I was going to provide for my daughter,
and I had no help from anyone. My mother, herself a single
mom of three, had made it clear that I was on my own. I was so
isolated that if there was help for me, I didn't know about it,
and I didn't even know how to go about looking for it.

At first, of course, I lived in crisis. I needed to provide my
daughter with the necessities of life: food, shelter, clothing. The
only job in my town that offered an uneducated teen enough to
meet those needs was factory work, so I went to work at the
rubber glove factory. As soon as I was meeting those basic
needs, I thought about the future: about freedom from fear of
factory layoffs, freedom from the monotony and misery of the
job. On one level I was hunkered down, determined to do whatever it took to get me out of my situation. On the other hand, I
was resentful and angry. Why was my dream of going to college
so unreal now? Why was my life over? How could I find the
way to become a person becoming someone? How could I still
be a part of my generation, not that of the mostly middle-aged
and older women who worked at the factory? I wanted to be
able to support my daughter but not feel bitter and angry and
trapped. I also knew I didn't want her to grow up in a factory
town with no prospects, no hope, and no possibilities except a
job like the one that I had.

The mom part of me wanted to provide for my daughter in
the best way possible. The teen part of me wanted to have my
own liberty and pursuit of happiness: to have a chance to know
what God's will might be for me, to find out what my potential
might be, to find out what my path in life was supposed to be. I
wanted to pursue the dream I had before I became pregnant. I
wanted to go to college, not only for myself but also for my
daughter.

I didn't have the slightest idea how to get to college. College
was something people went away to. I didn't know where it was
or where the road was that led there. No one I asked told me I'd

ever be able to get there. Instead they told me I had "ruined my life."

I was in a bad place. I had no idea where "better" or even "good" was, but I had to go on the road to find out. After three years of working in the factory, I saved enough to move to a place with a college, where I thought my chances would be better to find the way into it.

A young man who worked in the factory with me became my boyfriend and wanted to go with me. We bought a van and camping equipment and set off for what turned out to be bad luck for me. He battered me and kept me a virtual prisoner, with control over my money. I had to leave with nothing. There I was, back at zero, on my road to finding the way for my daughter and for me.

I moved to be with my closest friend in Colorado, where I found a waitress job and started to get back on my feet. There I met Jackie Ward, a single mom of two children, who told me about financial aid and the way to go to college. The minute I walked into my first Metropolitan State College classroom, my life and the life of my daughter changed from better to good to unbelievable.

Suddenly I too had a chance for life, liberty, and the pursuit of happiness.

I didn't even know what anthropology was, yet suddenly I was in a class discussing Lévi-Strauss's theory that men invented war and religion to upgrade their status in a matriarchal society. Suddenly I was asked whether I thought the difficulties that Hester Prynne faced in *The Scarlet Letter* are true today. Suddenly I understood the significance of the fact that the employees at the factory were mostly women. Suddenly I pondered the causes of the increase in single parenting. Suddenly I was on the equestrian team and my daughter was taking lessons in another ring of the indoor arena while I learned Hunter seat jumping. Suddenly all of my daughter's friends were the children of college professors and doctoral students.

Suddenly all my friends were pursuing their dreams: wanting to invent a new heart valve mechanism, wanting to protect the legal rights of Native Americans, wanting to find new ways of caring for the aged and ailing, or wanting to become medical illustrators. I began to consider that I, too, might find meaningful work.

I saw that when people settled for less than what they wanted, they assuaged their unhappiness with material things, or worse. I saw that many people found themselves excluded from finding the way to pursue their own true happiness, from finding what their purpose might be. And I knew that teen moms and single moms were just such a group.

I saw that if I provided my daughter with a role model of someone who was willing to keep her dreams ferociously before her, that perhaps she too would fight for her rights, pursue her dreams, and not give up. That seemed even more valuable than protecting my daughter from all of life's difficulties and challenges.

I decided to do what Jackie Ward had done for me. I started visiting GED programs, armed with financial aid forms and college applications, and I helped the young moms I met there with the process of applying to college. I wrote my novel, *The Amazing "True" Story of a Teenage Single Mom,* to inform and inspire other young and single mothers.

Even now, teen mothers do not have equal rights to education. If a teen mom drops out of high school or is coerced to leave, she misses out on guidance counseling, which would inform her about financial aid and the process of applying to college. Even if she overcomes the isolation and discovers the way to a GED program, usually no one there tells her about the process of applying to college.

Similarly, single moms do not have basic rights to equal opportunity in housing, fairness in the courts, employment, and education. I recently worked with the New York Civil Liberties Union in a class action lawsuit against the New York City Board of Education for coercing teen moms to leave high schools. Interns at NYCLU pretended they were teen moms and called twenty-eight high schools in the metropolitan area. Only six of those schools would allow the pregnant or teen mom to enroll without any restrictions. The others tried to divert those students to other schools, even though the interns explained that they wanted to go to a particular high school because it had a program they were interested in or was close to their home or day care.

Now I am working on a book examining the top three hundred colleges in the United States with regard to accessibility to mothers. The results of my research are dismal. Many colleges require that all freshmen live on campus but have no on-campus family housing. I found no college that would allow a mother to bring a child with her into a dorm. Many colleges call their family housing "graduate student housing" or "married student housing," thereby discouraging moms from considering themselves as qualified. The top schools are the worst offenders. Some colleges have token programs to help a handful of single moms for one year in a separate, almost segregated, setting, but have no mothers who are students or accommodations for mothers on the campus itself. The best schools are usually large state universities, where single mothers sometimes have access to the "married student" housing built for World War II veterans taking advantage of the GI Bill.

There is much work to be done to guarantee equal rights for women with children. I know that had it not been for Jackie, I would not have dreamed of having the right to my own life, freedom, and pursuit of what makes me happy—which is discovering and developing my potential. My child is still the most beautiful thing in the world to me. I am so proud of my daughter, who received her degree in sociology and plans a career in medicine. As my daughter has said, "If my mother can raise me, care for herself, and go to college, then I can do . . . anything."

Katherine Arnoldi *has a BA in art from the University of Arkansas and an MA in creative writing from City College in New York. She has received two New York Foundation of the Arts Awards (in fiction and in drawing), the Jerome Lowell DeJur Award in Creative Writing, and the Henfield Transatlantic Fiction Award. Her graphic novel,* The Amazing "True" Story of a Teenage Single Mom *(Hyperion, 1998), received an award from the American Library Association and was nominated for a Will Eisner Award.*

Jessica Allan Lavarnway

Things Aren't What They Seem to Be

The baby that would be mine lay in the backseat of the decrepit car. Pudgy and sleeping, she dreamed there in oblivion while I stared at her. Eight months old. Twenty-four pounds. Wearing a T-shirt and a diaper and little else.

I didn't even know what a baby was, really. My sole experience with children younger than myself included only a few poorly paid baby-sitting jobs years ago.

I glanced up at the driver of the car, my date for the afternoon, and sputtered, "Uhh . . . I didn't know you were planning on bringing her." I climbed in the car anyway.

He ignored the remark for a few moments while backing out of my parents' driveway, then said, "What was I to do with her?"

He had a point. Though I didn't realize it, he'd planned our date to go to the park and for ice cream around the condition— not the contingency—of having a baby girl with us. At that point in my life, I wasn't even conscious of the interruptions that an eight-month-old was capable of making. I knew Jason vaguely from work, and he and I had been flirting with increasing intensity until he'd offered to take me on a date. I accepted. I knew he had a daughter named Alicia, but I was unsure of the circumstances. I certainly never expected to see her.

We talked a little about my college, a bit about our work, and, though I kept on turning around and looking at her, I studiously avoided the subject of the baby. I couldn't believe she was there. Finally, I ventured tenuously, "Is there something wrong? Why is she sleeping so much?"

He glanced at her. "No, she's just napping." He took a look at the lingering shock on my face and said, "I hope you don't mind that I brought her, because if you do, I'll drive you home and drop you off. But that would make this our only date. We come as a package deal."

"I don't mind," I said quickly. And I didn't. I just had no frame of reference. I knew of single moms and married couples, but I'd never heard of a single dad.

At that moment as we were pulling into the parking lot of the local park—Alicia woke up. I expected her to scream. That's what babies did, right? No. She looked at me patiently. As Jason unloaded the diaper bag, he asked, "Can you unbuckle her from her car seat?" I had a feeling this was an in-your-face test: Can you handle the idea that I have a kid? Can you handle the fact that you're having a date with a guy and his kid?

I held my breath and proceeded to figure out the labyrinthine complex of straps and buckles and injection-molded plastic. All this time, she stared at me. I fumbled with a buckle and cursed under my breath. She giggled at me. I looked at her, really looked at this little baby laughing at me when I'd had enough culture shock for one day—and then I laughed right along with her.

We spent the day rolling in grass, letting her rip apart the contents of my backpack and throw them in the air, and eating soft serve ice cream. When Jason saw me at work two days later, he asked if I wanted to go on another date. I said yes, but with one stipulation.

"What do I have to do?"

"Bring Alicia."

It was a strange dating relationship. I was sixteen years old, on a hiatus during my second semester of college, working as a waitress. I knew that his daughter and he were very close, although I'd never met a twenty-year-old dad before. I'd only heard the media approaches to teen parents—the closest I'd ever been to one was when I read Kristin Luker's *Dubious Conceptions* in sociology class the semester before. I knew he was poor. At the restaurant where we both worked, I was waiting tables for something to do until summer semester started; he was doing it because he lived on the income.

About a month into our relationship, Alicia was placed in foster care with her paternal grandmother. When that happened, we both heaved a sigh of relief. Jason had been taking Alicia with him constantly, since he didn't have a safe place to leave her; now she would be safe. The court handed him a list of conditions to fulfill to reobtain custody. As he became more stable, living in a safer apartment and working better jobs, we were allowed to spend more time with Alicia.

I took more college classes, held Alicia's hand as she made tentative steps, and watched Teletubbies with her. Jason and I began taking her for regular overnights with us, then regular weekends, and eventually four- and five-night stretches. When she was fifteen months old, she called me "Mama." Her biological mother started to fade out of her life, but everyone—social workers, family members, acquaintances, doctors—excused her absence: "She's only seventeen, after all."

When I heard this, I bristled. Jason was providing for his child in the best way he could, and he was twenty. I was being the best stepmother I could (for by then we were engaged), and I was sixteen. Yet no one expected us to be able to take care of Alicia. Nevermind my education or his (he had enrolled in college in an attempt to improve his employment situation and his living situation in general). Nevermind our efforts to learn about parenting and child development, the agonized hours we spent attempting to decide what sort of relationship we should request from her biological mother, the long conversations into the middle of the night about where we'd move to so Alicia could have decent schools. Apparently we were only playing at parenthood. We needed adults to take care of us, to tell us what to do and what to say. We couldn't possibly be expected to be competent. We couldn't know what was best for our child.

When I was seventeen, Jason was twenty-one, and Alicia was nearly two, I graduated from college with my associate's degree. I felt committed to serving our country in the military, as most of my family has done. After many conversations about idealism versus rationalism, we agreed that I would serve in the Army Reserve and we would marry when I finished my six-month active duty obligation. Immediately upon my return home, we would file jointly for guardianship to be reinstated to Jason.

Alicia and I had a tearful good-bye from each other. Jason and I agreed that she would come with him to watch me graduate from basic training, and off I went. I called Alicia at every opportunity, and she always asked me, "Mama, will I get to see you soon?" I received lengthy letters from Jason describing every trial and tribulation Alicia went through—hand, foot, and mouth disease, for instance, or a distressing visit with her biological family. Friends from college said, "At least now you won't be tied down. You're only seventeen, you know." Of course. I'm only seventeen, so I should run screaming from the child whom I've comforted through midnight fevers, the child who looked at me triumphantly when she learned how to pump her legs on the swings, the child who snuggled up to me at 3 A.M. saying, "Mama, Dada, I had a nightmare." I'm only seventeen. Many of these friends went on to say in a confidential voice, "I still can't believe you got involved with a man with a *child*." Of course. Children are anathema, and if I help raise a child who loves me and whom I love, my life is over. I'll be condemned to a life of scrubbing carpets and cashiering at supermarkets.

I never realized before these conversations that children were considered a hedonistic result of selfish actions, as opposed to the next brave generation. To many of my acquaintances of all ages, a child was a purely private indulgence, like an SUV, not a person I had to guide through this world.

I dropped my associations with these individuals.

My time in the army was lonely, but it was all worth it when I came home for two weeks' leave at Yule. Jason and I couldn't hold off any longer; Alicia was happy to know that Mama and Dada were getting married.

I spent my wedding night watching videos and eating Chinese takeout. The next day I spent changing sheets, and Alicia asked what being married meant. I explained to her that it meant that Mama and Daddy would get to live together forever. She asked, "Can I live with you too?" I committed myself at that moment to filing for permanent guardianship and full custody.

Upon my discharge from the army, we filed for guardianship. I was just under eighteen and a half years old, but they never asked my age or commented on it. The judge sighed as he signed the papers authorizing Alicia to be returned to our full legal and physical custody, explaining, "This is what happens when children bear children." If the guy had glanced at birth dates, he'd have realized that the child who bore a child was more than a year older than the "child" who was now being given full parental rights. But, of course. Teen parents are bad parents by default. I must be older! Why else would I be acting responsibly toward a child?

After being granted guardianship, I walked outside with Jason, adjusting to the idea of actually having a permanent legal bond with Alicia. I was a couple of weeks pregnant with our daughter Julianne and trying to not puke every ten seconds. I asked him, "When was the last time that Alicia's birth mother visited?"

"Oh, it's been three, four months."

I recalled the long days I'd spent with law books, since we couldn't afford a lawyer to do the guardianship paperwork. I remembered flipping back repeatedly to a certain section, looking at it and wondering, *Maybe, maybe, maybe . . .*

I turned to Jason and said, "Hey, hold on a second."

"Sure. I saw the bathroom. Past the metal detectors, on the left."

"No, not that."

I strode into the probate court office and asked, "Could I have the paperwork for a petition for adoption and a petition for termination of parental rights?"

I went to the library, throwing up frequently and trying to keep Alicia at bay with a Magna Doodle. I looked up the statutes, found the relevant grounds, and wrote out the petition for termination. I also wrote out the paperwork for a stepparent adoption. The conditions for obtaining a stepparent adoption were relatively easy—no home studies, no guardians ad litem, just simple paperwork. Jason paid a visit to his ex, bringing the termination paperwork and the consent-for-adoption paperwork. She was several months pregnant with her second child with her new boyfriend.

"I'm sorry I haven't stopped by lately," she said, "I've been real busy. . . ."

That is all I know of their conversation. When Jason left, she went with him to a notary to sign over her parental rights in favor of the adoption. We had ample grounds at this point for legal termination of parental rights, but that would be unnecessarily complicated and painful, and it was a foregone conclusion.

Two weeks after her third birthday, at the courthouse, my daughter received her birthday present from me.

The judge asked us many questions. While we answered, I dealt with Alicia's many requests and complaints: Could she have a juice box? She was bored; what could she do? Where was her Magna Doodle? Were there any Goldfish to eat in my purse?

Finally the judge asked me if I was ready for "full parental responsibility."

I replied, "Does it look like I don't already have it?"

The judge smiled. He then asked Alicia, "You know that if I sign these papers, she'll be your mommy forever?" She smiled and said, "But Mommy already *is!*"

Two signatures and a stamp later, the paperwork was done.

I believe to this day that at eighteen years, eleven months of age, I am probably the youngest adoptive parent ever approved by the state, at least in recent history. People have criticized my path to becoming a "teen mother"—that it was too cushy, that I had too many opportunities to get out, that it was too gradual—but I was Alicia's mother long before the judge stamped our papers.

Jessica Allan Lavarnway *is twenty-two years old and the mother of six-year-old Alicia and two-and-a-half-year-old Julianne. She serves in the Army Reserve as a combat medical specialist, volunteers as a rape crisis counselor, works as an emergency medical technician, and studies history and political science with a specialty in international diplomacy. She also washes diapers, argues about bedtimes, cuts the crusts off sandwiches, brings fifteen juice boxes and Fig Newtons to Brownie Girl Scout meetings, has her teeth cleaned with a toddler sitting on her lap, and can continually operate on five hours of sleep. She aspires to a job in international affairs, getting out of student loan debt, and once, just once, experiencing sixteen consecutive hours of sleep.*

Rebecca Trotzky - Sirr

Scaling the Ivory Tower With a Baby on My Back

"came out" as a mom in front of some of the smartest and most talented eighteen-year-olds in the world. Standing before all one thousand of Stanford University's frosh class of 2002 as an official welcoming speaker, I introduced them to the "diversity" of the school by speaking about my three-year-old child. I was wholly nervous about the prospect of having the entire fresh-faced class's first impression of me be that I was a weird single mom. I was worried that they'd think I was not as perfect as they were. I don't remember all of what I said, as I was too excited. Mostly I commented about unwritten rules of elite education, ones that said that young moms on welfare were not as smart or as good as . . . well, Stanford students. Unwritten rules that defined excellence by excluding people like me, young single moms, from access to upper-tier education. But after the thunderous applause, I felt proud to be a young mama attending the "Harvard of the West."

Now, I'm not going to lie to you and tell you it was all peaches and cream—or sushi and mocha lattes, as the case may be. More often than not, Stanford's students and professors wavered between moderate hostility and blind ignorance of the issues I faced in order to attend school. There were the Little Things, like finding a way to get to the library to cram the night before an exam, or not eating breakfast in order to both get my child to preschool and not be late for my 8 A.M. class—again. Then there were the Big Things, like finding quality and affordable child care while living in Silicon Valley during the height of the dot-com rent inflation, or balancing working a part-time job or two while going to school full-time. Or sitting with a social worker who proclaimed, "Stanford University is not a job training program" and suggested I drop out of school to enroll in a certified job training program. Stanford ignored—perhaps intentionally, perhaps simply through oversight—the very real needs of students who were not a part of the traditional collegiate experience. This impacted no one more than us moms and kids.

Yet, I was really lucky to be in school as a mom. Frankly, if I had gotten knocked up during the summer of what would have followed my senior year in high school (except that I hadn't been in high school since I was fifteen) and preceded my freshman year at college, I wouldn't have done it. Had I found out that I was preggo a few months earlier, say during the winter college application deadlines, I would have been too scared to go ahead and apply to colleges. Any later, when I was already attending college, I would have been pressured into thinking that I couldn't possibly be a good mom and a good student. But when I found out I was pregnant, right after I hopped a freight train to freshman orientation, I was already committed to going to school and not yet initiated into academia's perception that being a mother is a liability.

Besides timing, I had a number of other privileges throughout my pregnancy: I was smart, healthy, and over eighteen, and thus able to make my own medical decisions. My babydaddy was "in love" with me, we'd been together for a few years, he didn't physically abuse me, and he had a good job due to the fact that he was college-educated and more than seven years older than me. I had a mom who cared about me and who worked hard, with little help from my father, to provide a good foundation for her kids. And I was (still am) white. While these factors didn't always make for smooth sailing, I never had to deal with racism, complete poverty, and legal issues that many young mamas face every day.

Needless to say, my mom was not initially thrilled to find out that she was going to become a grandma. To her, I was finally getting my act together after a tumultuous and adventurous adolescence, and now I had just "gone ahead and ruined my life." I had spent the four years between high school and college living the activist life, hopping freights and hitchhiking to the movement of the moment. I learned more geography hanging with hobos, more history from activist Judi Bari, and better Spanish in Mexico than at my underfunded high school. But my mom worried about me.

My then-boyfriend was also not thrilled by our unplanned pregnancy. But, by that time I was also not thrilled with the then-boyfriend and was tacitly ready to stake my own claim on life. I had met my boyfriend at an Earth First! meeting, but two years later realized that despite his anarchist T-shirt collection, he acted a lot like a workaholic corporate banker. Even though his work consisted of politics I agreed with, he put his work before everything else, including me. I told him that it was my body and my choice. His choice was whether to sign or not sign the birth certificate acknowledging his responsibilities as a father. While he eventually did sign the birth certificate, it is dubious whether he ever assumed the responsibilities of fatherhood. Throughout my pregnancy we were involved in a relationship that consisted of me conspiring to escape his grasp and him convincing me that I was insane for not wanting to be with him.

Personal drama aside, I was the punk rock preggo girl on campus. Everyone knew who I was. I dove into my studies, focused. In case anyone had any misplaced sympathy for me, I founded an anarchist student union. Bringing speakers from revolutionary struggles in Mexico and movements to reclaim democracy in the classroom, I waddled through my first two trimesters of my pregnancy and my first two trimesters in college. Barely squeezing into the classroom desk, I would take notes from a Nobel Prize–winning neoclassical economics professor about how welfare distorted the economy. Right after, I would meet with my welfare caseworker.

I recall stepping into that professor's leather couch–red carpet–personal secretary–corner office during his office hours to inquire about a minute detail in our text. As he glanced up from his old-growth redwood desk, first confusion and then horror spread across his face. I could read the question in his eyes: "*Are you a* freshman? *Are you . . .* pregnant?" I could almost hear his internal analysis of . . . sigh . . . my food stamp and medical assistance check distorting our economy . . . right this very second! His monotone voice rumbled in my head: *You see, the tax shifts the labor supply curve moving from the optimal wage creating a dead weight loss in the economy.* In that instant, all I could think was that my progeny *Would. Never. Be. Dead. Weight.* I think my intensity in his class and my frantic pursuit to understand the justification behind his neoclassical madness scared him.

By my third trimester, I had figured out that: 1) My baby was due a week before finals, so I could finish the academic year if I worked like crazy; 2) In a few weeks my life would be dramatically and unpredictably different; and, 3) If I didn't graduate, I would be seen as another statistic—a young, unmarried, poor mom—so I'd better haul ass.

On May 20, 1999 I helped organize a campuswide discussion of creativity in activism. Afterward, I went to see the just-released *Star Wars, Episode 1,* knowing it would be my last chance to see any movie for a while. That night I wrote in my journal, "I'm bigger than a house/elephant/whatever. Everyone's scaring me cuz I haven't done Lamaze. I just think birth is gunna be intense no matter what. And I'll be able to cope no matter what." I never went to bed that night. By seven the next evening, my son was born without Lamaze and without any drugs. It was the most intense twenty hours of my life. The best part about my labor is that I don't remember it. Hurrah for natural endorphins!

When I looked at my scrawny new baby boy who smelled like the ocean, I finally found that strength to do whatever it takes to get it right, realizing that it ultimately meant ditching an emotionally vacuous relationship that I'd been in and out of since I was fifteen. I was scared to dump my boyfriend, but I knew that I deserved to be loved *and* respected. I knew that I needed to be alone in order to grow into the person I wanted to be, not the person he wanted me to be. Birth brings a universal wish to make the world a better place to raise our children. I used this momentum to become the woman I knew lurked behind the boyfriend. Just about everyone I knew blamed my decision to break up with the father of my child on my hormones. Yet, hormones or not, through childbirth I had finally found the power and agency to do what I had always wanted to do: be my own woman.

Scraping together my kid's and my survival was possible, but paying for school was another matter. I prayed for a miracle. That quarter, I received a slightly larger needs-based scholarship, but that and my loans did not cover the costs of room and board, books, or child care. How was I going to make $580 per month of child support or pay my room and board fees of $1,200 per month? How was I going to pay for books? How much longer could I bring a precious nursling to class before the nursling turned into a rowdy, crawling baby? How could I possibly afford to pay for child care? How would we eat if I wasn't working?

It was the height of the Silicon Valley bubble. I knew that I was living among the richest people in the world. I knew that the questions I had were pebbles next to the boulders of racial and economic inequality in my larger community. But I also knew that I had a source of power to change and question things: I was an exalted Stanford student. I had immediate access to institutional clout and resources.

I searched and searched for other mamas at Stanford. Despite being told that I was "the only one," I found nearly two dozen undergraduate parents like myself at Stanford University. We were the valedictorian who gave her high school graduation speech five months pregnant, we were the couple who fell in love at Stanford and decided to start a family, we were the mom who zooms around campus in her motorized wheelchair with her two-year-old in her lap, and we were the sixteen-year-old mom who was the first in her Texas family to go to college. Together we enumerated our shared challenges and identified those that the university could do something about.

Top on our list was decreasing the financial barriers to our education. Since Stanford purported to be a "needs-blind" institution, it prided itself on its belief that all its students—regardless of financial hardship—had equal access to education. We started looking at specific barriers that the university maintained that prevented student parents from having equal financial footing with the traditional, childless students. For example, while undergraduates could live anywhere on campus, those with kids were required to live in twice-as-expensive family housing. At the same time, undergraduate parents (who were mostly student mothers) were denied a proportionate increase in financial aid to reflect our mandated pricey housing costs. Digging deeper, we learned that graduate student parents (most often fathers whose wives stayed at home with the kids) had financial aid packages adjusted for child care and increased family housing costs. Like most unjust policies, this one hit our poorest moms the hardest. Some student moms, isolated from family and friends, were dependent on abusive partners for money and support. Some moms dropped out of school. Changing this one policy, we knew, would dramatically increase an undergraduate parent's ability to be able to go to school without the hardship of choosing tonight's dinner over tomorrow's rent.

We met with the student body president, who immediately recognized the urgency of our situation. He arranged for the student newspaper to do a feature story about us, complete with cute pictures of our kids. Within the week the situation of student parents became the topic of dorm room conversations. Shortly thereafter, we had a sit-down with the provost of the university. It was, perhaps, the first and only time that three single moms on welfare have ever met with a man in charge of a nine-billion-dollar institution.

We moms wondered, *Would he be able to understand our lives?* We worked at using simple illustrations, such as, it's really hard to focus on homework when you're worried about whether you can buy groceries or a birthday present for your kid. In the end, the meeting went really, really well. The administration responded rapidly with positive changes that created more equitable financial aid packages, making it possible for student parents to attend school. We won the fight to reclaim our education, sending a message to other moms at other schools that they can do it too.

Despite our success in making Stanford more accessible to moms like me, I grappled over whether I should even have attended an institution that by its mere existence creates elitism through exclusion. As a single, poor, young mama with access to the upper echelon of power, I was an outlier. Was I deluding myself, believing that I could change inequalities from the inside of a fundamentally biased institution?

Yet, I do have the ability to change the distribution of power. While I did learn a lot from Stanford, I believe that Stanford learned a lot from me. Every professor whom I met with my boy in tow now realizes that young mothers aren't statistics, that we can be honor roll students. The administration now recognizes the need to eliminate financial barriers to education for pregnant and parenting students. I sparked a broader discussion about maintaining a work-life balance in the traditionally male-dominated realm of academics. My classmates have seen mothers succeed in demanding university careers. Students who will be the world's future bosses and managers have been introduced to the challenges of building family-friendly policies and have heard about the institutional benefits of ample, affordable, quality child care. Preeminent researchers were introduced to brilliant welfare moms. The entire freshman class of 2002 heard from a pro-choice mama.

Along the way, I earned an MS in engineering while getting a BA with honors in urban studies—all within four years. It kicked my ass, but I kicked theirs harder. As a young mama, I used my education and my degree from Stanford to amplify my voice, to send out a louder call for justice. Many young moms I meet say that having a kid radicalized them. Having my kid focused and concentrated my energy to fundamentally transform the way we build our future. I better understand the righteous anger of marginalized moms and kids as, despite all odds, we keep trying to pull ourselves up. I feel the urgency to create a sustainable world as the demon of poverty breathes down my back.

Having a child changed my revolution, making it far more personal. Yesterday, it meant confronting fat phobia and disordered eating with a group of young mamas. Today, being a revolutionary mom means talking to the next generation of mamas still in high school, reading over their applications to college, working to end the discrimination that pregnant teens face from their high school teachers, demystifying financial aid forms, and showing them that if I can do it . . . they will too. Tomorrow, though, being a revolutionary might just mean working as the engineer that I am trained to be. Because for me, having my degree from sanctified Stanford University is inexorably intertwined with being young, single, poor, and a mother. And to me, that is a small revolution.

Rebecca Trotzky-Sirr *is a smarty-pants mama and a spoken word artist who believes that grammar rules are meant to be broken. Her preschooler, Zev, is a rock star who likes to roller-skate through the financial district. Rebecca wants to let everyone know about needs-blind financial aid policies at elite universities so that you too can scale the ivory tower.*

In 2002, Rebecca graduated from Stanford University with a BA in urban studies (with honors) and an MS in construction engineering; yes, she knows far too much about steel and concrete. Rebecca lives in the Midwest, where she recently cofounded the Revolutionary Anarchist Mom and Baby League (RAMBL), strengthening the voices of marginalized mamas in the movement for social justice.

Rebecca is looking forward to attending medical school in the year 2004. She wants to become an OB/GYN who provides quality reproductive health care services in underserved communities to women of all ages. Her clinic will have really great toys and plenty of children's books in the waiting room. She wants to hear from you at nerd.girl@stanfordalumni.org.

Speak Out!

If you could wave a magic wand and change one thing to improve the lives of young mothers, what would you do?

Eliminate nasty stares.

Create villages full of women to help nurture, raise, and discipline our children when we're losing our mind.

Imbue us with self-confidence and strength.

Give them absolute support, love, and acceptance from their families.

Erase the prejudice that says a woman can't be a good mother if she's young. I would wave it over teenage fathers to have as much responsibility as the moms. Add a mute button to babies so mothers still in school can get homework done. Show them that they can be everything they have ever dreamed they could be.

Make Money!

Make access to high school and college easier.

I'd make communities feel a sense of love and responsibility for all their children.

Provide an "invest in our future" package of free education, living expenses, and day care.

I would have us be respected and admired for our strengths.

I'd give each mom patience for when blood, sweat, and tears don't seem to be enough.

> Increase the welfare rate for young moms who are in school, trying to better their lives.

Offer limitless educational opportunities and career mentoring programs.

> I would like each young mother to have a positive role model who can guide, influence, and encourage her in positive ways.

Give every young mom a full night's sleep.

Index